FLIM FLAM

FLIM FLAM

The Truth Behind the Blind-Faith
Culture that Led to the Explosive NCAA
Investigation of Ole Miss Football

By Steve Robertson

Library of Congress Control Number: 2017951087

ISBN: 978-0-692-92182-1

Manufactured in the United States of America.

Distributed to the book trade by:

Foxx House, LLC
P.O. Box 718
Jackson, MS 39041
601-533-8595
www.flimflamthebook.com

Dedication

I didn't have to think long about who to dedicate this book to. From the moment I agreed to write *Flim Flam*, I knew whose names I wanted on the dedication.

My father, Freddie Robertson, raised us all to be Mississippi State Bulldog fans. He grew up on a dairy farm in Ellisville, Mississippi, and then spent his career working to help families and farmers as well as the American taxpayer.

He taught me about hard work and taking value in the job you do. He shared with me the importance of accountability, and how grown folks accept responsibility rather than make excuses.

I lost him in 2005. The last words he ever spoke were to his wife and children. He cleared his throat and said, "I love all of y'all." He was my best friend. I miss him every single day.

My mother-in-law, Pat Hill, dreamed of being a published writer someday. She had a sarcastic wit that I appreciated. She was well read and loved the Mississippi writers. I know she would be proud to know I have completed my lifelong goal of writing a book.

She was an unbelievable grandmother to my children. I believe she really found her groove as "Granny Pat," a name she never wanted, but warmed to easily. She loved Crime TV, The Phantom of the Opera and the music of Collective Soul and Ozzy Osbourne.

While she was my wife's mother, Pat was my friend. We had a connection that I feel was more special than most in-laws. She treated me as if I was her own child. I miss her terribly. She was the second-best Rook player in our family.

Daddy and Pat helped me become the person and writer I am today. This book is dedicated to their memory.

Preface

I've been asked countless times why I wrote this book. The answer can often be very complicated. The concise answer is I didn't think anyone else would.

After being approached about tackling the challenge of writing this story, I felt it was important to document what has transpired, and what it all means to college football.

Hugh Freeze is a wildly popular coach who has taken Ole Miss football to heights not seen in generations. The personable coach with the downhome charm, reminiscent of Andy Griffith fresh from Mayberry, evoked strong reactions from fans and foes alike.

Rebel fans see Freeze as a local boy "done good," while his detractors see him as a coach with a persona that looks a little too good to be true.

As rumors began to spread the NCAA was looking into the recruiting practices of the Ole Miss football program, I expected the in-state media coverage to really take off. It didn't. In hindsight, I should've known better.

I didn't ask to be an authority on this topic, but at the same time I'm incredibly grateful to those with information who crossed my path or reached out to me to share what they knew. Without them, there's no story to tell, at least not a very good one.

Many people had something to say, but simply didn't want their names mentioned in connection with such an explosive topic. As I have learned over the course of the last three years, there're many who're willing to look the other way as long as the wrong doing doesn't inconvenience them, or hinder their favorite football team from winning on Saturdays.

They don't want to be involved, but they don't mind

telling you what they've heard as long as there're no personal ramifications for them.

Gossip is quite often the bed partner of good journalism. It's a jumping off point for the truth, anyway.

This story at its core is about college athletics, and how the desire to field a winning team trumped just about everything, including the contents of a person's character. It's about academic fraud, arrogance, betrayal, burner phones, cash payments, cover-ups, lawsuits, lies, looking the other way, manipulation of the media, recruiting through boosters, and eye-roll ignorance. This is a case of reality outstripping a novel.

To summarize, this book is the true story of the false narrative.

At times, I wondered if I'd ever get this book into print and onto bookshelves. Just when I felt like the story was winding down, something new happened, new villains emerged, and the story took a new twist.

I've been threatened with lawsuits, financial ruin and even death. Yes, death. I've been lied about, slandered and conspired against. All of that only providing fuel for the journey, and evidence I was really onto something.

If I'd been wrong, why would they have cared? As the old timers say, "A hit dog hollers."

My hope is you will enjoy the ride this story provides. I believe everyone who's followed the Ole Miss NCAA case understands program-changing sanctions are on the way for the Rebels. By telling this story, I want to give folks an opening and an invitation to take some time and learn more about the twisted tale that brought the Freeze era from the "promised land" to probation.

I made a lot of friends along the way who lightened the

load a bit, and shared the walk for a while. Their cooperation and kindness won't be forgotten.

Many of them provided helpful information, but did so under the condition of anonymity. They simply wanted the truth told. There were lots of things shared that appeared credible, but simply couldn't be proven.

To put it bluntly, there's more to the story than can be told here. Sometimes sources were reluctant to attach their names to information or would only go so far. Whether it be a fear of retaliation, a lack of trust or something else, some sources simply never felt comfortable enough to tell the full story.

I've done my best to share my sources' stories in this book, and I thank them from the bottom of my heart even though, at their requests, their names won't appear in the acknowledgments.

There'll be Ole Miss fans who'll think I've gone too far, but everyone outside of Hotty-Toddy Nation will think I didn't go far enough. I've gone only as far as the facts I can verify will allow.

In some situations, the facts didn't match up with my own suspicions. In others, the facts blew the self-serving spin from Ole Miss defenders into confetti. I've done my best to bring the truth to light, and allow the chips to fall where they may. It's up to you to decide.

It's amazing how adversarial some of the relationships were at the beginning of the writing process, and how in some cases old foes became new allies in the final stages of the book.

I've learned a lot about myself through all of this. My skin's a couple layers thicker. I've also received an education on how hard others will work to conceal the truth, all in the name of college athletics.

Some of the things you read will disappoint you, and likely

cause you to see some people in a new light.

You'll learn new things about open records laws, and the tricks some people will use to get around them.

I never thought I'd write a book about Ole Miss football. It simply wasn't on my radar, but I believe it's important to get an unvarnished view of the facts whenever we can.

While others ran from this story, I saw it as an opportunity. In my opinion, this scandal is one of the biggest sports stories in the Southeastern Conference and one of the most important ones in the history of college athletics. Certainly, in the state of Mississippi.

It's also a story many people didn't want to see the light of day. It's embarrassing for many and redemptive for others.

My sincere hope is this story is both entertaining and informative.

There's a lot to unpack, so let's get to it....

Introduction

A graduate of Mississippi State in 1969 in Agri-Business, daddy went to work for Farmer's Home Administration. When talking about job security, he used to say that there'll always be a need for clothes and food, so there'll always be a need for farmers.

Growing up Robertson, we learned to have a healthy respect for the man who farmed his land and tended his fields for the betterment of the community. It was honest work. It was hard, hot work, and often low paying work, but it was honorable labor.

I still marvel at the lessons my daddy shared growing up as one of Otis Robertson's baker's dozen in tiny Ellisville, Mississippi. For every lesson learned there was a story told.

After spending a couple of years at Jones County Junior College, he headed for Mississippi State. Newly married, my parents lived on campus in marital housing. While many other college students enjoyed a rich social life with frat parties and tailgates, my daddy was up early to run the street sweeper around campus before commuters and professors found their daily parking spaces.

He used to tell me that he felt at home at Mississippi State. He shared with me the love he had for Starkville and the values of the Bulldog family. We were a blue-collar lot who saw value in a solid day's work, dinner on the grounds after Sunday service, and the satisfaction of doing things the right way.

During my childhood years, a Mississippi State game on television was a rarity. We had four channels those years with one of them being the Mississippi Public Broadcast channel. If you wanted to see the Bulldogs play, then you usually had to go see them.

The first Bulldog football game I ever attended in person was November 1, 1980. We beat Bear Bryant and No. 1 Alabama, 6-3. We sat on the Alabama side among the Crimson Tide football parents. Daddy bought three tickets from a scalper just before kick-off.

As a father with children of my own, I can look back on that day and understand why it was so important for him to make those memories with his boys.

Mississippi State freshman quarterback John Bond became my hero that day.

I see John from time to time on the sidelines at State games and sometimes I get a little misty eyed. Daddy's gone now, but when I see John it reminds me of that day. It reminds me why it all means so much. It reminds me of a single father trying to share a memory with his sons.

After seeing Mississippi State end Alabama's 27-game winning streak, and leaving Jackson's Memorial Stadium with a grin from ear to ear, I felt like the Bulldogs were the best team that ever could be. Hollywood could not have written a better scene for a movie script of my life than fate did on that day.

Contents

Dedication

Preface

Introduction

Chapter 1: Turning Back the Tide 1

Chapter 2: Are You Ready? 8

Chapter 3: Freeze Hired, Trouble Brewing 18

Chapter 4: NCAA Enforcement 101 30

Chapter 5: Sifting Through Sources 41

Chapter 6: Catfishing – It's Electric! 52

Chapter 7: Catfish Noodling 67

Chapter 8: Skinning the Catfish 82

Chapter 9: A Voluntary Gag Order 88

Chapter 10: Praying for Peace, Readying for War 104

Chapter 11: One of us was Wrong 120

Chapter 12: Draft Night 130

Photo Album..143

Chapter 13: A New Day and a New Worry 151

Chapter 14: Tunsil-it-is 163

Chapter 15: Red Flags and the Memphis Blues 178

Chapter 16: Hacked 192

Chapter 17: Scapegoat Herding 202

Chapter 18: A Funeral Procession 214

Chapter 19: A Probation for a New Rebel Generation......221

Chapter 20: Robertson vs. The University of Mississippi ...232

Chapter 21: Hot in the Shade 244

Chapter 22: Pushing Forward Back 259

Chapter 23: Freeze Escorted Out 267

Freeze Escort Document 280

Epilogue

Acknowledgments

Chapter 1

Turning Back the Tide

October 4, 2014

With 37 precious seconds left in the game and Vaught-Hemingway Stadium at near capacity, more than 60,000 fans held a collective breath. Hugh Freeze's Ole Miss Rebels were a booth review away from knocking off the No. 1 team in the land — National Champion Alabama.

Not since the days of Eli Manning had those who wore the powder blue been able to enjoy a win over the Crimson Tide.

The Rebels needed a reversal of the on-the-field call ruling Ole Miss senior cornerback Senquez Golson out of bounds with Alabama quarterback, Blake Sims' pass in hand for an interception.

If the Rebs could pull this off, it would cap a nearly perfect day in Oxford.

ESPN brought their "A" team to Oxford for the very first time to broadcast their *College GameDay* show direct from the Grove (the most hallowed of all tailgating grounds, at least to the Ole Miss faithful). Lee Corso sat in the same patch of grass that famed Rebel signal caller Archie Manning strolled across four decades before on his way to class.

Kirk Herbstreit offered his picks with pop superstar Katy Perry. She was invited to Ole Miss as a guest picker to attract publicity for their football program.

The weather was Chamber-of-Commerce quality and expectations on both sides were at an all-time high. Alabama and Ole Miss entered the game with unblemished records at 4-0. Winners of their first in-conference games, both teams were looking for a 2-0 record in the Southeastern Conference, and a solid leg up in the race to Atlanta and the SEC title game.

Atlanta! It's the place no football Rebel has ever been as an SEC Western Division champion. A win over Alabama could pave the way to the gridiron Holy Land of the South with Freeze playing Moses leading the children of Manning out of the captivity of mediocrity.

Could this be the year?

A pair of 4th quarter Bo Wallace touchdown passes had Ole Miss in the lead despite struggling on offense most of the day. The Rebel defense kept the dream alive as they entered the final stanza, down just 17-10.

A 36-yard strike to Vince Sanders helped pull the Rebels even at 17. On the ensuing kickoff, Alabama return man Christion Jones collided with Ole Miss reserve defensive end Channing Ward resulting in a fumble recovered by Kalio Moore. Wallace and the Rebel offense went back on the field.

The possession ended with a 10-yard toss to Jaylen Walton just inside the pylon for the go-ahead score. Alabama was able to block the point after, but still needed a touchdown to win.

Down 23-17, Sims methodically worked the Crimson Tide down the field. What seemed like a dream day was in danger of becoming another "wait-'til next-year" story.

After a rare Alabama holding call, Sims called the cadence on 2nd and 13 from the Ole Miss 32-yard line. The senior quarterback looked to future All-American tight end O.J. Howard, the player flagged for the hold to make the game saving play.

Howard was bracketed on the play with safety Cody Prewitt underneath and Golson playing over the top. Sims' pass sailed long and high; Howard failed to elevate to meet it. The result was Golson appearing to make the game-clinching interception, but Alabama got the call.

As Howard himself called the play incomplete, the back judge signaled in agreement. Golson was ruled out of the end zone nullifying the interception.

The replay booth officials took a second look at the play. Rebel fans were optimistic their guy caught the ball in bounds, but they'd been here before. Long-suffering Rebel fans remember another tight contest between the two programs that was, for all intents and purposes, decided by a booth review.

In 2007 on 4th and 22, Seth Adams laid one up deep inside the Alabama 20-yard line for wide receiver Shay Hodge. Hodge came down with the ball inside the Crimson Tide five-yard line with just seven seconds left.

Trailing 27-24, Ole Miss could've lined up for a game tying field goal or for one more play for all of the marbles. Instead, instant replay official Doyle Jackson, a name still cursed in Oxford, not only overruled the call, he assessed a penalty and the game was over.

Now, seven years later, those same feelings of dread and conspiracy began to well up within the souls of Ole Miss fans who simply knew that the officials were going to do it to them again. The sacred elephant of the SEC, Alabama, would be spared once more.

Just as anxiety began to intersect with "Here we go again," the call came down.

"After further review, the ball was intercepted in the end zone...."

The rest of the message was of no consequence; Ole Miss won! The reigning king of college football, Nick Saban, had been vanquished by a former girls' basketball coach from Tate County, Mississippi. It was the stuff movies were made of.

Ole Miss had just won only its tenth game over Alabama in 120 years of Rebel football, and its first win over a team ranked No. 1.

Rebel fans rushed the field, tore down the goalposts and paraded them around town, reveling in their victory until they simply couldn't take another step.

For a program and fan base that places a premium on pomp and circumstance, the new generation of Rebels had graduated. No longer did they have to hear of the days of yore, they now had their own moment. Freeze had ushered in a "new normal" where the Rebels were no longer an "also ran" in the greatest football conference in all of college football.

They were contenders.

Due to a quirk in the SEC schedule caused by expansion within the league, Alabama avoided a trip to Oxford for two years, 2012 and 2013. The Crimson Tide had not played at Ole Miss since 2011. In that contest, Alabama tuned up the Rebels 52-7.

The Rebels were more competitive in the two games in Tuscaloosa that followed, 33-14 in 2012 and 25-0 in 2013. Yes, the Tide won comfortably in the final margin, but it required a much greater effort than they demonstrated in 2011; Houston Nutt's final year at the helm.

The question that persisted around the conference, and eventually the country, was, "How did they get this good this fast?"

Freeze's first class in Oxford didn't make a lot of headlines on National Signing Day. In fact, the Rebels signed just one player ranked four stars or above - Channing Ward of nearby Aberdeen, Mississippi.

While the 2012 18-man class didn't reap much in the way of national acclaim, the grouping included future quarterback Bo Wallace, NFL wide receiver Cody Core, head-hunting safety Trae Elston, defensive back Mike Hilton, and offensive line contributors Ben Still and Robert Conyers.

There were others who failed to make a noticeable demonstration in the motherland of Oxford, but looking back, the Rebels hit on more than they missed in that first official class under Freeze.

The real face lift for the old girl came on signing day 2013, when a .500 regular season Ole Miss team reeled in perhaps the greatest recruiting class in school history. In the final tally, the Rebels had secured the services of four five-star prospects and seven four-stars as part of their 25 inkings.

The Rebels were no longer just competing for the No. 1 player in their home state or even their border states. Suddenly, Ole Miss was a finalist for the top prospects at their positions nationwide.

Laremy Tunsil, the top prospect in the state of Florida, was also considered the best offensive tackle prospect nationally.

Five-star wide receiver Laquon Treadwell was ranked as the top prospect in his home state of Illinois, and fifth nationally at his position.

Blue chip defensive tackle Robert Nkemdiche was not only the top prospect in Georgia, and the top defensive tackle in the country, the Grayson High School superstar was considered by many to be the top player in the nation, regardless of position.

Five-star Tony Conner of nearby South Panola, an Ole Miss stronghold just 20 minutes down the road from the Oxford campus, inked with the Rebels, too. The talented safety led Ole Miss in tackles with 10 on Oct. 4, 2014, the day that changed everything.

While Conner's college destination came as no real surprise, some of the other decisions raised more than a few eyebrows.

The national recruiting networks rank thousands of college football recruits annually using a five-star system. The higher number of stars, the more talented the prospect projects to be on the college level.

A five-star designation is reserved for the best of the best. Players who look to have real NFL potential are found in this category.

Scout.com awarded just 42 high school prospects a five-star rating for the 2013 signing class, and five of those blue chippers signed with Ole Miss.

Headlines everywhere featured the dazzling stars of the Rebels' new class on that February morning. Only reigning SEC National Champion Alabama inked more five-stars than did the Rebs, signing six.

Freeze's Ole Miss staff signed more five-star players than college blue bloods Florida State University, Louisiana State University, University of Notre Dame, Oklahoma State University, Ohio State University, and Penn State. The 2013 recruiting haul at Ole Miss was a consensus top 10 class.

People took notice.

Who could really blame them? To put things in perspective, Ole Miss has only signed five high school players with a five-star rating in the past 10 years. Suddenly, Freeze and the Rebels weren't just competing with the most storied football programs in America for five-star talents, they were plucking them right out of their own backyards.

Allegations of cheating ran rampant. While there were some who may've had real concrete evidence of wrongdoing, most fans around the SEC simply knew something was amiss. In their minds, there was simply no way a program a year removed from a winless conference slate could entice some of the top college prospects in America to join a team riding the momentum of a 7-6 season and a win in the Birmingham Bowl.

Freeze heard the whispers, and felt the need to respond to the allegations publicly. Rather than simply turning a deaf ear to his accusers, and beating President Trump to the Twitter punch, Freeze turned to Twitter to voice his frustration with the insinuations regarding his program's impressive recruiting haul.

The popular coach certainly found favor with his intended audience. Ole Miss fans were quick to respond to the bravado and defiance of Freeze. The Rebels were emboldened by the brash nature of their coach, who essentially called out his accusers, daring them to suggest that the signing class of 2013 was the result of some shady dealings.

While it played well to the home crowd, Freeze's detractors were all too willing to oblige him on his request. While Freeze maintained that he and his staff were doing things above board, there were more than a few people willing to call his bluff.

The Rebels continued to win and recruit at a high level, and Ole Miss fans were more than willing to stand behind the coach that had given them reason to be proud. They were all too willing to go along with the narrative that Ole Miss is simply a magical place where legends are born.

In their minds, the Rebels had arrived and they were ready for their moment in the SEC sun. Even if the story was a little too good to be true, it was time for a new generation of Ole Miss fans to have their moment.

Cheers for "Hotty Toddy" never had more gusto. The phrase became more than just a school tradition. It became a rallying cry to many and simply signified now was the time.

Chapter 2

Are you Ready?
....
Hell Yeah! Damn Right!
Hotty Toddy, Gosh Almighty,
Who The Hell Are We? Hey!
Flim Flam, Bim Bam
Ole Miss By Damn!

I suppose all college football programs have their own rallying cries that are unique and special to their supporters. In Alabama, the state is split down the middle with half of the population yelling "Roll Tide," and the other "War Eagle."

In the Mississippi of my youth, the Magnolia State had three passionate groups of fans. "The Big Three," Mississippi State, Ole Miss, and Southern Mississippi, own the allegiances of most Mississippi residents.

Each program had their own traditions, but attempts to market the respective universities led to official declarations to give each school an identity of its own.

Mississippi State branded itself with "Hail State" in the past decade as an ode to the Bulldog fight song by the same name penned back in 1939 by Joseph Burleson Peavey.

The Golden Eagles of Southern Miss followed a similar path to nomenclature by taking the first line of their fight song from 1955 "Southern to the Top" and modernized it to "Southern Miss to the Top."

The longest standing in-state tradition for a school cheer or unofficial greeting among fans belongs to Ole Miss. The phrase "Hotty Toddy" is synonymous with the Rebels.

For as long as I can remember, I've seen the phrase on bumper stickers, buttons, pendants, and T-shirts. I have heard it more times than I can count.

While the Bulldogs and Golden Eagles can easily trace the history of their athletic mottos to their respective band halls, Ole Miss' famous phrase provides a little more mystery.

Hotty Toddy, in effect, refers to the full cheer that Rebel fans use to identify one of their own.

"Are you ready?"

While legend is often more fun than fact, the first official record of the cheer appeared in the Ole Miss student newspaper, *The Daily Mississippian,* in November 1926.

That rough draft of sorts began "Heighty, Tighty" in the same vein as Virginia Tech's Regimented Cadet Band who began operating with the nickname "Highty Tighties" in the early 1900s. The Hokies also had a football cheer encouraging their ball carriers to hold the ball "high and tight."

Any witnesses to the genesis of the Ole Miss cheer have long since passed on, so we're all left to conjecture rather than fact. The roots of Hotty Toddy may lie in Blacksburg, Virginia, but all we have to base that on are our assumptions and some deductive reasoning.

In both the original and current version of the cheer the phrase "Flim Flam" appears. A rather strange inclusion in a college cheer to say the least.

Merriam-Webster defines Flim Flam as "deceptive nonsense or deception, fraud."

The phrase dates back to Scandinavian origins as early as the 1500s. Throughout history, the one word or two-word forms both signify deceptive practices.

So why is it in the cheer?

While there is no official explanation, the common school of thought is that Flim Flam simply fit the rhyming pattern for the cheer that already had the final line written, "Ole Miss by Damn."

Flim Flam once followed the phrase "Rim Ram" in the original cheer and now precedes "Bim Bam" in the modern version.

While Rim Ram alone has little in the way of an actual definition, Rim Ram Ruf is defined in the Oxford dictionary, of all places, as "clumsy or unsophisticated poetry."

Alternatively, "Bim Bam" can be traced back to the German word bimbam as the sound that Hell's bells make similar to the English phrase "Ding Dong."

There may've been no intended double entendre or secret meaning to any of it. In the end, the author may've simply thrown it all together, because in his or her mind it just sounded right.

Over the years, Heighty Tighty gave way to Hotty Toddy and Bim Bam replaced Rim Ram, but Flim Flam has stood the test of time. Rebel fans have shouted "Flim Flam" for generations. Given the current state of affairs, it seems ironic that fans of a college football team would cheer for deceptive practices.

While many have no idea what they're yelling, there's a segment of the Ole Miss fan base that has no problem wearing the "black hat" if that's what it takes for their beloved Rebels to have on-the-field success.

By and large there's been no shortage of Rebel boosters ready to step up and aid in the Ole Miss recruiting efforts. Rather than just put on a powder blue polo shirt and cheer, some choose to involve themselves in the business of benefits for student athletes and run afoul of NCAA rules.

There has been a laundry list of dirty deeds alleged:

Allegations of improper contact between boosters and recruits.

Charges of boosters providing clothing, gifts, lodging, and meals.

Talk of a booster possibly providing an automobile to a recruit.

An Ole Miss staffer reportedly offering cash in hopes of getting a prospect to commit.

Arrangements for a deferred loan and a loaner car.

Unethical conduct by the head football coach and lack of institutional control.

Pretty serious stuff for 2017, but how about for 1994?

What you've just read are most of the charges levied at Ole Miss in their mid '90s appearance before the NCAA's Committee on Infractions, their second in 10 years. Throw in some trips to a Memphis strip club and you have a pretty good understanding of what Coach Billy Brewer's Rebels were accused of doing.

When the final verdict was read, Ole Miss got absolutely hammered.

The NCAA placed the Rebels on probation for four years, banned the program from post season play for two years (1995 and 1996), prohibited Ole Miss from playing on television for the 1995 season, and cut both scholarships and official visits. A pair of Rebel boosters were disassociated and Brewer received a four-year show cause. A "show cause" penalty is handed down by the NCAA for administrators, coaches, and staffers who've been found to have committed major violations of NCAA by-laws. The penalty essentially prevents a coach from simply leaving the school facing sanctions for greener pastures with another program.

While not a ban per se, the show cause penalty makes it incredibly difficult for coaches to slip out the back door of one school and avoiding personal sanctions for wrong doing and accepting a job at another school.

In fact, a new school would have to appear before the Committee on Infractions to show cause why an individual should be or could be hired at that institution. More times than not, schools simply avoid these candidates and find other coaches not under the scrutiny of the NCAA enforcement staff.

After 11 seasons, five bowl appearances and two NCAA cases, Brewer was finished at Ole Miss.

Brewer, who played for former Ole Miss coaching legend Johnny Vaught, coached the final game of his 22-year career on the road at Mississippi State, a 20-13 loss, ending the 1993 season with a 6-5 record.

When the Committee on Infractions delivered its final report on November 17, 1994, Brewer and his boss, Athletic Director Warner Alford, were both long gone.

Alford resigned, but then University of Mississippi Chancellor Dr. Gerald Turner, the former NCAA chairman of the sub-committee for Presidential Leadership of Internal and External Constituencies, fired Brewer after two major NCAA cases during his tenure as the Ole Miss head football coach.

It took Ole Miss less than two weeks to file their appeal in an attempt to lessen the sanctions leveled at their football program. The legal challenge suggested that penalties were "harsh" and "unwarranted."

The chairperson of the NCAA Infractions Appeals Committee was a gentleman by the name of Michael L. Slive (later became commissioner of the SEC).

In the final report, the overwhelming majority of penalties were upheld. The committee wrote:

"Imposing significant penalties in this case provides a clear message to the institution, its athletics department administration and the representatives of its athletics interests that any repeat violations of NCAA rules will cause great harm to the institution and its football program. It also serves to deter staff members, student-athletes and friends and supporters of other institutions from becoming involved in activities that might harm the programs that they wish to assist."

The NCAA clearly wanted to send a message to Ole Miss and others that the enforcement process was to be taken seriously.

One of the factors noted in the appeals committee's decision was the similarity in the infractions from the 1986 case and the one being sanctioned in 1994.

In the '86 final report, Ole Miss was placed on two years of probation, banned from post season play in both 1987 and 1988.

The alleged transgressions involved cash benefits, clothing, transportation and free football camps at Ole Miss. Investigators uncovered more of the same types of violations in the case that ultimately unseated Brewer.

It was clear there was a pattern of behavior when it came to recruiting the Rebel way and the NCAA aimed to change that.

Two years after Alford and Brewer left their posts in Oxford, Chancellor Turner would follow suit.

With declining enrollment and trouble afoot with the Rebel football program, Ole Miss turned to one of their own, Robert Khayat, to help them right the ship and navigate the University into calmer waters.

Khayat, a Mississippi native, was a two-sport star at Ole Miss during his college career earning All-SEC honors for his play on the baseball diamond and named an Academic All-American in football as the Rebels' kicker.

Once his professional football career with the Washington Redskins was over, Khayat earned a law degree and opened a legal practice on the Mississippi Gulf Coast before returning to Ole Miss as a law professor.

The Moss Point, Mississippi, product would leave Oxford

twice over the next decade; once in 1980-81 to earn a Masters' Degree from Yale and again in 1989 when he was named President of the NCAA Foundation.

Three years later, as NCAA investigators were closing in on the Ole Miss football program once again, Khayat returned to Oxford to take a position with the Ole Miss law school.

In 1995, Khayat was named the 15th Chancellor of the University of Mississippi, a post he'd hold until his retirement in 2009.

When legendary SEC commissioner Roy Kramer announced his retirement, Khayat was mentioned as a possible replacement to sit in the big chair in the big office in Birmingham, Alabama.

While Khayat withdrew his name from consideration, he found himself on the search advisory committee charged with finding the right candidate to continue the successes of the Southeastern Conference.

Many believed that SEC Associate Commissioner Mark Womack was a shoe-in for the job as he'd served as one of Kramer's most loyal lieutenants. Womack had served the league since 1978 and had tons of support, but in the end the league went outside of its headquarters for its new leader, Michael Slive.

Slive had plenty of experience. An attorney by trade, the Utica, New York, native served as the first commissioner of The Great Midwest Conference from 1991 to 1995.

In 1995, Slive was named the first commissioner of Conference-USA, a position he held for nearly eight years before being tabbed as the new SEC boss in 2002.

Slive took over as the SEC commish in July of 2002. His tenure ended on July 31, 2015.

With Slive's wealth of experience with the NCAA enforcement process after serving on various committees, including the Infractions Appeals Committee, it appeared that the folks from the land of "sure everybody cheats" were about to learn that there was a new sheriff in town.

There were twelve schools in the SEC when Slive took the job. He vowed to clean up the league's outlaw image and ensure that NCAA by-laws were followed to the letter.

During the Slive era, 10 of the initial dozen programs under his supervision spent some time on the NCAA naughty list. Only two SEC schools avoided probation during the time Slive served as SEC commissioner: Vanderbilt, who has just one infractions case in school history, and you guessed it, Ole Miss.

Despite those 13 years of maximum allowable scholarships free from NCAA scrutiny, the Rebels couldn't take advantage. In fact, Ole Miss had more losing seasons (seven) during this stretch as they did winning campaigns (six); only posting a winning record in-conference just three times (2003, 2008, 2014).

The SEC split the conference into two divisions in 1992. Every charter member of the league's Western division has appeared in the SEC Title Game in Atlanta, except for one... Ole Miss.

The frustration associated with getting close in 2003 only to see Eli Manning trip on offensive lineman Doug Buckles' foot on the Rebels' final offensive snap against LSU has left a lasting memory.

Back-to-back Cotton Bowl wins under Coach Houston Nutt appeared to signal brighter days ahead. Instead, the Rebels would win just one SEC game over the course of the next two seasons leading to a coaching change.

To make matters worse, the Golden Egg, and all of the bragging rights that go with it, had resided in Starkville on the campus of Mississippi State for three straight years.

Coach Dan Mullen had arrived on the scene brash and full of bravado refusing to call Ole Miss by their desired name. That "Yankee" dubbed the Rebels "The School Up North" and beat them on the field home and away.

The Bulldogs' three-game winning streak was the longest streak for State in the series since the 1940s when Coach Allyn McKeen's teams beat the Rebels four straight times from 1939-1942.

Mullen found a way to get under the Rebel skin cheering every Bulldog win over Ole Miss regardless of the sport. If the Mississippi State scrabble club earned a victory over somebody in an Ole Miss pullover, the Bulldog football coach tweeted his support and feelings of solidarity.

Maroon and White billboards popped up all over Mississippi declaring the Magnolia State Bulldog country in a very unique way. One of the first scenes travelers saw as they crossed the state line was a picture of Mullen waving and welcoming folks to "Our State."

Needless to say, these advertisements didn't sit well with the Ole Miss faithful. It was bad enough that the Bulldogs had the better of it on the football field, but Rebel fans couldn't even drive to work without being reminded of it.

Something had to be done.

The momentum in state had shifted in a major way towards Mississippi State, and Bulldog fans were feeling their oats. The Rebels had to do something to counter.

Enter Rebel legend Archie Manning. Manning would be the co-chair of the Ole Miss search committee assembled to hire a football coach to change the culture and direction of the football program.

While it seemed like a foregone conclusion long before the committee was announced on 11-11-11, Coach Hugh Freeze was eventually hired as the 37th head football coach at the

University of Mississippi.

A native of Independence, Mississippi, and a graduate of Southern Mississippi, Freeze was a hot name after a 10-2 season and Sunbelt Conference Championship at Arkansas State in 2011.

A former Ole Miss assistant under Coach Ed Orgeron from 2005 to 2007, Freeze knew Ole Miss and Ole Miss knew him. He understood the culture and as a Mississippian he understood the expectations.

For better or worse, the Rebels had their man. Danny Hugh Freeze Jr. would look to lead Ole Miss into the promised land of college football.

Chapter 3

Freeze Hired, Trouble Brewing

When Hugh Freeze accepted the head coaching position at Ole Miss, trouble was already brewing around the football program. There were some academic concerns about a few of the Rebel signees that had already made the rounds, and the late decisions of blue chip players left some looking at the Ole Miss program with a little suspicion.

A handful of football recruits, mostly from out of state, who had inked with Ole Miss during Houston Nutt's tenure had shown up at The Education Center in Jackson, Mississippi, a school without residence halls, to take the steps necessary to earn their certification by the NCAA Clearinghouse.

The clearinghouse process is not just a rubber stamp deal. Each college bound prospect must have an acceptable grade point average in sixteen core courses determined by the NCAA and a corresponding standardized test to gain clearance.

The NCAA clearinghouse reviews the transcripts and test scores of all players who signed a national letter of intent to ensure that they meet NCAA entrance requirements.

Some prospects elect to take these courses in a non-traditional classroom setting, which was the case with this group of college football hopefuls bound for Oxford.

Where would they live? Who would prepare their meals? How would they get back and forth for classes? Perhaps the best question of all was: How did this all come to be? Just weeks after finishing up their senior seasons on the field, these signees were in Jackson for the spring semester.

In addition to the eyebrows raised about the players attending the Ed Center, rumors began to circulate about out-of-state Ole Miss recruits electing to take the ACT in tiny Waynesboro, Mississippi. One could possibly understand a home-state player making that move, but why would players from as far away as Florida and Georgia go to the expense and trouble of taking a standardized test in small town Mississippi hours from home?

None of that seemed to matter on Dec. 5, 2011, as Freeze was introduced to a packed house at Ford Center on the Ole Miss campus.

When it was clear there'd be a changing of the guard on the Rebel sidelines, many Ole Miss fans threw out high profile names like Mike Leach, Jon Gruden, and many others as potential coaching candidates.

Freeze was a bit of a dark horse candidate, but one who moved the needle with many due to his previous recruiting successes under former Coach Ed Orgeron. His remarkable one-year turnaround at Arkansas State ended with a 2011 Sunbelt Conference championship and the Red Wolves' first bowl appearance since 2005.

Ironically, when Orgeron was sacked following the 2007 season, Freeze stayed on as the "transition" coach as Nutt's staff got acclimated to Oxford. Weeks later, Nutt elected not to retain Freeze. As fate would have it, Nutt would be replaced by the very coach he was reluctant to keep.

With private talk of sins on the recruiting trail by Nutt's staff still smoldering, Freeze was brought in to redeem the Rebels. Part of that redemption involved winning the Golden Egg trophy away from Mississippi

State. The Egg symbolized in-state supremacy, and that spoils of rivalry games had resided at Mississippi State for three straight years.

Freeze was no stranger to the importance of winning that Magnolia State blood feud, on and off of the field. In the final game of the Orgeron era at Ole Miss, Freeze stood helpless on the sidelines as five-star defensive back Derek Pegues, a player Rebel fans expected to sign with Ole Miss, returned a fourth quarter punt for the Bulldogs that led to a come-from-behind victory sending State to the Liberty Bowl and Coach O and his staff to the unemployment line.

Being relieved of his duties was a new experience for Freeze, who'd been a successful football coach at Briarcrest Christian School in Memphis, Tennessee, for 13 years, and the last decade as the Saints' head man.

The program experienced some unprecedented success in the final years of Freeze's tenure winning a pair of state championships in 2002 and 2004.

Big-time results only come as a result of big-time players. A pair of Freeze's seniors, kicker Justin Sparks and five-star All-American offensive tackle Michael Oher, signed with Ole Miss on Feb. 2, 2005.

Three weeks later, in a move that would be impermissible today due to new NCAA legislation, Freeze was hired by Ole Miss as an off-the-field football staffer. The official title on the new business cards was Assistant Athletics Director for Football External Affairs.

On Feb. 1, 2006, the Rebels would sign another Briarcrest star in defensive end Greg Hardy.

Nine days later, Hardy's former high school coach, Freeze, was promoted to an on-the-field coaching position at Ole Miss. The following week, it was learned not only would Freeze coach the tight ends, he would also serve as the program's recruiting coordinator.

In about 15 months' time, Freeze walked out of Vanderbilt Stadium with a 24-0 state championship win over Evangelical Christian School, and then moved into an assistant coaching position in the SEC where he was responsible for helping the head honcho find football players to compete in America's toughest football conference.

While that run in Oxford was short lived—just three seasons—and provided forgettable results, many Ole Miss fans found themselves enamored with Freeze. Many remembered how badly he wanted to stay on and hoped at some point down the road their paths would cross again.

Freeze may not have been the Rebels' first choice to replace Nutt, but he was determined to prove he was the right choice, and the experiences gained in his time away from Oxford in recent years had prepared him for a successful run as the head man.

With a handful of assistants following Freeze from Arkansas State to Ole Miss, the task of piecing together a recruiting class in the final weeks proved to be very difficult.

There were 18 new Rebels in the first "official" class under the new head coach. Scout.com ranked the new haul as the 58th best class in the country - good for dead last in the Southeastern Conference for the 2012 recruiting cycle.

Had local hero, and five-star defensive end Channing Ward of Aberdeen, signed elsewhere, Ole Miss would not have signed a single player who garnered more than a three-star rating.

Rebel fans were hopeful, but to be fair, that wasn't

a lot to feel good about. Ole Miss had not won an SEC football game since knocking off Kentucky on Oct. 2, 2010.

The 2011 Rebels won just three games and went winless in the league. In fact, Nutt's tenure ended with seven consecutive losses including a 20-point loss at home to Louisiana Tech, a 52-3 blowout loss to Louisiana State University on the Rebels' senior day, and a four-touchdown whipping at the hands of Mississippi State, 31-3.

People were aware a rebuilding process was in place, but having some successes on the recruiting trail had to be a big part of that.

Just as fans were getting their hopes up about the 2012 football season, it was announced that former four-star and U. S. Army All-American wide out Tobias Singleton was leaving the program.

Singleton wasn't the only defection. Earlier in the year, Freeze announced blue chip wide receiver Nickolas Brassell wouldn't return after the spring semester. Days after the Singleton news was official, offensive lineman Mitch Hall declared his intentions to transfer to Missouri.

Not only were the Rebels struggling to add talent to their roster, beaten down by two years of misery, they were seeing departures from players expected to aid in the program's rebuild.

Good, bad or indifferent, Ole Miss was going to play football for Hugh Freeze in 2012. Expectations were tempered, at best, when fall camp began. But, Rebel fans were happy to have some on-the-field news to look forward to.

The Rebels began the season with four straight non-conference games and came out the other side with a 3-1 record. The lone blemish was a 66-31 route on the road at Texas.

Ole Miss lost to Alabama and Texas A&M in back-to-back weeks as a reminder there was still some steps to take. But optimism soared after SEC wins against Auburn and Arkansas brought the Rebel season record to 5-3 with four games to play.

Freeze and his staff were just a win away from bowl eligibility in their first season in Oxford, a feat that anyone with a Red and Blue argyle sweater vest on their Christmas list would gladly take.

A road loss to Georgia didn't help, but narrow misses against Vanderbilt and LSU gave fans hope that better days lay ahead.

Archrival Mississippi State rolled into Oxford nationally ranked. The Bulldogs began the season with seven straight wins, but found some adversity in the back half of their SEC schedule.

Cowbell clangors of the world hoped that a 45-14 blowout over Arkansas the week before had given their team confidence. It was their chance to win a fourth consecutive Egg Bowl.

Mississippi State wasn't able to capitalize on some of the early Ole Miss turnovers, and a strong second half by quarterback Bo Wallace gave the Rebels their sixth win and a bowl berth.

The win returned the Golden Egg to Rebel hands. Ole Miss fans rushed the field in celebration. There was joy in Oxford. Freeze was a hero, and there was hope for brighter days ahead.

Ole Miss defeated Pittsburgh in the Birmingham Bowl, 38-17, ensuring the Rebels a winning season for the first time since 2009. With just four weeks until National

Signing Day, Freeze and his staff had momentum. They also had a ton of work to do to improve their talent level and make a run up the SEC standings in years to come.

It looked like Ole Miss had positioned themselves for a strong close, but just how good? The Rebels were among the finalists for many of the nation's top talents, but was a .500 regular season and a minor bowl win enough to lure true blue chippers to Oxford, Mississippi?

Some steps had been taken in previous recruiting classes to give the Rebs more than a puncher's chance when it came to prize fighting for some of the top talents at their respective positions for the 2013 signing class.

Interestingly enough, a pair of late signees in both the 2011 and 2012 signing classes gave Ole Miss some solid connections and real insight into the courtship of two of the top players nationally, five-star wide receiver LaQuon Treadwell of Crete, Illinois, and the nation's top prospect five-star defensive end Robert Nkemdiche of Loganville, Georgia.

Houston Nutt and his staff had the forethought to sign Nkemdiche's older brother, Denzel Nkemdiche as part of their 2011 recruiting haul. A late academic qualifier, the elder Nkemdiche inked with Ole Miss in May of 2011, more than three months after national signing day. That decision would later pay dividends for Freeze and his staff when they began their efforts to land the consensus No. 1 player in the 2013 talent pool.

Nearly a year later, Crete-Monee High School corner Anthony Standifer elected to join the Ole Miss roster as part of the 2012 class. Despite reported "offers" from nearly two dozen programs including Northwestern, Notre Dame and Pittsburgh. Somehow the 6-1, 180-pound corner went unsigned until he elected to accept an offer from the Rebels a month after national signing day.

A close friend and former high school teammate of Treadwell, Standifer helped get Ole Miss into the game with the highly touted pass catcher who was already considered one of the big fish in the 2013 recruiting pond.

Just down the road from the Ole Miss campus on Highway 6, five-star safety Antonio Conner had the Rebels sweating just a bit. Conner was a product of South Panola High School - a perennial state champion program, and considered by most around the state of Mississippi as an Ole Miss stronghold.

Unlike many of his Batesville, Mississippi, peers before him, Conner elected to forego an early verbal declaration to Ole Miss and simply wait out the process. While the Rebels were considered a favorite from start to finish, the hard-hitting safety took official visits to Alabama and Mississippi State in addition to his trip to Oxford. In fact, the Bulldogs hosted Conner the weekend before signing day.

It made sense that the Rebels would be a factor with Conner, Nkemdiche and Treadwell due to personal connections. The talented trio all had friends on the inside at Ole Miss who could tell them about life and times as a college football player at the University of Mississippi.

As the process moved forward, Freeze and his staff suddenly became a real threat to the University of Georgia, and the Bulldogs' chances of signing the nation's top offensive tackle, Laremy Tunsil, a five-star blind side protector from Lake City, Florida.

The late rush from the Rebels appeared to come out of nowhere. Long considered a Georgia "lean" Tunsil's decision provided some real intrigue down the stretch. The Columbia High School product took official visits to

Alabama, Georgia, and Ole Miss in the final weeks before making his decision official.

Prior to making his first ever trip to Oxford, Tunsil made a return trip to Athens, Georgia, where he was hosted by future NFL running back Todd Gurley.

The weekend before, Tunsil and his mother sat down across the table from Coach Nick Saban and discussed playing for national titles and preparing for a professional football career.

On signing day, Tunsil signed with Ole Miss, citing his relationship with Rebel assistant coach Chris Kiffin and an eye-opening visit to the Ole Miss campus.

Following Tunsil to Oxford was Conner, Nkemdiche and Treadwell. Freeze and his staff closed with a flurry of four five-stars and drew national attention for their sudden recruiting prowess.

A program that struggled to land a class in the top half of college football was now the talk of college football after signing a top 10 class a year later.

In addition to the four late five-star additions, the Rebels flipped four-star offensive lineman Austin Golson out of Prattville, Alabama, away from intentions with Florida State.

Former Clemson commitment cornerback David Kamara of Buford High (Georgia), the same high school as the Nkemdiche brothers, chose the Rebels over Kentucky.

In the days prior, four star running back Jordan Wilkins of Cordova, Tennessee, chose Ole Miss over reported offers from Alabama, Auburn, Michigan, and home-state options from both Tennessee and Vanderbilt.

Wilkins joined one of Mississippi's top running backs, Kailo Moore, in the Rebel class. Moore, a long-time Mississippi State commitment, was the subject of rumors throughout the process.

The West Bolivar High School standout denied the back room whispers all the way up until the moment he committed to Ole Miss.

All told, the Rebel coaching staff signed 11 of scout. com's top 300 players. It was an impressive undertaking. Fresh off of a mediocre season with just six regular season wins, Ole Miss was going head-to-head with the big boys of college football and beating them on the recruiting trail.

The Rebs had both attention and momentum. Social media was a flood of mixed messages from people both impressed and suspicious. Ole Miss fans soaked in the moment and took pride in the fact that they were the center of attention again even if it came with a few raised eyebrows.

While the four- and five-star boys fueled the Rebel rise up the recruiting rankings, we later learned that some less heralded prospects were about to be caught up in some drama that'd prove to be a major concern for all involved.

Ole Miss was already recruiting against the back drop of an NCAA investigation in multiple sports including football, but on Feb. 6, 2013, none of that seemed to register.

As the Red and Blue faithful gathered at signing day parties around the state to celebrate their day in the sun, a storm was brewing close to home and close to Freeze.

When Freeze first arrived in Oxford he worked for Orgeron, who was determined to build a proverbial fence around Memphis in an effort to land the town's top talents. Perhaps Freeze's connections and experience in the River City played a role in his first opportunity on the college level.

Now, some of those ties to the city that Elvis Presley called home were under scrutiny. The NCAA had already been asking questions and the probe was about to grow in a major way.

The Plantation wasn't on fire just yet, but the brush fires on the back forty were nearly out of control. The overwhelming majority of Ole Miss fans had no clue what was taking place behind the scenes, and there was little effort being exerted to uncover it.

Many wondered how a head football coach with just two years' experience on the FBS level as a program CEO could be such a quick study in major college recruiting. How could Freeze attract top shelf talent to a program with six losing seasons in the past decade?

Even the great Eli Manning struggled to win big at Ole Miss. During Manning's four years in Oxford, the Rebels won more than seven games just once in 2003 and struggled to recruit at a high level despite having the best signal caller in a generation on campus.

Manning seemed like ancient history as Freeze became a media darling. TV and Radio personalities were all too eager to hear the stories of how Ole Miss went from an SEC also ran to rising contender. By hook or by crook, the Rebels were back in business.

Chapter 4

NCAA Enforcement 101

Most fans of college athletics only have a passing interest in NCAA enforcement. It is safe to say that the average fan has a very a limited understanding of how the investigative process works.

Having a level playing field is paramount in sports. Rules are in place for a reason; to protect the integrity of the game. Winning and losing are part of competition, but all participants want to be sure that they had a fair opportunity in the contest.

While headlines are made when news breaks regarding the existence of an on-going investigation, or when the final report is issued and the sanctions are handed down, there are always people at work behind the scenes to get the truth.

Message board and social media trolls thrive on a juicy rumor, but the men and women of the NCAA enforcement staff are searching for the truth in all matters involving intercollegiate sports.

For much of the past three decades, one of those fact finders has been David Didion. Now in his second tour of duty in the compliance office at Auburn University, Didion has seen the best and worst of times for the NCAA enforcement division.

Didion served as an NCAA Director of Enforcement from 1987 until April of 2013 when he left to return to Auburn. Over the course of his tenure in Indianapolis, the Ohio State graduate had his fingerprints on several major infractions cases.

One case of interest to fans of the Southeastern Conference would likely be the probe into the Tennessee's men's basketball program and former head coach Bruce Pearl. Didion was the lead investigator on that case that ended with the Volunteers on probation and with a three-year show cause penalty for Pearl.

Just over a year after Auburn hired Didion to head its compliance efforts, the Tigers hired Pearl to revive a struggling men's basketball program. Before Auburn athletics director, Jay Jacobs, made a serious play for Pearl, he checked with Didion.

Known as a hard-nosed administrator with strict standards for compliance, Didion reportedly gave the green light on the Tigers' pursuit of Pearl.

While the on the court results to date may not have been exactly what Auburn fans have been hoping for, Pearl has kept his nose clean and the Tigers free from the crosshairs of the NCAA.

I reached out to Didion to bring credibility and show the seriousness of the NCAA allegations I've outlined in this book. While I am sure many would enjoy reading old "war stories" from days gone by, I was mostly interested in the NCAA side of things as it relates to an enforcement case.

Four years removed from his post as NCAA police chief, Didion now makes it clear that his code of ethics remains in place. Any talk of cases that he may have investigated throughout his career remained safely off limits.

My quest for knowledge centered on the investigative process from start to finish behind the closed doors of the NCAA. Just how does an enforcement case begin? Who decides which cases to pursue and what does that process entail?

"The rumor and innuendo has to be backed up by some facts," Didion said. "There has to be some corroboration and a lot of it. It just sort of comes up from the incoming information heap.

"The director and the department head get together and they decide that this looks like it warrants an investigation, so they make it an active case and begin looking into it."

An enforcement case is only as good as the evidence that supports it. Many times, that information is obtained from student athletes and coaches who are subject to NCAA bylaws. All such individuals have a duty to cooperate with investigators.

The situation gets a little more complicated when third parties are involved. Private citizens cannot be sanctioned by the NCAA, so their involvement in the process is undependable.

"It really depends on how powerfully you can persuade people," Didion explained. "If you have the power of persuasion and people can help you, then they will. If you don't, they won't.

"One way to do it is to go through the University and get help from the university if it is someone that is recognized as their athletic booster or their athletics representative.

"You can ask the university for their help to compel that person to cooperate with the investigation."

The matter can be complicated further by fans of athletic programs that have no direct ties to the university. Third parties who never purchase season tickets or never make financial contributions to the school can be more difficult to track down.

"Sometimes it's someone who is not known by the institution," Didion said. "They may not be a booster or a representative. It may be just a fan or just somebody who wants to get involved. They may want to provide benefits to somebody.

"The only way you can get them to cooperate is through the power of persuasion. You can't always compel somebody like that to help you."

When it comes down to the student-athletes, their cooperation with the enforcement staff is mandatory. A player can't simply plead the fifth and refuse to answer difficult questions.

"The student athletes have a duty to cooperate," Didion said. "If they decide that they're not going to tell the truth in an investigation, then that is up to them.

"You can explain to the student athletes and you can explain to their families what the ramifications are. If they are interviewed by a representative from the NCAA or from a conference and they choose not to provide truthful information, it will have an impact on their eligibility. It absolutely will.

"That has to be a reason for them to cooperate, but sometimes they don't. If they choose not to provide truthful information, then that's the risk that they run if they chose to go down that path."

In some instances, the NCAA enforcement staff can provide student athletes who may be unwilling to talk about sensitive issues with a grant of limited immunity. This step permits the athlete to come clean about potential violations without the possibility of reprisal from the enforcement staff provided that the information from the athlete is accurate.

"If the NCAA has reason to believe that the student athlete knows some information but is reluctant to cooperate, then the NCAA can speak with that student athlete and his family about limited immunity," Didion said.

"If the student athlete agrees to a situation with limited immunity, then the NCAA representative has to go to the Committee on Infractions and request limited immunity. They have to present the reason why they are requesting limited immunity. The Committee on Infractions has to approve that arrangement.

"If they do, then the student athlete understands that

anything that he or she says is not going to be held against them as far as their eligibility is concerned, but they have to tell the complete and the whole truth.

"If they withhold information or they don't provide the complete truth, then they are still eligible to be charged with unethical conduct for failure to cooperate or for providing false or misleading information."

Didion reports that the process of seeking a grant of limited immunity for a student athlete is neither a frequent or rare occurrence. The long-time NCAA staffer does share that the penalties for athletes who fail to uphold their end of the arrangement are extremely serious in nature. An athlete's eligibility can be reduced or completely revoked.

As part of the interview process, the school being investigated can have representatives present during questioning. In some cases, member institutions are active partners in fact finding even before a formal investigation is launched.

"The institution can be involved from the start if they are aware that there are questions being asked about the institution's program," Didion shared. "Nothing rises to the level of an allegation until there is serious information that develops. It's the kind of information that people consider when conducting serious affairs. It has to be reliable, it has to be probative and it has to be complete.

"It can't be just information like 'Oh, I heard this happened'. It has to be more than that. It has to be substantial information.

"When it gets to that point that there is an indication that a violation occurred, then it's likely that the enforcement staff is going to come forward with an allegation."

The formal process of compiling a Notice of Allegations to an NCAA member institution is not a casual undertaking.

The results of the investigative process are reviewed by both the Director of Enforcement and the lead investigator assigned to the case before an actual charge of wrong doing is made against the University.

After the allegations are forwarded to the University, there is a response from the school answering the charges made against them. The NCAA enforcement staff will then respond to the school's defense and a hearing before the Committee on Infractions is set.

There is no negotiation between the Committee and the school. There is no plea bargain. There is no chance to turn state's evidence in hopes of lessening sanctions.

In fact, there is no communication between the Committee and the University until the hearing begins.

"They are not involved with the investigation in anyway unless there is a request for limited immunity," Didion said of the committee. "In that case, their involvement is just for that issue.

"Once the enforcement staff completes the Notice of Allegations, the notice is then sent to the institution and the committee on infractions at the same time.

"The Committee on Infractions will receive all of the supporting information that the enforcement staff relies on. They will receive the institution's response. They will receive the enforcement staff's position on that response and any information that the institution wants to provide after that as well.

"All they know is what is presented after the Notice of Allegations. They don't know anything before that. They are armed with the information from the enforcement staff and from the institution when they come into the hearing room to commence the hearing."

Multiple parties have told me that the hearing before the

Committee on Infractions is an extremely difficult day. There aren't many friends in the room and unlike a court of law, there is no presumption of innocence.

Yes, the enforcement staff has to make their case, but the NCAA is a voluntary organization. Administrators, coaches and student athletes are well aware of bylaws regarding their conduct long before any charges are made.

"It's really serious," Didion said. "You're there because it's a serious matter to be considered by the Committee on Infractions. There is a lot at stake for the people in the room.

"For coaches, it's their reputation and their livelihood. For the institution, it's their reputation and their ability to continue to field teams to win championships. For the enforcement staff, it's to make sure that all of their information is considered by the Committee on Infractions and that all of the information they want to share and every position they want to take is known by the committee.

"They want to provide everyone a full and complete opportunity to be heard. It's a pretty serious atmosphere."

Once both the enforcement staff and the member institution have had a chance to present their arguments to the committee, the hearing concludes and deliberations begin.

"The committee goes off on their own. They're sequestered from everybody," Didion explained. "The enforcement staff has no role to play in developing a penalty or making a finding.

"The only role the enforcement staff has is to bring up the evidence that has been collected, to present their arguments and then let the Committee on Infractions take it from there.

"The committee goes off by themselves and they deliberate on everything that they've heard. They deliberate on all of the evidence that they have been presented and then they decide if they are going to make findings of violations.

"If they do, then they are going to decide what the penalties are going to be, but they do that on their own. "

The process of determining fair and just penalties has been simplified. In years past, schools complained that sanctions were not uniformly applied. In 2013, the NCAA rolled out a new penalty structure that made the process less arbitrary and provided schools what amounts to a plug and play matrix that removes much of the mystery.

"They wanted to provide some consistency with penalties that the Committee on Infractions levied," Didion said. "In addition to case precedent, they will look to see what the severity of the penalty was, whether there were mitigating circumstances or aggravating circumstances. They will come up with a reasonable penalty based on that circumstance and the consistent application of the rule."

Over the course of the last few years, the NCAA has looked to reinvent itself. Employee attrition, lawsuits and a change in leadership has brought reform to an organization looking to convince its membership that it means business.

Didion shares that the enforcement staff underwent a facelift, but that there are still some challenges that face the "New and Improved" NCAA.

"I think credibility is an issue," Didion said. "There are a lot of people that like to criticize the process and they like to criticize the individuals involved. There are a lot of people who think that they can do a lot better job without knowing what the evidence is or what the circumstances are.

"There are people in this business who know what they are doing. The investigators that develop the information, they know the case. The directors that supervise them know the case. The head of the enforcement department knows the case. The Committee on Infractions members, they know the case. They know what they're doing.

"They know the nature of the seriousness as opposed to the talking heads who get on television who like to criticize the process.

"I do believe that the committee reaches fair conclusions and in the way that they administer penalties based on the evidence that is presented to them.

"It's easy to be an armchair quarterback when it comes to infractions cases. They have no idea what the evidence was that was presented to the committee involving those violations."

While Didion is supportive of the NCAA enforcement process, he believes there is still some work to be done between those who investigate potential wrong doing and the schools that make up the membership.

"I think that there has to be a trust level that the enforcement staff has to regain," Didion said. "I don't know how far along in the process it is. There is a credibility issue with the enforcement staff.

"The only way this process works is that the membership believes that it works. If the membership has faith in it and if they believe that they selected the right people for the committee, the right people are working on the enforcement staff and in the national office, then our system is going to work. The cases are going to be adjudicated fairly.

"People don't like it when their school is penalized. I understand that, but if violations occur, then violations occur.

"In order to be fair to all of the member schools that don't cheat, then you have to administer a penalty that fits the violation."

Many have opined that the NCAA enforcement staff picks on certain conferences and schools, while other programs are protected and not subjected to the same set of rules.

Didion disagrees with that line of thinking in a major way.

"Oh, that's bullshit," Didion said. "There has never been a case of selective enforcement that I have ever seen.

"When I first started working at the NCAA, I heard a lot of people say that they will never put Notre Dame on probation or that they will never put USC football on probation.

"Well, within the first few years I was there, both of those schools were on probation. There is just no such thing as a sacred cow. There is no such thing as a case that can't be touched.

"If you violate the rule and the information surfaces and it's reliable and it's credible and it's persuasive then it doesn't matter who you are. You are going to be judged by your peers."

Didion has devoted his working life to fair play and providing a level playing field for athletes of all types who choose to compete on the college level. A career in enforcement sort of happened by chance.

"I have always had an interest in intercollegiate sports," Didion shared. "I just kind of fell into it. I had no reason to believe that anyone at the NCAA national office would ever respond to a letter that I wrote.

"I just took a shot and I wrote them a letter. I asked them for a job back in the late '70s. They had an opening and they responded. I interviewed, I got lucky and I got the job.

"That's how it happened and I had no reason to believe that it was going to work, but it did."

Looking back over his career with the NCAA, Didion reports that he had a simple approach to dealing with his job and the people he served.

"The one thing that always served me well when I was working in enforcement was that I always tried to be fair," Didion said. "If I told someone I was going to do something, then I did it. If I told somebody I couldn't do something, then

I couldn't and I didn't.

"I always did my best not to lie to anybody and I was always fair, I think even when I had to deliver bad news. That's just the nature of the job. I just tried to be fair and deal with people honestly and I think it worked."

While Didion didn't want to discuss any specific case, one of his comments really hit home, and that was the one about being fair to the other schools who didn't cheat.

Some have joked that if the NCAA didn't do something about Ole Miss' recruiting practices that the enforcement staff was going to have to apologize to SMU for giving the Mustangs the death penalty.

At the end of the day, providing a level playing field is job one for the NCAA. Rules are in place for a reason. If you break them, you should be punished.

As you will learn over the course of this book, Ole Miss cut corners in just about every way imaginable. The Rebels received a competitive advantage through various pursuits to circumvent the protocols put in place by the NCAA membership.

The NCAA has a responsibility to every program to punish offending programs. There are violations at every school, most unintentional, that never make the newspaper, but they still have to be reported, and in some cases sanctions have to be levied.

When it comes to this case, the overwhelming allegations stem from willful disobedience. Many violations involve staff members who clearly thought they were invisible and invincible.

It appears there was an undercurrent of arrogance that fueled the caper and led staffers to believe they'd never be caught. They were wrong.

Chapter 5

Sifting Through Sources

My wife's the real runner. She gets such joy out of the experience of putting one foot in front of the other, but my favorite part of running is finishing. Sure, I have a good time just getting away from it all, but the real chore for me is to commit to getting in a long run.

As I trained for the Frost Bite half marathon, I struggled to find time to get out there and get some mileage in.

I was settling in to a new town, working more than I ever have and trying to finalize the sale of our house in Baton Rouge and the purchase of our new place in Starkville.

The fact that Dak Prescott and the Bulldogs were making a run to No. 1 in the country for the first time in program history made work a lot more demanding and rewarding.

On this particular morning, it was cold and windy. I laced up my Asics running shoes, put in the ear buds and started the therapeutic pitter patter along the roadside.

After about a mile or so, Old Man Winter reminded me that I had failed to put on my gloves. The thought of pressing onwards seemed like a bad idea. I circled back and declared the run finished at two miles.

With throbbing hands red from the elements, I grabbed my phone to see what I missed.

In my line of work, there is always a question to answer, an e-mail to respond to, a call to return and no shortage of folks who have something to share. As I sorted through the recent messages one piqued my interest.

A friend from Tupelo, Mississippi, had a simple directive, "Call Me! Important!"

It has been my experience that just about everybody

considers what they have to say as important. Sometimes you have to prioritize who of "importance" to call based on available time and opportunity. I had the place to myself for a couple of hours, so I made the call.

Just for fun, we will call the Tupelo informant "Elvis."

Elvis seemed nervous as he answered my call. I probably had to offer him assurance that I would never mention his name a dozen times. Like a lot of people, Elvis was in love with what he knew and could not wait to share it.

It turns out that Elvis had a friend who was an Ole Miss booster who had been contacted by the NCAA enforcement staff. This booster apparently felt that by being on the NCAA radar he had achieved some new self-esteeming notoriety.

Elvis talked. I listened.

To hear Elvis tell it, his friend had regular interactions with Ole Miss' players and coaches. He mentioned Ole Miss assistant coach Maurice Harris by name more than once and shared that he'd seen text message conversations between the booster and current Ole Miss players on more than one occasion.

It was clear that the booster had some connections and wanted everyone to know it. There is a lot of bluster that goes along with these type of folks, so you never really know how much truth is in their commentary.

Elvis spent the better part of an hour relaying the story to me and going into great detail about many of the claims his friend had made including essentially boasting that he was on the phone with Harris when the NCAA investigator showed up for a face to face discussion.

If the NCAA was in fact conducting interviews in Tupelo, Mississippi, that right there was proof positive something more was going on than just a cursory review of blue chip athletes. With smoke mushrooming out of Waynesboro,

Mississippi, about potential ACT fraud, it was clear that there were a lot of questions being asked about Ole Miss football coaches, past and present.

Elvis would end up calling back and sharing more details about things his friend had to say. It appeared that his pal wore the fact that the NCAA knew his name like a badge of honor. While most people would recoil at the thought of causing potential problems for their favorite college program, this guy appeared to believe that the greater sin was holding his tongue rather than his wallet.

People like Elvis weren't hard to find. They usually found me, one way or another. One of the profound truths of life is that people love to tell their story. I am awfully happy to listen.

Once people realize that you won't burn them, then they will tell you almost anything if their names are kept out of it. People love to share information and people love to compare notes. Gossiping about a story of this magnitude was certainly common place. I believe the fact that a scandal involving integrity on the recruiting trail only added to it, because so many people wanted, and were hoping, that Ole Miss' "too good to be true" rise to be, in fact, too good to be true.

You bet, there were a lot of tall tales, but a lot of people knew things that were more damning to the University than they realized. Often times, they wouldn't know the full context of the situation or they would have a piece of information that paired up with something else I had heard elsewhere. But, it made for bad news for Ole Miss.

Throughout the process things popped up, like talk of a huge effort to get the Rebel class of 2013 to Birmingham for the bowl game between Ole Miss and Pittsburgh. Someone, somewhere, decided this needed to happen, so there were a few future Rebels who found their way to the bowl game and saw the team win.

Dear reader, please know that those putting on bowl games do not provide free tickets to prospects. During home games, member institutions generally allow prospects complimentary tickets to enjoy the game day atmosphere and have a chance to get a feel for everything. These trips are classified as unofficial visits by the NCAA, meaning that the prospect must provide his own transportation and lodging. There is no limit to the number of unofficial visits players can make to a prospective college.

An official visit allows the school to provide lodging, meals, transportation and reasonable entertainment. A recruitable athlete can take as many as five official visits, but only one per school.

Any recruit being courted by the Rebels would have had to make his own way to Birmingham for the bowl game, buy his own ticket and be treated just like a garden variety fan.

Rumors began to circulate that some prospects got a free trip, and actually some face time with members of the Ole Miss coaching staff during their time in Birmingham.

It is worth noting that all of the rumors that began to circulate at the end of 2012 did so against the back drop of an on-going NCAA investigation. While the initial charges did not implicate Freeze and his newly hired assistants, there were rumors of academic impropriety running rampant about current and former Rebel football players.

Multiple sources who spoke under the promise of anonymity claimed that some out of state Rebel signees had made their way to Jackson, Mississippi to improve their chances of qualifying for freshman enrollment in Oxford later that fall.

Why they would elect to leave their hometowns and high schools for an unfamiliar place raised eyebrows to say the least.

There was talk of irregularities involving the ACT and where certain out-of-state Ole Miss signees elected to take that standardized test.

These were serious allegations, if there was any truth to what people were saying. We weren't talking cash and cars just yet, but the sanctity of the process was at issue here.

Were there efforts to circumvent the NCAA Clearinghouse and the qualifying process by committing fraud in the educational process of student athletes? There seemed to be some credence to that line of thinking. One of the biggest questions going forward would be, why would Freeze and his staff take these kinds of chances, knowing that the eyes of the NCAA enforcement staff were already on Oxford for indiscretions involving a previous coaching regime?

I got a great tip that the probe into Ole Miss had reached another college campus, The University of Louisiana-Lafayette.

Coach David Saunders, a three-time Ole Miss football staffer, left Oxford for an on-the-field coaching job at Louisiana-Lafayette. Saunders coached cornerbacks for Coach Mark Hudspeth from 2011 to 2014.

Questions about some potential misdeeds at Oxford bubbled up to the surface in Cajun Country at the end of 2013, leading the NCAA enforcement staff to conduct face to face interviews with Saunders.

On Dec. 16, 2013, NCAA investigator Mike Sheridan and the Ole Miss legal counsel sat down with Saunders at ULL to reportedly ask questions about some activities that took place during his time at Ole Miss, including a time span shortly after he left the University.

The presence of the Ole Miss attorney is of great importance. Had the questions been strictly about the coach's activities at ULL, then only the attorneys representing ULL would have been allowed to be present.

Ole Miss was allowed to participate in the interview process, because their school was the program being investigated for wrong doing. ULL was able to be present, because their assistant coach was being interviewed.

In a ULL document dated Aug. 20, 2015, it was apparent to the ULL associate athletic director, Jessica Leger, that the enforcement staff was quizzing Saunders about potential violations that had taken place at Ole Miss.

The immediate issue involved some prospective student athletes who were reportedly advised to take the ACT at Wayne County High School in tiny Waynesboro, Mississippi, population 4,962.

Saunders reported that he developed a bit of a professional relationship with then Wayne County High School ACT proctor Ginny Crager. Crager is an Oregon native who studied at the University of Southern Mississippi back in 2006 as the Rebel coaching staff was recruiting five-star defensive tackle Jerrel Powe of Waynesboro.

Powe signed with Ole Miss and was denied initial NCAA clearance. The talented big man enrolled at Hargrave Military Academy in hopes of preserving his full four years of eligibility rather than attending a junior college program.

On Feb. 1, 2006, Powe once again signed with Ole Miss. Hopes were high that a year of prep school and some personal tutoring from Crager would boost the chances of passing NCAA academic review.

After close to a dozen online courses offered by Brigham Young University and proctored by Crager were rejected by the clearinghouse, Powe was deemed a non-qualifier for the second time.

In a statement on the matter, the NCAA admitted it had questions about the coursework submitted on Powe's behalf offering that a significant amount of coursework had been completed "in an unusually limited amount of time."

The former U.S. Army All-American was later allowed to enroll and prove himself in a college classroom at Ole Miss after being denied admission the two previous years.

The Buckatunna, Mississippi, native put together back to back All-SEC seasons for Ole Miss in 2009 and 2010 and was drafted in the sixth round of the 2011 NFL draft by the Kansas City Chiefs where he played three seasons.

While Powe was finishing up his Ole Miss playing career, Crager and Saunders remained in touch about "stand-by testing" for the ACT.

Stand-by testing is essentially a process that allows test takers who missed the normal cut off dates for registration to register with no guarantee of a seat at the testing center. Similar to stand-by travelers at the airport, students show up with photo ID and stand-by papers in hand, hoping to be included in the testing group.

Crager reportedly supervised the testing date in question, June 12, 2010. The NCAA enforcement staff alleges that three Ole Miss signees had their answer sheets altered enabling them to post fraudulent scores.

In documents made available by ULL, it is alleged that the practice of sending prospective student athletes to Waynesboro to obtain a favorable score began while Saunders was at Ole Miss and continued once he joined the coaching staff in Lafayette.

One of the principles in the ULL NCAA case was a former Ole Miss defensive end Delvin Jones. Jones signed on with Ole Miss as a four-star standout from Palmetto High School in Miami, Florida.

Jones claimed scholarship offers from Alabama, Florida, Florida State, LSU, Michigan, Nebraska, Oregon, and Tennessee among others.

Just three weeks before National Signing Day, Jones elected to back off of a six-month verbal pledge to Tennessee after former Volunteer head coach Lane Kiffin headed to USC to accept the post vacated by Pete Carroll, who had taken the head coaching job with the NFL's Seattle Seahawks.

Now scrambling to find a solid landing spot, Jones re-opened his college recruitment. Complicating matters was the fact that Jones did not have a standardized test score on file with the NCAA clearinghouse, a requirement for college bound prospects to take official visits.

As Signing Day approached, Jones found his options rather limited. Ole Miss' "big game hunter" Chris Vaughn had been the primary recruiter for Jones and several other Rebel targets in South Florida including future Rebels running back Jeff Scott of Archbishop Carroll High School and linebacker Ralph Williams of Miami-Southridge High School.

Despite the fact that Jones reported a healthy offer sheet, Ole Miss essentially "won" Jones' Signing Day autograph by default.

In fact, the talented pass rusher signed with Ole Miss having never seen the campus in person. Jones would get his first look at Oxford when he made the trip to see the Rebels' spring game that April.

Shortly after that visit to attend the 2010 Grove Bowl, Jones made the move to Jackson, Mississippi, to enroll at the Educational Center in hopes of improving his chances of earning NCAA Clearinghouse approval.

"It was cool. Everybody was family oriented down there in Mississippi," Jones told me from his home in Texas. "It made it easier for me to be away from my family."

The relocation and fresh Mississippi air appear to have agreed with Jones who was able to gain certification from the NCAA clearinghouse qualifying him for freshman enrollment at Ole Miss.

Jones' freshman campaign yielded just two combined tackles against Fresno State and Kentucky for the Rebels, who went 4-8 on the 2010 season. Six months later, the highly heralded pass rusher was flushed out of the Ole Miss program following a violation of team rules.

The south Florida prep star enrolled at Coffeyville Community College (KS) to give his playing career a reboot. After earning his associates degree, Jones transferred to ULL and rejoined Saunders.

Despite being more than seven years removed from his signing with Ole Miss, Jones is still getting inquiries about the months that led up to his enrollment in Oxford, and the issues raised about his recruitment and clearance at two college programs.

"They have an investigation going on with Ole Miss," Jones said. "I have had a bunch of people calling me and asking me a lot of questions about Ole Miss.

"All types of people—media folks, lawyers, and investigators, and a lot of them. It's been a bunch of them. There's been a lot of people asking me questions."

With a criminal justice degree in hand, Jones has elected to give his football dreams another try, and push past the memories of a promising college career that is now lost. He wants a new beginning, once and for all.

"One of my friends hooked me up with an agent," Jones explained. "I went out there to Iowa (Arena Football) and I liked it. This past year was my first year. I just started back playing football this past year.

"It's cool. I just have to get totally back into football. I haven't played football in like, four or five years."

Jones has moved on with life, and is far removed from any potential penalties assigned to the college programs who managed to sign him. The manner in which he was recruited and managed to earn his college eligibility remains a matter of discussion, and a rather serious one for the coaches responsible for their school's courtship of him.

Make no mistake about it though, Jones was not an isolated incident.

Rumors surrounding Ole Miss signees, mostly from out of state, setting up residence in Mississippi's capital city spread like wildfire. How did all of this come to be? Clearly, it wasn't all by happenstance that a group of out of state college bound football players showed up at an alternative learning center to live and study together and work towards their collective college eligibility.

It was obvious that a scheme was in place, but who was behind it? Who was paying for it? Where would these players live? Who would feed them? Who would pay the light bill?

While there was plenty of smoke around the ACT prep classes in Jackson, was it improper for these student athletes to seek out academic support? The bigger question would be, why did they elect to do so in Jackson, Mississippi, rather than at home?

As I began to talk more openly about the probe into Ole Miss football, people began coming out of the woodwork with what they knew. Some valuable information, and some not.

I was even provided with a picture of a cashier's check rumored to be for the purchase of a luxury vehicle by the father of two prominent Ole Miss players. I encouraged all who would listen to not post that picture on social media for two reasons. First, it's a financial document that contains sensitive information, and secondly, the check, in and of itself, is only proof that somebody bought a car.

I suspect I had upwards of 50 people send me a picture of that check. It was everywhere, and proof in some people's minds that hellfire and brimstone would soon raineth down upon the heads of the unjust in Oxford.

The blood lust soon hit a fever pitch once fans of other schools came to the realization that something was truly happening. This was no fire drill. The smoke was real, and the fire was blazing on many fronts.

Chapter 6

Catfishing – It's Electric!

When I was coming up "catfishing" meant heading to the water for a day of fun and fishing. Whether I was running trotlines in the Pearl River or going to an all-you-can-eat restaurant, the word "catfish" brings back a lot of good memories.

Nowadays, catfishing is a contemporary intrigue that means something entirely different. Social networking sites identify it with a group of fish, which also sport a big mouth and sharp fins that will stab you if you're not careful.

By today's social media definition, a catfish is no longer a fish at all, but a human being. They're a person who assumes a fake online persona for the purpose of luring someone into a relationship of some type; typically, it's done to bring a person into a romantic entanglement for the sake of exploitation. Catfish gain the love and trust of their targets, then start asking for help in the way of gifts of money.

Catfishing is also a form of cyber-bullying. Leave it up to a bunch of tech-savvy thugs to find new and creative ways to impact the sport of catfishing.

Here's maybe the first catfish on steroids—a famous Notre Dame athlete tricked by pictures of a beautiful woman and words he believed were hers. Remember Manti Te'o? He's the All-American linebacker from Notre Dame who back in 2012 was duped into an online relationship by a fictitious woman.

Te'o led Notre Dame to the BCS championship game against Alabama, and was runner-up for the Heisman Trophy in 2012. But, what people remember about him is what tarnished Te'o's career forever. He fell in love with a nonexistent woman online, and told the whole sports world about it.

National media focused on the drama surrounding Te'o's implausible saga. ESPN, *Sports Illustrated* and other national media were constantly updating the public on the complex and layered hoax perpetrated by Te'o's fake girlfriend, "Lennay Kehua," who turned out to be Ronaiah Tuiasosopo, a 22-year-old California man.

Tuiasosopo created a false online identity—Lennay Kehua—by utilizing multiple social media outlets such as Facebook, Twitter, and Instagram. He then conned his 23-year-old friend, Diane O'Meara, into sending him her photograph, which he used as the face of Kehua. Beginning to get complicated, right? That's the nature of these catfishing soap operas.

Let's not go into every sordid detail, since it would waste good ink. It's worthy of revisiting the highlights, though, so here's a thumbnail sketch of Te'o's tale:

Te'o "met" Kehua on the internet and fell in love with her only to have her die months later. The two lovebirds communicated through social media, and even talked on the phone. The two even fell asleep at night texting each other. How Tuiasosopo managed to masquerade as a girl is still very fishy, to me. Nevertheless, the Kehua saga was full of ups and downs, and close calls with death.

First, Kehua was in a nasty car wreck that left her near death. Then, after she recovered from the wreck, she was diagnosed with terminal leukemia. A bone marrow transplant followed. All along, this was just a pack of lies, and of course it became "fake news" before such a hashtag was ever a twinkle in Putin's eye.

The drama was stretched out over several months as Kehua and Te'o continued to exchange private messages, and talk frequently on the phone. Her bogus plight was reported by media as the tragic story of Te'o's long-distance girlfriend and he received sympathy notes from across the country. Te'o was strung along from 2009-2012, nearly three years, before the whole twisted ball of yarn began to unravel.

Then came the coup de grâs: On or about Sept. 11, 2012, just when it looked as if Miss Lennay had recovered from her bone marrow transplant, her creator, and the perpetrator of the hoax, Tuiasosopo, dropped the hammer by faking Miss Lennay's death, only six hours after Te'o's real-life grandmother, Annette Santiago died.

During the catfishing saga, Tuiasosopo also set up another phony person—a brother named Koa—who had the heavy job of informing Te'o that the love of his life, Lennay Kehua, had died.

Fueled by a willing audience the national and mainstream news and sports media reported the sad story about the famous athlete's girlfriend. The heartbreak of Lennay Kehua's death reverberated in hearts across America.

A few months later, the Te'o family began to put the pieces together and realized Manti had been hoodwinked. It didn't help that Te'o had broken off the relationship. Perhaps as revenge, Tuiasosopo killed off the Lennay persona.

"I would say I was naïve, and I was just unlucky," Manti Te'o said. "This is incredibly embarrassing. I was naïve in that I trusted this 'person.' But a lot of things just happened."

The fake love affair is a brand seared into Te'o's hide that will mark him the rest of his life. Although Te'o was the victim here, it's his name that's been drug through the mud. Some think he was involved, in some degree, with the scandal.

It's still unclear why Ronaiah Tuiasosopo masterminded the cruel ruse. What were his motives? What was the condition of his psychological health, which would not only allow, but compel him to commit such a fraud upon the tender-hearted

American? Was it insecurity, jealousy, revenge, loneliness, or some other emotional need?

There're many subspecies in the catfish family. They can come in all sizes, genders, and motives. They can come from fans, from haters, from players, and they can also come in football recruiting. That's right, football recruiting.

The National Collegiate Athletic Association has always held strict ethical policies on communications between boosters and recruits. Contact is flatly prohibited. These bylaws weren't ready for the explosion of social media.

Today, recruits are only a mouse click away from a fanbase hungry for infotainment, and from boosters hungry for the next superstar athlete. The policies were put in place because the temptation has always been there to communicate to desirable recruits, even before social media's onslaught. In some cases, it can become an unplanned and ugly situation. The internet is the wild, wild West, and the NCAA is struggling to maintain order.

With the wide-open, and unpoliced space Twitter, Instagram, and Snapchat provide, social media mavens are being born every day. The selfie, the hashtag, and the follow have all become a big part of our lexicon in this modern age of technology.

As a result of this era of availability, it's much easier to communicate with people we know, or think we know, or just want to know someday.

To their credit, NCAA officials have adjusted their by-laws to address the compliance challenges created by this new form of often clandestine communication.

13.1.2.1 General Rule. All in-person, on- and off-campus recruiting contacts with a prospective student-athlete or the prospective student-athlete's relatives or legal guardians shall be made only by authorized institutional staff members. Such contact, as well as correspondence and telephone calls, by representatives of an institution's athletics interests is prohibited except as otherwise permitted in this section. {D} (Revised: 8/5/04, 10/30/14)

The general rule on booster-to-recruit contact hasn't changed much. All interaction remains off limits.

When asked for clarification on the NCAA's stance specifically about fans contacting prospective student athletes on Twitter, and similar forms of social media, NCAA assistant director of public and media relations Meghan Durham explained, "Fans can tweet generally about a current student-athlete who is enrolled at the school, but cannot tweet at a prospective student-athlete."

So, in the eyes of the NCAA, tweeting at recruits is also out of bounds. Of course, it's extremely difficult to police this activity. Especially when it's nearly impossible to prove just exactly who is on the other end of the connection, and these are people who are interacting with high school players and college prospects, who in turn, are trying to make up their minds about which college they are going to attend and play ball.

Those youngsters already have enough "information" flying at them from the usual channels. Now, add unsolicited contacts from, well, who knows who, and the waters get muddier than a hog wallow.

Such was the case with a rising star appearing on the internet as "Analesa Presley," a.k.a., "AP." This Presley figure first came to public view around the year 2012, and claimed to be a die-hard Ole Miss fan. She was well-known enough to get a birthday greeting from Ole Miss head coach Hugh Freeze. His tweet to her:

Happy birthday to one great Rebel @**FinsUpAP**

— Hugh Freeze (@CoachHughFreeze)

Presley claimed to be a native of tiny Tremont, Mississippi, a reported graduate of Itawamba Agricultural High School, a one-time freshman at Ohio State, and at some point, a student at Itawamba Community College. Most significant, she claimed to be a former Ole Miss student and posted photographs of a 20-something-year-old adorable blue-eyed blonde, Southern belle.

AP, who portrayed herself online as "@Rebel_AP," "@Rebel_AGP," "@FinsUpAP," and others, was a rock star of an Ole Miss booster. She took the stage on Twitter, Facebook, Myspace, Pinterest, Snapchat, and Instagram, where she did nothing but flimflam Ole Miss athletics, and enticed potential Ole Miss student-athletes to sign with Ole Miss.

So how does a random Twitter account make the move from obscurity to being one of two Ole Miss fans followed by Rebel head football coach Hugh Freeze?

In the case of Analesa Presley, her profile got a solid boost by doing some pro-bono writing for an upstart website and podcasting outfit called *Make It Rain Sports.*

The genesis of this venture took place in 2011 when a pair of lifelong friends from Florence, Mississippi, Acey Roberts and Jake Wimberly, elected to get into the business of sports coverage.

"Neither of us was known at the time, or had an 'in' with any other sports website," Wimberly shared. "I enjoyed writing. I had covered high school football for a south Mississippi newspaper years before.

"The goal of MIRS (*Make It Rain Sports*) was not only to make it a fun website, full of content about Mississippi State, Ole Miss and the SEC, but also a more edgy site where we didn't hold back on our opinions and created conversation.

"We fronted our own money, started a website and began doing tabletop podcasts on random nights on blog talk radio, again buying our own gear, and figuring out how to podcast."

While Roberts saw the pursuit as more of a hobby, Wimberly hoped his efforts would lead to something more substantial, and perhaps a break through as a sports journalist.

"Our motivation probably differed, but my motivation was I always wanted to break into writing and radio," Wimberly explained. "I really didn't have any guidance in how to do so, but felt I could be successful in it, and this could be my only shot.

"I had the mentality that I can be better than anyone out there, and this was my chance to make it work. Once I realized I could just do it myself, with the advent of a website, a mic and social media – I decided, why not? Let's literally bring this thing out of the ground and give it a go!"

As full-time employees at the Mississippi Department of Transportation, the part-time bloggers needed some additional help to drive content and page views.

Their decision was made to reach out to others who had an interest in doing some freelance writing, with a ringing emphasis on FREE.

"Rebel Analesa a.k.a. "AP" Presley came on board because we decided we were going to solicit for writers to build more content," Wimberly said. "We put out on social media 'you could come write for us, while albeit free, but a chance to write if you've ever wanted to.'

"The goal in mind was to drive enough content for good page views for future advertising. We both received several tweets and messages on various social media platforms about people interested in providing content."

Wimberly explained that their screening process left a lot to be desired, but at the end of the day, this was simply a group of folks wanting to talk sports, and hopefully one day, have a little side income, too.

An opportunity to build an audience without much scrutiny laid the foundation for a catfish like Presley, who was operating under the guise of a false identity.

"This Miss AP had no job application to fill out, and no background check to be run," Wimberly explained. "All it took was a "Yes, I'll do it," and a nice profile picture and this Presley figure was writing for us.

"We let just about anyone who could formulate an opinion on paper come on board, and at one time we had as many as 10 people providing content."

"She contacted Acey and wanted to cover Ole Miss and at that time I never questioned it – why would I? "She had a cute smile, a little flair about her, and why not? Page views were what we wanted and having a face easy on the eyes never hurts in that regard."

In an attempt to create buzz, and push traffic to their blog postings, the MIRS crew took to social media to engage in some targeted discourse.

Hot takes led to spirited discussions, and eventually some real questions about who was pulling the strings.

Wimberly explained how things began to unravel:

"MIRS was full of people at one point who used real and pseudo names on Twitter. To get conversations going we'd seek out others to confront in a friendly albeit sometimes edgy banter. We would contact people from opposing fan bases and just general people. The idea was to interact with as many fans as possible, create conversation and promote our brand."

"Rebel AP" was interacting with Ole Miss fans, MSU fans and more! But, then she began to become more of an unofficial mouthpiece for Ole Miss recruiting.

As time went on, people started to question why she was so dialed into recruiting. They were wondering why she received a follow from Ole Miss head football coach Hugh Freeze, and why she never posted any photos of herself with friends at games. There were more unanswered questions, too.

It just so happened that at about the time, MTV's hit series *Catfish* came out, people started asking questions like: Was she a real person, or the person she said she was?

She appeared on radio show *Head-to-Head* to try and clear up questions surrounding her identity.

Presley went on to defend herself and the false narrative she had created quite successfully on the call-in radio shows. Her back story then became well known to both Mississippi State and Ole Miss fans alike.

Wimberly, like a lot of other people, were suspicious of the pretty co-ed from Tremont, Mississippi. While the "young" lady talked a good game, she didn't behave like a 20-something-year-old on social media.

Something was rotten in the house of MIRS, and it stunk bad enough to knock a buzzard off a gut wagon.

"I became skeptical after we had a few MIRS meet-ups at some football games and local establishments and she never showed," Wimberly said. "She was supposed to, but didn't and she proclaimed she loved MIRS.

"Also, I began noticing her photos more and more and how her face and color seemed to change, and she got sloppy in what she chose to post.

"I also didn't believe any female could love recruiting that much. While many women love football, I had never seen a girl that in love with recruiting.

The final straw was no selfies ever of her and friends nor pets or anything, and what girl her age this day and age does NOT do that? After she was challenged to just take a photo with a paper and the date of the day and never came through,

I thought there is no way she is who she says she is."

I was not aware that there was a whole Egg Bowl Twitter thing. In my mind, Twitter for me wasn't a place for me to communicate with friends, family, and subscribers. It was really just a chance to make funny comments and then tweet out stories.

I'd tweet out news, and hope to get reads, and collect some likes on my videos. So, it really was more of a medium for me to communicate my work and that of our *Scout.com* staff. It wasn't a place to have an internet persona.

Analesa Presley grew in prominence. I didn't follow her on Twitter, but occasionally I'd see her mentioned or she'd come across the timeline and people would retweet it.

One day I got a message from a guy who worked at one of the Mississippi State blogging sites. He asked if I knew about *Make It Rain Sports* group and this Analesa Presley person.

He suspected the whole thing was a fraud. He was trying to chase it, but the site he worked for told him to leave it alone. But, he knew something was there.

"They told us to leave this alone, but I really wish you'd look into this," the guy told me.

I had no interest in it whatsoever. Zero. It wasn't in my scope of journalism. I didn't see a story there, so I didn't care. I didn't care about it at all!

Then, while watching the 2015 Super Bowl, I noticed people were bickering back and forth on the *Make It Rain* group on Facebook and Acey Roberts and Analesa Presley were right in the middle of it. I didn't really know much about the group. I'd been on their podcast before, which Jake Wimberly handled like a poor man's Head to Head.

As I watched the back and forth, I remembered the whole thing about my colleague thinking something just wasn't right with Rebel AP.

I went back and looked at her timeline. She made some comment about the lesson learned is to tell recruits the truth before signing day. It was one of those truisms that didn't even need to be tweeted.

So, I quoted her tweet and I said, "Well, the catfish has a point." I was basically calling Analesa Presley a catfish. And I really was just trying to stir the pot.

I unknowingly stepped into something I wouldn't be able to scrape off my shoe. I hadn't been aware of the fact that this had been an ongoing feud and accusation by Mississippi State people that Analesa Presley was a fraud.

Now the State folks were surely thinking, "Steve sees it. She *IS* a catfish." But, I didn't fully recognize it at that point in time. I went after her nevertheless.

Analesa defended herself so vociferously I finally said, "I'm not interested in this. So be it. Be what you want to be, whatever."

I hadn't really done any research or anything about her persona at that point. It was an interchange on Twitter. You have those every day with people you don't know. They don't really go anywhere. Who cares? Right?

Well, the next day when I got up, one of the very first notifications I got on Twitter was from Acey Roberts. He tweeted at me that I needed to leave little girls alone. I was offended.

I mused, *number one, this is just inappropriate. You know this is not a little girl.* They were claiming she was a 23-year-old former college student and a former Ole Miss student. I thought his tweet was in poor taste, and was really an attempt to impugn my character. I felt I needed to defend myself. That became a watershed moment.

Funny how these "debates" get started on social media, stuff that really gets me going. Somebody says something snide, and I gotta go get 'em. He made those criticisms of me so I started looking a little closer. *These people are right,* I realized. *This thing is a fraud. There's no way this girl is who she claims to be.*

I even said that day on social media to Acey, "Hey, if she's using a fake name and a fake picture for security everybody will understand. Just tell the truth. Just say, 'Hey, she's had some issues in the past. She wants to get out here and interact with Ole Miss fans and have a good time and just talk sports and she doesn't want to have the issues off the field with drama.'"

If she was protecting herself everybody would've gone along. I even gave him the mulligan. I said, "Look, just admit it; if that's the situation everybody's okay with it."

But no, they dug in their heels and proclaimed, "Nope, she is legit. She is exactly who she says she is."

Then it became kind of a joke to me. Next, Rebel AP threatened to contact my employer, *Scout.com*, and basically accuse me of harassment. That I was harassing her! How can you harass a fake person?

It only pinged my radar a bit, because there's always somebody complaining about something. If somebody doesn't like what you write, or have to say, they'll try to find a way to get you in trouble. So, I didn't pay a whole lot of attention to it. But, there were some higher-ups in the Rebel camp that were paying attention.

Later, while I'm traveling to Louisiana to bury my wife's grandmother, I get a text from Chuck Rounsaville, publisher of *The Ole Miss Spirit*, chastising me for hurting this young girl's feelings on social media. He said she was in tears and so beside herself. "I just want to know where you're coming from?" he asked.

That statement, or half-ass question, insulted me. Number one, I'd rarely communicated with Chuck Rounsaville. I don't recall if he'd ever texted me in my lifetime, and then this is what he texts me about? This fraud? This nonsense?

"You know, we've been working together for all these years and this is what you contact me about?" I asked. I found that a little bit curious. Then, I created a little fiction to hide my search for the truth. I said, "Well, as far as I'm concerned Chuck, I'm done with it. She can be who she wants to be. I don't care. But I'm going to tell you this girl isn't who she claims to be."

I didn't want him to know I was going to keep digging. The fact they were threatening to contact *Scout.com* and file a complaint against me for "inappropriate contact" put me into motion, and caused me some concern about my job.

I knew this was a fraud. My communications were only in a Twitter response. I told myself, *it's not like you've done anything inappropriate, that you hurt anybody.*

Just in case, I had to defend myself, I wanted to have my ducks in a row. I thought, *I'm going to have to protect myself.* I just didn't want any drama. My investigation left the launch pad.

Very quickly into my look beneath the photographic surface of the Rebel AP persona I really started to get suspicious, because I saw Rebel AP's account was followed by Hugh and Jill Freeze, Ross and Sonya Bjork, the Ole Miss Department of Compliance office and the Ole Miss coaching staff.

Well maybe Analesa is who she says she is, I thought. Surely these people won't be following some fake account. This is probably somebody who has some connection to the football program in some form or another and maybe I have overstepped my bounds. Maybe I've made a huge mistake.

But, I kept looking, and the more I looked, the more I realized this isn't the typical college girl Twitter account. I've got girls of my own. They change their profile pages like they change outfits, they're constantly adding pictures and taking new profile photos.

I pondered, *she's had the same profile picture for months. Most of these college girls are always going to the beach or the park and taking pictures left and right. There's always something new. They're always doing something to let their friends know what they're up to. Rebel AP does none of this.*

Then I noticed there were never any pictures of her with friends. It wasn't passing the smell test for me. My conclusion was: *This is bullshit!*

I was talking to my wife one day and I said, "You know, one of the things I'm most fearful of is, what if I get to the end of this and Analesa turns out to be a special person who has some type of major issue? What if I get to the end of it and I find out she's handicapped or heavy-set, or maybe she's just a person who is awkward socially, and I take this from them? I don't know if I could forgive myself."

"Could you be any more dramatic," my wife snapped me back into reality. "These people are lying and they're coming after your job, and they're threatening your livelihood, and they're trying to get you in trouble, and the whole thing is a big fraud!"

My digging revealed several interactions on social media between Rebel AP and Hugh Freeze. There was even "happy birthday to a great Rebel," Freeze tweeted.

There were other tweets, too. He'd send out his thought for the day, and tag her in the quote. I thought, *this is clearly somebody he knows. Why is she so special?* I mean, Hugh Freeze only followed a couple hundred accounts, and the majority of them were players, or recruits, or staff members.

There were only two people who I'd call civilians—just fans—that Freeze followed, and Rebel AP was one of them. It didn't make a lot of sense. Why her? Why would he be following her? So, I said to myself, *I've got to figure this thing out.*

Chapter 7

Catfish Noodling

By now you're surely wondering: Why did I put forth so much effort over a twisted tale that was unlikely to impact any school football program anyway?

My business is built on personal contacts with high school and junior college players, their coaches, their families and local newspapers. The internet has made recruiting coverage a source of information and entertainment to hundreds of thousands of college sports fans that reaches far beyond what print magazines and newspapers could provide.

Recruiting reporters are only as informative and entertaining as our sources make possible. That requires a level of trust. When individuals passionate to "help" their school inject themselves into the recruiting process, nothing good happens, and sometimes bad things do. That's why schools and conferences provide information on what boosters can, and moreover, cannot do. It's why compliance offices keep an eye on those covering their school's recruiting.

Now, we can see in this case an example of potential new trouble for the NCAA, conferences, and schools to begin guarding against. Because, for all our technological prowess it remains fact: On the internet, you can be whoever you say you are and nobody else be the wiser.

I faced opposition from Ole Miss fans, as one could imagine, the more I tried to get a straight answer out of Analesa Presley. I attempted to track her down through information I could find in online media posts and podcasts. I had plenty of folks tell me, "Analesa is who she says she is."

I was told this repeatedly by Rebel fans who'd go so far as to even tell me they'd gone on dates with her, or they'd had lunch with her. Even Acey Roberts defended her by saying, "She is who she says she is. I've met her."

As the trail got a little warmer he started backing off that statement. He really didn't know who she was, but just like everyone who was binge drinking the Hotty-Toddy Kool-Aid, he defended her. And, the more they told me I was wrong, the more determined I was to prove I was right. Maybe it's just me and it's a character flaw, but I just felt like, who're these people to tell me I'm wrong, and to leave her alone?

Folks were even calling her an Ole Miss icon on the radio, and talked about how she had become a big part of the culture.

She had thousands of Twitter followers. She even gave gift ideas to Rebel moms looking to buy stuff for birthday parties.

It was incredible how this person just came from nowhere, and because she was some cute girl that talked trash about college football, she became an internet phenomenon people sought to follow.

I pulled up a couple of podcasts she was a guest of, and transcribed them, noting anything she said about herself. Then I scoured through those tweets and Facebook messages, and saved any personal information she revealed. Then I began to systematically pick it apart.

She said she went to Ohio State. Then said she graduated from Itawamba Agricultural High School in Fulton, Mississippi. She supposedly grew up down the road in Tremont.

I figured, this was pretty easy to solve. I contacted a friend who works in college admissions. "What can I find out legally from a university about a student?" I asked. "What is public knowledge?" I learned it's actually anything a college would put in a student directory that's available and accessible.

When the subject of her identity first came into question, Presley elected to go on-air (in voice only via telephone) with the state-wide *Head to Head* Radio talk show hosts Matt Wyatt and Richard Cross, both of whom have extensive experience in sports and media.

A day later, April 30, 2013, she appeared on the *Make It Rain* podcast in an attempt to validate herself. During the on-line show, Presley reported she left Mississippi shortly after high school and enrolled at Ohio State University.

According to Amy Murray-Goedde, the assistant director of University Communications Media and Public Relations, there has never been a student enrolled at Ohio State with the name Analesa Presley.

"I also checked our alumni database and there's no one by that name, either," Murray-Goedde reported by e-mail correspondence.

The inconsistencies increased as digging went deeper. I contacted Maikhail Miller, an Ole Miss football player, a guy I liked and knew well. He was the only person I knew who'd gone to Itawamba Agricultural High School.

"Hey, Maikhail," I said, "do you have the yearbooks for these particular years?" And he said, "Yeah."

A trip to Fulton, on March 12, 2015, provided me with the chance to review some yearbooks from Itawamba AHS. Miller and I met at a Chinese restaurant in Fulton and he handed me the yearbooks. "I'm just going to tell you man, there ain't no Analesa Presleys," he said.

"Well listen, I just need to look through 'em to see if anybody looks familiar," I said.

I went through the yearbooks, and there was nothing. There were a few students named Anna, and even one Ana, but no Presleys, and certainly no Analesa Presleys.

Miller thought it was hilarious even though he was a guy who used to play at Ole Miss. He wondered, why of all the places, would somebody say they were from Tremont,

Mississippi, and went to Itawamba.

"Why didn't they say they were like from Memphis or something?" Miller asked.

"That's a great question," I said. "Why be so specific, and involve a small town? They didn't think it through. They probably should've just said they were home schooled, and were from Memphis, and there would've never been any trail to follow."

I knew I had her then. It's like when you clear that first hurdle and you know you're in the race. And even though you know you've got some hurdles to jump, you see the finish line ahead.

My first stop in the hamlet of Tremont was at a gas station where the owner couldn't have been more helpful. I showed him and a few customers the current profile picture of "Analesa." None said they'd seen her. One gentleman agreed to call his wife, who worked at the Tremont Attendance Center for her entire adult life. That helpful lady reported no recollection of an Analesa Presley attending during her tenure.

One gentleman told me to check across the street at the floral shop, because the owners were genuine Ole Miss fans. If there were others in town, they'd certainly know them. Folks there made time for me, and they, like those at the gas station, had never seen the young lady pictured on Analesa Presley's social media accounts.

Another hurdle jumped.

Before leaving town, I stopped at Tremont Grocery, sitting conveniently in a fork in the road towards Fulton. I arrived just before a couple of local businesses shut down for lunch, and most made their way over to the small country store. One 23-year-old lifelong Tremont resident, Carey, told me, "I wish there was a girl like her around here, but there ain't. I would've remembered her." That response and others came from residents living in a town with a population of about 465 people.

I kept clearing hurdles.

After a trip to Itawamba County, it was clear there were more questions than answers as it pertained to Analesa. Everything that had been reported as facts of her life were all turning into dead ends. Not only did we have an account contacting recruits via social media, it appeared they were doing so under false pretenses.

While I was confident this social media profile was fake, there was very little information about who was controlling the account or whose smiling face appeared in all of the profile pictures?

As fate would have it, a tip came from a guy on the MSU side of that whole "she's a fraud" argument, he messaged me and said, "Dude, I got something." He'd found the girls whose pictures were being used by Rebel AP.

Our perpetrator was actually using two sisters' photos— Ashley and Bailey Sims of Dalton, Georgia.

I found the sisters on Facebook and messaged them. Bailey Sims agreed to an interview. Bailey's pictures had a striking resemblance to those of Analesa Presley. In fact, all of the profile pictures on every form of social media for Analesa Presley turned out to be either Bailey Sims or her sister, Ashley.

"It all just creeps me out," Bailey said. "I can't believe something like this would ever happen."

Ironically, this wasn't the first time something like this had happened with the Sims sisters and Presley.

"We were just talking about this about a week ago," Bailey said. "We don't go around telling people my sister got 'catfished,' but a couple of years ago, this account with the name Analesa Presley used a bunch of my sister's pictures. I can't believe she did it again!"

As it turns out, Presley stopped using Ashley's pictures and began using one of Bailey's as her primary picture on all forms of social media.

"It just gives me chills to think about that," Bailey said. "What if I went somewhere and they thought that was me from that Twitter account. It's kind of scary to think about somebody using your pictures like that."

If her concern for safety sounds absurd or over-the-top, think again, it certainly isn't when you consider the passion SEC football provokes in die-hard fans.

The Sims family is unsure who'd be involved in taking their pictures and creating a profile on social media under an assumed name.

"I don't know Analesa Presley and we're not even Ole Miss fans," Bailey said. "We're Auburn fans, so "War Eagle!" I don't even know any Ole Miss fans that I can think of."

I was ready to go face-to-face with Rebel AP and find out who was really behind the bombshell. Possessed of enough facts to push the issue, I found her on Facebook and messaged her.

"Analesa, it's time you and I had a talk," I wrote

"Why would I want to talk to you?" She asked. "I don't want to talk to you; leave me alone."

She didn't want to talk, but she agreed to answer some questions through the Facebook messaging system.

After several rounds of denials, I finally laid my trump cards out on the table and illustrated everything I'd found, from Ohio to Tremont.

"You're a fraud!" I unloaded on her. "Everything you said about yourself is a lie."

I took her down the list until she finally said, "Look, I'll just go away if you'll leave me alone."

"It's too late for that," I said. "I gave you that opportunity a couple of months ago, but instead of you going away, you went and contacted Chuck Rounsaville. And, you tried to contact my employer, *Scout.com.* You tried to smear me. You and your friends tried to make me look bad. You went after my job and tried to attack my credibility, and so now I've got to write the story. It's not just for me, but for these poor girls whose pictures you've taken."

Faced with the facts, the architect behind these social media accounts admitted the pictures and persona weren't her own. And, now, she was ready for this entire episode to be over.

Upon reading my absolute refusal to not publish the story, Presley deleted every trace of her "existence." As quickly as she'd grown to prominence, she was gone.

The afternoon wasn't over before Twitter, Facebook, Pinterest, Snapchat and Instagram accounts belonging to Analesa Presley were all gone. Once labeled an "Icon," the person nicknamed "AP" was no more. Before deleting the final account, AP asked me not to write the story. I wrote the original article March 15, 2015, for Scout.com.

On the other hand, Bailey Sims was adamant about me writing the story in hopes the publicity around the incident would protect her and her sister from any future run-ins with a person who has knowingly used their images more than once to perpetuate some self-esteeming exercise without their consent.

I did some soul searching, I thought maybe just embarrassing the catfish would be enough. I thought, *well if I just tell her, "look, I've got all this on you; just go away. Don't go away mad; just go away or I'm gonna expose you.*

But then after speaking to the Sims girls, I knew I had to finish the deal.

The Sims sisters encouraged me to go after the perpetrator,

holding nothing back.

"I want her shamed into knowing she can never do this again," Bailey Sims pled. "You have to do this for us."

I can't feel sorry for the villain. I've got to think about the victims, I thought to myself. Not to mention it's gone on multiple times.

I knew this story was going to spread like wildfire and I tried to approach it with that in mind. As I began to detail out the narrative in my head, I quickly realized this was going to be an emotional story for a lot of people. It was emotional for me. I had a good sense of the drama this story would create.

My wife reinforced the Sims' desire. "Don't chicken out on this," she insisted. "Don't pull any punches on this. You got to finish the deal."

As much as I wanted to feel sorry for AP, there had to be some accountability.

Before publishing "Coming Undone: A Cautionary Tale," I contacted Jake Wimberly to give him a heads-up that the truth was about to be published.

In the beginning as a favor to Wimberly, I left Acey Roberts out of the story. Based on Roberts' behavior since then, I regret doing that. The fact of the matter is, Roberts is responsible for a lot of the damage done by the account. In fact, it was a posting on Roberts' blog that drew his head coach, Freeze, in and into public ridicule for promoting Presley as some Ole Miss super fan.

Make It Rain Sports podcast was taken off of the air within hours of the story being published. While the blog remains available on line, most contributors have moved on to other things.

Wimberly now hosts an afternoon sports show in Jackson, Mississippi, and writes for *Gridiron Now.* It appears his goals of being more involved in sports have been reached. While Roberts' and Wimberly's career paths have headed in opposite directions, Wimberly still maintains a friendship with Roberts who eventually left Mississippi for an engineering job in Tampa, Florida.

"When all of this started boiling over and I could see the end coming, I told Acey and those with MIRS this is on you when it comes down, and I will not defend any of it," Wimberly told them.

"At the time, I told them I didn't think she was real, while several still proclaimed she was in fact a real person. I told them countless times I will not defend this if she ends up being fake." Once the cat was out of the bag, there were some quiet times between us, but never any bad times.

"We have maintained our friendship to this day, and I would like to think we are bigger people than to let some internet story of a girl stealing someone's identity mess up a friendship. I know on my end, there have never been any hard feelings, I just stuck to my guns and wouldn't comment or get involved in it. How do you defend something you felt was never real to begin with? I've never had a second of anger or hostility towards him and hope and assume those feelings were returned and I believe they were. It's a topic we just do not discuss."

The next morning the story hit and it was incredible! The response was immediate. Media requests came from all over the country. Gene Swindoll called me and he'd gotten a call from the National News desk at *Scout.com* wanting to know why we didn't send the story to them to market.

I didn't think they'd be interested in a story like this. At its heart, it's just a story about a fan who let her passion for her team exceed her ability to use common sense. And, she got caught up in the internet identity, and the attention that went along with it. Low and behold, she ended up getting the attention of her head coach. She got some interaction with Freeze, and as a result it became intoxicating.

They wanted to know on the National News desk of *Scout. com* why we didn't market the story, because it was basically outpacing the entire network... that one story alone. We had people pick it up. *Deadspin* picked it up and *Sports Illustrated* picked it up. We had several other entities that picked it up or referenced the story.

I made several national radio appearances; all over a Twitter account. A person might think to themselves: *Where are we as a society that a story like this becomes such a big deal?* I know I did.

The reason that it became such a big story is the national news desk at *Scout.com* added the tweet where Hugh Freeze wished her a happy birthday. That action took things to a different level.

There we were; a college football coach not only wishes this girl a happy birthday, but has a rather regular correspondence with her openly on social media, and she turned out to be such a complete fraud.

At the end of the day, I didn't put her name out there, because she's a middle-aged woman with three adult kids. I thought to myself, *if we put her identity out there it's her kids and her husband who pick up the tab.* Her husband has no idea any of this stuff is going on. I can't even begin to imagine what her husband would feel if he found out.

It's funny, but we're still in contact with one another. I still hear from her occasionally.

Ironically, she said, "the one person who did the most to destroy me actually freed me from the people I thought were my friends who are no longer in touch with me."

I think at her heart she's a good person. It just got away from her. I think all she really wanted to do was to get out there, talk some trash, and just enjoy talking about the teams, and then for some reason, she decided to use that cute girl's picture. That act resonated with people, and some of them are creeps.

The flip side of catching this catfish are some of the stories have never been told. There were so many people who'd contacted the catfish to try to begin a romantic or sexual relationship. Some of these men are married. Their behavior hinged on a picture, because a cute girl was talking football. It just demonstrates how desperate people are to have something, some type of connection.

I had five different guys contact me afterwards who thought they were in a relationship with her, but had never met her. They'd never had any physical contact with her, obviously. They'd talked to her on the phone, but most communication was texting.

One guy told me he'd been texting her every night for six months. He thought she was his girlfriend. He even drove all the way up from south Mississippi to Tremont to surprise her on her birthday.

He gets to Tremont and goes to where she's supposedly going to get her hair done. His plan was to show up with flowers and gifts and sweep her off her feet. Well, come to find out, that hair salon had been closed for a couple of years.

He gets her on the phone and asks, "Hey, where are you?"

"Oh, I was getting my hair done," she answered.

"Well, I'm in Tremont. I wanted to get together."

"Oh, I'm so sorry my girlfriends are taking me to Memphis and we're getting ready and we're on the way. I'm so sorry, I wish I'd known you were coming."

It hit him then. He knew he'd been played.

He was willing to pay me for her name, because he was so embarrassed, so humiliated. Here he was thinking he had a relationship with this cute girl only to find out the whole thing was a sham.

There were five or six of those guys who all thought they were in varying degrees of a relationship. He's the only one I know of who actually made that kind of effort, who drove all the way up there.

The other part of this story belongs to the girls whose pictures were stolen. When the creeps found out who the real girls were, and they really were cute 20-somethings, suddenly the Sims sisters started getting unwanted attention.

The same creeps who were chasing Analesa Presley were now chasing these sisters in Georgia. Some guys started sending them money. The Sims sisters didn't like Ole Miss and didn't really care anything about college football. They were just good ole country girls.

When I first began to get critical of the catfish account, before I even broke the story, Jill Freeze tweeted to Analesa Presley and wrote, "Stay strong. It's an audience of one." I'm assuming referencing God.

I had one woman email me and say she hated me. She wrote, "I feel like a kid. I feel like I've been completely duped." She said, "I'd rather have just lived with my illusions than to have you pull the curtain back on this."

Consider the cited examples of people who were duped by the fictitious Analesa Presley on social media and online sports news outlets. Now multiply that by the thousands more who followed her like sheep. Studying this sociological pathology reveals the same mindset that easily fell for Ole Miss leadership's "the investigation is over."

After my story broke, Chuck Rounsaville called.

"Hey brother, we need to talk," he said.

We're not brothers. We don't have that kind of relationship.

My first two impressions about Rounsaville's response to my accusing AP of being a catfish: first I thought, *I've struck a nerve here. I've hit pretty close to home; second, there's somebody probably involved with the Ole Miss coaching staff who has reached out to Chuck to find out what's happening.*

"Oh, I was talking to Hugh," Rounsaville said, confirming my suspicion. "Man, we just think that girl was crazy." It's funny, but they didn't think she was crazy when they personally contacted me to tell me I should leave her alone. They thought they could shake me down, and that I'd take the story off *Scout.com.* I wouldn't.

Something in me changed after that experience. I've spent some time thinking about being a risk taker as a sports journalist.

I've always stopped short of anything that might embarrass somebody else. If there was potential collateral damage I've always erred on the side of caution. In this instance, I had to defend my name, reputation and credibility, so I went all in and wrote the story.

I had some people contact me afterwards to say Analesa Presley had contacted some recruits, and there's a couple people in media who she shared information with, "just trying to be a good Rebel."

It's important to note Analesa was so good at what she did that she got the entire coaching staff and administration involved. Those people retweeted articles she wrote. Analesa Presley created a convincing persona, which they all just bought into. They all just took it hook, line and sinker.

Whatever was wrong in the life of our dearest catfish could

be made right when she logged on and became Analesa Presley and was the Dixie maiden of Ole Miss.

The catfish story was cute, and it helped me to sharpen my chops and maybe gain the allies I needed to pull off a story about this NCAA investigation. I earned some credibility, because Analesa didn't want to be found. She was enjoying a great existence.

The story gained some complexity because a lot of those guys wanted to sleep with her. Many of the women involved wanted to be her, because she was this cute girl who knew so much about football and all these guys loved her. That's the part of this whole thing that can't be thrown out on the conference table for discussion, right, but it is a part of the motivations behind what people were saying and doing when it came to Analesa.

Little did I know that investigating the catfish story was just a dress rehearsal for what was coming next—digging into the NCAA violations story. Finding my way through this catfish story I gained the confidence to trust my instincts. I learned with breaking a story that more informants would come out of the woodwork. I didn't ask these people to contact me, but I'm glad they did.

There were married readers who either sent money or offered to send money to the Sims sisters. That's absolutely despicable. But, I'll never disclose their names. That is their story to tell if they so choose. Bottom line, I learned a lot about people.

Analesa Presley wasn't the only fake involved in this story. There're a lot of other people who are involved who are as fake as she is. The only difference is she's not using her name in the picture. They're phonies too. They're just doing it behind the scenes, like the *Ashley Madison* dating website.

There's a part of me that feels sorry for the woman who portrayed Analesa Presley. Not that she lost the Analesa Presley personality, but the fact she thought she thought she needed the Analesa Presley persona at all. There's something obviously missing in her life that Analesa's presence fulfilled in her. That makes me sad. I go to bed at night feeling good I didn't do anybody a disservice. I think I exposed a lot of people who were willing participants in something that was ridiculous on many levels.

In the end who's at fault here? The person portraying Presley found herself with a byline as a sports writer and a radio guest. She claims those parties sought her out, which brings up a new angle entirely. Should there not be a vetting process in place to ensure people are who they say they are prior to publication? I would say so.

When all's said and done, it's impossible to create a back-story good enough and strong enough that will hold up to scrutiny when it's nothing but a house of cards. It's like a Ponzi scheme in a sense, because it's only a matter of time before it all comes crashing down. Everyone involved holds some sense of responsibility, which is an indictment on what we consider media these days.

Chapter 8

Skinning the Catfish

One of the things that made the catfish story of Analesa Presley so unique is how many people fell for it. Her popularity on Twitter and other social media was boosted by her participation in radio shows, podcasts, and writing some blog posts for the walk-on media outfit *Make It Rain Sports.*

I have my own personal feelings about the woman on social media known as Analesa Presley. She'd invested countless hours to set up and manage accounts on Twitter, Facebook, Myspace, Pinterest, Snapchat and Instagram.

There was an awful lot of work and effort wrapped up into creating an internet persona with the face of the girl next door, who had the on-line wit of a salty barfly.

In some twisted way, I admired her hustle, I simply had to know why.

I reached out to the woman a.k.a. Analesa Presley to find out what her true motives were when this all began.

"I had never been on Twitter before," AP shared. "I didn't understand the hype of it all. I knew celebrities used it, but I didn't know of anyone I knew who was on it. I created it just to see if I could get a famous person to follow me. Just something for fun on a boring day. I never had intentions of talking to people."

As she began to develop a better understanding of the Twittersphere, AP took to it like a duck to water. Before long, the AP account was off and running and suddenly a must-follow for Ole Miss fans.

"Since my beginning objective was to get a famous person to follow me, I tweeted Shepard Smith of Fox News fame," AP explained. "All I said was 'Hotty Toddy.'" "He tweeted back and the Rebel fans followed. I remember hitting 100 followers and felt honored.

"When some of the larger Rebel accounts found me, I started getting more and more.

"I often tweeted trash talk about football and it just grew and grew.

"Once, I wrote a blog post about how happy I was to have Coach Freeze at Ole Miss. I tweeted it to him. He followed me after that.

"So of course, when he followed, I got more and more followers, including the staff.

"Included in those new social media contacts were Jill Freeze, the wife of Hugh Freeze, Athletic Director Ross Bjork and his wife Sonya, most Ole Miss assistant coaches, and the Ole Miss compliance department of the "If you have evidence of a violation…" fame.

With a growing audience of people who Rebel AP respected; her message about the Ole Miss athletic programs took on a more rah rah slant.

"I was always positive, I was tweeting encouraging things to players, staff and yes, to recruits," she admitted. "But, I *never* hit on a recruit. I discouraged that." One of the girls I followed worked at Ole Miss. She and I became Twitter friends. Several students who worked in and around the athletic department followed me and talked to me."

As her popularity among the Ole Miss fanbase grew, the pretty girl from Tremont, Mississippi, was becoming a bit of a commodity. With talk of enrolling at Ole Miss as a student making the rounds, a job offer of sorts was extended for AP to become officially a part of the Rebel football program.

Despite being flattered by the possibility, AP had to pass on the opportunity of a lifetime, because she wasn't who she claimed to be.

"There was a graduate assistant, who is no longer there, told me if I wanted to do it when I moved to Oxford he would help me," AP shared. "There weren't any details discussed, because I knew I wasn't going and didn't want to lock myself into something I knew I couldn't do."

With that matter settled for the time being, AP continued to operate the social media accounts in an unofficial capacity. A rising interest in recruitment paved the way for hungry fans looking for good news about their program. A set of folks who're used to getting the best, and getting what they want when they want it must have been the perfect set up for a carefully crafted narrative.

"It was recruiting season and that is what everyone was talking about," AP said. "What's funny is I got ALL of my recruiting info from Twitter and radio talk shows. Except I got what some called 'inside' info, and all it amounted to was stuff I got from their message boards. I didn't tell things people told me. I didn't leak things if someone told me not to tell. I was trusted.

"I came across *Make It Rain* before *Make It Rain* really existed." "They were just three guys, Matthew Faulkner, Acey Roberts and Jake Wimberly on Twitter with fun banter. I picked on Jake and Jake gave it back. Obviously, they were Jake and Acey on Twitter at the time. They each had anonymous accounts, both of them, not just Acey.

"It was all in fun. This was all before the radio thing was created. Once they got started, I tweeted about them, because it was all in fun and I wanted to see them be successful.

"When they started the blogging page, Acey asked me to write some things. I did, but it was intended to be fun and drive banter on Twitter."

Much of the banter on social media centered around the true identity of the person running the Analesa Presley persona. Many suggested perhaps Faulkner or Roberts was pulling the strings behind the scenes and the whole charade was an internet creation.

Roberts, of course denied any involvement, but defended his new "star" despite having never laid eyes on her.

"No, I didn't meet any of them," Presley said of her blogmates. "My biggest regret with the whole thing is the way people blamed them. AP was created long before *Make It Rain* was."

Dubbed an "Ole Miss Icon" by now retired blogger and podcaster Acey Roberts, Presley transitioned from a self-described "brat" on Twitter to a person some within the Ole Miss media placed confidence.

"There were some media that trusted me," AP explained. "If I knew something about a recruit announcing a certain way, I kept my mouth shut. I didn't hint around to anything before the kid announced. If someone told me something in confidence I made sure I kept that confidence. I had one recruit tell me, while he was committed to an out-of-state, non-SEC school, he was flipping to Ole Miss and told me not to say. He was a fairly big-name recruit. I kept my mouth shut and let him have his day. I would never take that away from a kid."

While those intentions seem noble, interaction between boosters and recruits is strictly prohibited by NCAA bylaws. Much of the contact between Presley and recruits took place publicly in exchanges on social media, but there were some private conversations, too. Conversations between a middle-aged mother in Mississippi and teenagers making one of the first adult decisions of their young lives.

"Usually I would tweet a hype-type tweet about them, and I'd mention them in the tweet," AP explained. "Believe it or not, right or wrong, some recruits like the hype and attention.

"Some would send me a message flirting, but I tried to derail things like that. I was asked to 'party' with them and I always responded, 'I'm not that kind of girl' or 'I don't do the party thing.'

"I rarely sent a private message to someone who had not already contacted me. There was a kid who had gotten hurt who I sent a message and told him I hoped he healed quickly. Things like that. Always, encouraging things.

"I did talk about Ole Miss, but I always encouraged them to talk to their family and do what was right for them. I intended for my tweets to be more hype and all rah, rah, rah! Encouraging more than anything."

Before the whole story fell apart at the seams, the cover story nearly unraveled long before Presley came to prominence in the Magnolia State. Somehow, someway the pretty blonde behind the AP persona, found out her pictures were being used without her knowledge.

"I was caught by Ashley. It was all over her Facebook, but nobody ever saw it," Presley admitted. "I hated it. I wanted out then, but I had people defending me that I didn't even know that well.

"I honestly tried to just be nice to everyone... most of the time. I wish it wouldn't have gotten so big. I often wondered, *why in the world do people care what I think?*

"Well, I wish I'd never done it. I wish I'd have just been anonymous. Funny, once I deleted all of the accounts, I thought I'd miss it, but now I don't care about Twitter."

Why did Analesa Presley capture the imagination of the whole Rebel fanbase? If she would've come on the scene as the middle-aged mom with the snarky remarks and bright banter, would she have still gotten the same opportunities and credibility? I'd like to think, yes, but I guess we'd have to wait for the real person, the real brains and wit behind the Analesa persona, to step forward and give us a demonstration.

While there was a certain satisfaction that went along with cracking the "case," there was a lot of empathy from me. I know many people hate the person who played AP, but in the end, I just felt sorry for her.

I've had countless of people contact me believing they had identified the person behind the internet persona, but just about all of them were wrong. I finally stopped responding to people about it, especially the handful who were correct in their guesses.

Maybe it makes for a better story not knowing who she really is and letting her fade off into Egg Bowl Twitter history. I hope so. I know also what a sad state of affairs this whole fiasco exposed. A lot of well-educated people volunteered to be victims of someone they never met, because she was willing to tell them what they wanted to hear about college football recruiting.

Chapter 9

A Voluntary Gag Order

The 2014 college football season was one for the ages. Both Mississippi State and Ole Miss began the season winning their first seven games. The Bulldogs and Rebels were both undefeated and ranked in the top 10 nationally. The two archrivals even shared the cover of *Sports Illustrated*. These were good times in the Magnolia State.

While many cheered for their own team and spent a portion of their nightly prayers asking for the other to lose, others in Mississippi simply enjoyed having the spotlight on their home state football programs.

The more leisurely fans simply wanted to see Mississippi represented well, and see both teams succeed.

The more die-hard fans weren't happy about sharing the moment, though. They wanted their team to have a moment in the sun all their own.

One clever Mississippi State fan wrote, "Cheering for Ole Miss just because they are from Mississippi is like cheering for the devil, because he's in the Bible."

The Rebels were the first to lose that year as they wound up on the short end of a 10-7 affair in Death Valley at LSU. Bayou Bengal running back Leonard Fournette simply owned the fourth quarter, and for the first time in a long time, a Tiger win over Ole Miss was considered an upset.

Ole Miss dropped from No. 3 to No. 7 in the Associated Press college football poll.

A weekend later, the Rebels fell at home to Auburn, 35-31. In perhaps the cruelest loss ever, Rebel star wide receiver LaQuon Treadwell was tackled at the goal line racing his way to score the winning touchdown for an Ole Miss victory.

On the play, Treadwell suffered a season ending injury. A mad scramble inside the five led to an awkward tackle by Auburn linebacker Kris Frost, and ended with a broken leg for Treadwell.

To add insult to injury, Treadwell fumbled on the play. After an official review, it was determined the ball was loose before the touchdown was recorded. The call was reversed, Auburn was awarded the football and, in turn, the win.

On the other side of the in-state rivalry, Mississippi State ascended to its first ever No. 1 ranking in football, a perch it would sit atop for five consecutive weeks.

Led by future Dallas Cowboys' quarterback Dak Prescott, the Bulldogs knocked off three consecutive top 10 teams; LSU, Texas A&M and Auburn. The lights in Stark Vegas never shined brighter.

The Bulldogs run at No. 1 ended on the road at Alabama, when Nick Saban and his Crimson Tide spoiled another State winning streak with a 25-20 victory in Bryant Denny Stadium

A week later, Dan Mullen's team rebounded and destroyed Vanderbilt, 51-0. Even with that lopsided margin, the score isn't indicative of how dominant the Bulldogs were that Saturday evening.

Bulldog fans who normally avoided road trips to Oxford, elected to lift their self-imposed travel ban in hopes of seeing Mississippi State win in Vaught Hemingway Stadium. A win would be the second time in their three most recent tries, and give Mullen another win in the series over "The School Up North" (TSUN).

Ole Miss quarterback Bo Wallace entered the game nursing a handful of ailments including an ankle injury that was expected to limit his mobility.

Mississippi State still had an outside chance of staying in the FBS playoff top four, thus keeping their narrow hopes of a rematch with Alabama alive. While Ole Miss was out of the playoff picture and playing for no better than third place in the SEC Western Division, the Rebels could play spoiler.

In State's finest season in generations, the Rebels could dash any hope of conference or national championships for their in-state rival Bulldogs. While no season in Starkville is complete without the Golden Egg, the 2014 campaign and the high stakes remaining made the game even more important.

Wallace completed just 13 of his 30 pass attempts, but he made each connection count, throwing for 296 yards. A 46-yard connection to tight end Evan Engram set up the game's first score, and gave Ole Miss an early 7-0 lead.

With 9:37 to go in the third quarter, Prescott scored from a yard out and gave State a 10-7 lead.

Engram would later become a 2017 first-round draft pick for the New York Giants.

The Wallace to Engram connection once again proved successful for the Rebels as an 83-yard catch and run set Ole Miss up inside the State two-yard line. Three plays later, an Ole Miss touchdown gave Freeze and the Rebels a lead they wouldn't relinquish.

The clock struck all zeroes with a final tally of Ole Miss 31, Mississippi State 17.

Mullen nearly walked out of the post-game press conference without answering a single question calling the loss "devastating." Bulldog players willing to talk to the media were in short supply following the disappointing loss to their bitter rival.

On the other side of the stadium, Ole Miss fans rejoiced, having protected their home turf and removed every possibility of Mississippi State advancing to the SEC title game and more. It certainly made for a good senior day.

Both programs advanced to New Year's six bowl games

and both lost. Mississippi State advanced to the Orange Bowl for the third time in school history, but fell to Georgia Tech, 49-34. Ole Miss played in the program's second Peach Bowl game ever and got steamrolled by a Texas Christian team, 42-3. The TCU Horned Frogs were left out of the playoff in the final rankings and took an SEC skin as a parting gift.

Despite the disappointing loss, hopes were high the next year in Oxford. Gone was the program's record-setting quarterback Bo Wallace. But Freeze and his staff had managed to win the signing day autograph of East Mississippi Community College junior college national champion quarterback Chad Kelly.

Kelly, the nephew of former NFL great Jim Kelly of the Buffalo Bills, had a checkered past. Dismissed at Clemson, Kelly made the decision to enroll at EMCC to give his college career a reboot. The pass happy scheme fit Kelly's skill set perfectly. The Lions roared with Kelly under center and outscored their competition 515-38 in the 2014 regular season.

Rebel fans were hopeful their offense would simply pick up where it left off with Kelly following Wallace, who also thrived in Scooba, Mississippi, as a national champion quarterback at EMCC.

Before Kelly was to report to Oxford, an ugly incident unfolded in the wee hours of a December morning. Initial reports said Kelly threatened to shoot up a night club after a member of his entourage had reportedly been kicked out of the establishment earlier in the evening.

Accounts of the incident varied, but they all ended with Kelly in handcuffs and hot water. There were a lot of questions about the Rebels honoring the scholarship extended to the troubled signal caller, but in the end, Freeze followed through and stuck by Kelly.

Many of the initial charges were dismissed, with Kelly electing to plead guilty to a disorderly conduct charge. There was a price to pay, but with the ugly incident now behind him from a legal point of view, Kelly was set to bark the signals for Ole Miss in 2015.

Just as Rebel anxiety had subsided, another incident took place that'd prove to have more lasting consequences.

Star offensive tackle Laremy Tunsil was charged after a family dispute reportedly got out of hand. Tunsil was accused of punching his then stepfather, Lindsey Miller, several times. The initial report out of Oxford was that Tunsil was defending his mother after Miller allegedly shoved her during an argument.

Miller claimed Tunsil was the aggressor and that he was trying to protect Tunsil's amateur status by keeping agents and their representatives away.

Tunsil was projected as the top offensive tackle in the 2016 draft and the battle to land him as a potential client was intense. A true blind side protector is a real commodity at any level of football, but in the NFL, bona fide left tackles command a hefty salary.

Miller and Tunsil pointed fingers at each other. Charges were filed against both parties and the makings of a true soap opera were in place. No matter where the blame lay, this was trouble Ole Miss didn't need.

In what turned out to be a mistake that Freeze and Ole Miss fans everywhere would pay dearly for, the official statement from the Rebel football program painted Miller out to be the bad guy.

"Laremy realizes he could have handled it differently, but I am proud of him for standing up for his mother and protecting his family," Freeze said. "Laremy and his mother have also pressed charges against the stepfather. As we gather more facts, we will make decisions accordingly."

If there was ever a time for a "no comment," this was it. Rather than playing it cool and simply saying he was aware of the incident and that they would gather facts before commenting, Freeze rushed to get out in front of the situation.

Painted by many as an abuser, Miller struck back looking to protect his reputation and share his side of the story. Once he started talking, it took some real effort to keep him quiet.

Within hours of the incident, pictures of Miller's swollen face appeared on TMZ.com. If Freeze and Ole Miss expected Miller to go quietly, it looked as if they were going to be disappointed in a major way.

As is the case in most disputes, there was an emotional reaction by all involved and certainly by those who cheer for Ole Miss. Their franchise left tackle was wrapped up in a family affair gone way too public. At some point, all families argue and some get physical. Rarely, do these issues make the headlines of the local newspaper.

Due to his status as a potential first round draft pick, Tunsil's issues made ESPN's *Sportscenter* and just about every other major sports show or periodical. This was big news.

The allegations themselves, a domestic violence simple assault, were bad enough, but as the details of the incident came to light there were questions about the Florida native's status as an amateur football player.

Painted as the bad guy in the initial reports, Miller had his own side of the story to tell and it appeared he was willing to share it with whoever was willing to listen.

Riley Blevins of *The Clarion-Ledger* was among the first to get an interview with Miller about the night in question and the circumstances that led up to the confrontation.

Miller claimed Tunsil was interacting with pro football agents and expressed concern over the possibility that, handled improperly, the future first rounder's college eligibility could be impacted.

Tunsil's account of the event involved an allegation of Miller pushing his mother, thus sparking the altercation.

No matter who was at fault, both sides agree a fight ensued and in the end a family was irreparably broken.

One of Miller's sons, Derek, watched as his father and the step-brother he looked up to came to blows in their Oxford, Mississippi, home. According the police report, Derek fell as he ran to a neighbor's home looking for help, skinning his knee.

A sad story unfolded in the family during a time that should've been the best of times, and it was played out on a very public stage for all to see.

Both sides filed charges.

Before the matter was settled, Miller did his part to air the dirty laundry, alleging Tunsil had accepted impermissible benefits and gifts from pro agents or their representatives.

Blevins continued to provide Miller with a forum to share his comments about Tunsil, the criminal charges and some less-than-flattering talk about Ole Miss and their handling of things.

Much of that could likely be pushed aside and labeled sour grapes as comments from a stepfather now being pushed out of the family, and out of a potential financial windfall, once Tunsil signed a pro-contract.

Many Rebel fans took that exact stance, and some of those became increasingly critical of Blevins and *The Clarion-Ledger* for giving any credence to statements made by Miller.

Even some members of the Ole Miss media beat turned on Blevins and made their attacks both personal and public.

"No one was ever outwardly unkind, at least not to my

face," Blevins shared with me. "I wasn't there long enough to form relationships with anyone, anyway, nor did I place much emphasis on that when I arrived to be fair.

"Everyone was trying to do their jobs and had different opinions of what that looked like," he said.

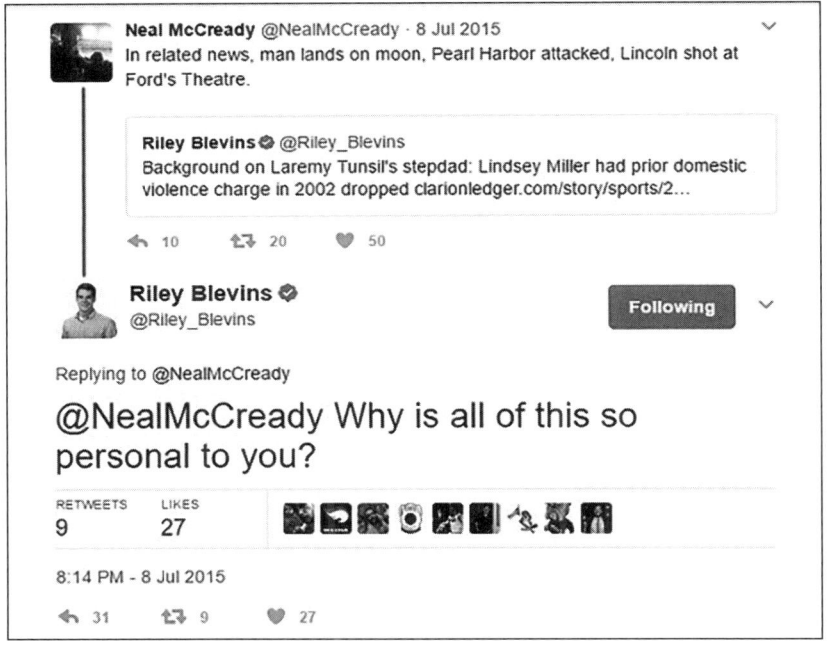

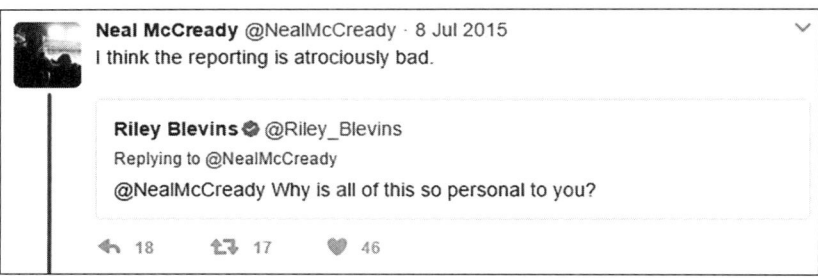

Living in Oxford became a real matter of inconvenience for Blevins who was serving as the Ole Miss beat reporter for Mississippi's largest newspaper. Locals began to confront him in grocery stores and even one during a quiet evening meal with his girlfriend.

The undertow of social media trends turned on Blevins and threatened to pull him under as punishment for shattering the Rebel illusion that all was well in Oxford. The fact that Blevins allowed some room in his column for the other side of the story, rather than the cookie cutter Pollyanna journalism Ole Miss fans had grown to expect, made for a real problem.

How could this be happening, many wondered?

For 60 years, the Magnolia State got its morning news from the Hederman-owned paper. The Clarion-Ledger, a Mississippi institution once owned by the Hederman family, was Rebel to the core.

In 1982, Gannett purchased *The Clarion-Ledger* and began moving forward into a new age of publishing. Old habits die hard in this neck of the woods. While there may've been a change in leadership, the reputation of being a "Rebel Rag" still exists in the hearts and minds of many around the state.

Rebel fans called for Blevins' ouster, while others suggested that Ole Miss-owned businesses should pull their advertising dollars or use their influence with connections at the paper to settle down the young "loose cannon" aboard the battleship Freeze.

To hear Blevins' side of the story, the actions of the vocal minority did little to deter him from doing his job and chasing the truth of the matter.

"The paper was in a time of transition when this happened, which made it a little harder I suppose," Blevins explained. "I had support. I talked to our editors for hours on what to do, how to proceed, etc. They wanted to chase the story as bad as I [did]."

The story stayed in the public eye for weeks. There was a hearing to remove a protective order filed on behalf of Miller against Tunsil. There was the arraignment, and then eventually a dismissal of all charges against all parties.

While the criminal portion of the soap opera was over, there was still the matter of Miller undergoing a series of interviews with the NCAA enforcement staff about potential violations involving Tunsil as part of his college recruitment and impermissible benefits provided to the former five-star talent during his time on the active Ole Miss roster.

This was no longer about a dust-up on the front porch; this could have further [or, far reaching] reaching implications. These were the types of allegations that end careers and derail programs.

As the news of Miller's cooperation with the NCAA began making the rounds, many looked to discredit him, while the more level headed Ole Miss fans wondered if the NCAA had found a smoking gun that would lead to the Rebels undoing.

NCAA enforcement staff reportedly met with Miller on or about July 1, 2015. An Ole Miss spokesperson reportedly told Blevins the program was unaware of the meeting between Miller and NCAA staffer, Chris Howard.

Less than a week later on July 7, Ole Miss released a statement regarding the matter.

"The University of Mississippi department of athletics is aware of the allegations made by Laremy Tunsil's stepfather regarding potential NCAA violations involving Laremy. As we do with any allegation, we initiated an internal investigation last week and have offered the NCAA our full cooperation. We take the obligations to the NCAA and SEC very seriously, and we will continue to educate and monitor and enforce all applicable rules. Any other reports are speculation until the process is complete."

Miller became public enemy No. 1 in the eyes of Rebel fans. In many respects, Miller breathed new life into an NCAA case that was winding down.

The keyboard cowboys that comprise the Ole Miss message board and social media community continued to bash Blevins for allowing Miller the chance to speak out and defend himself. It became very personal and widespread.

Right or wrong, Blevins was giving both sides an opportunity to tell their story. Granted, Ole Miss was rather limited in what they could say due to NCAA bylaws regarding on-going investigations and potential civil liability.

Once word spread that the criminal complaints against both Miller and Tunsil were no longer active, many Ole Miss fans deemed the matter completely over and done, as if the local courts held some sort of magical jurisdiction over the NCAA enforcement process.

I shared a few notes with Blevins during his time on the Ole Miss beat. I liked him long before he was an employee of *The Clarion-Ledger*. Before getting his start in print media, Blevins worked some for the *Scout.com* Tennessee site, *InsideTennessee. com.*

The Illinois native would make the move to Jackson and begin his tenure with *The Clarion-Ledger* as a prep reporter working alongside award-winning journalist Courtney Cronin.

He worked hard and had real talent. He was promoted to the Ole Miss beat in a matter of months. Blevins replaced Hugh Kellenburger, who'd covered the Rebels for nearly four years before taking a post in Jackson as a statewide columnist.

The grind of covering an SEC beat, the backlash associated

with chasing an unpopular story, and being away from family appears to have taken a toll on Blevins.

On August 18, 2015, Blevins announced he was leaving his post at *The Clarion-Ledger* for a job in Chicago, Illinois, outside of journalism.

"There was a lot of pressure on me during all of it, most of which I placed on myself," Blevins admitted. "It all got me thinking. Is it worth it? The low pay? This stress? The long hours? The lack of job stability? Being far from home? Missing moments with people you care about?

"And my answer was, no. It was clearly, no."

Conspiracy theories made the rounds shortly after Blevins left *The Ledger*. Many suggested Ole Miss had the young beat writer "processed" out, but the chance to work close to home with better pay and hours was too much to pass on.

"I laugh so hard every time I see theories of being run out by *The Clarion-Ledger* or Ole Miss," Blevins shared. "I left on my own accord and probably shocked a lot of my co-workers and bosses in doing so.

"I'm honestly glad it happened just as it did. I wouldn't change it. I learned valuable lessons that made me a better person both personally and professionally. I'm very happy today."

With Blevins no longer in the state and asking questions that provoked uncomfortable answers, I was pretty much the lone dissenter in Mississippi media reporting on the big storm brewing in Oxford.

What's also of note is the sports editor who hired Blevins, Zachary Creglow, would part ways with *The Clarion-Ledger* shortly after seeing his department reel in a handful of Associated Press Sports Editors awards for some tremendous work on the prep beat.

I'm not sure if we ever got an official explanation on whether Creglow jumped or was pushed, but the man who replaced him as head sports editor of the state's largest newspaper was the same reporter who Blevins replaced on the Ole Miss beat, Kellenberger.

Kellenberger had earned a reputation as being a bit of an agent' provocateur and a reporter who didn't mind taking shots at Mississippi State unnecessarily in what appeared to be a running attempt to curry favor with the Ole Miss readership.

Perhaps the one Kellenberger column that drew the most reaction was a hit piece on Mississippi State iconic quarterback Dak Prescott who was considered a potential Heisman trophy candidate by many sports pundits around the Southeast and the nation.

Kellenberger took the hatchet to Prescott essentially calling his candidacy a farce and his magical fourth quarter comeback win over Ole Miss in 2013 a fluke. The Appalachian State-educated reporter referenced some "almost interceptions" to support his faulty premise that Heisman voters need not waste their time with Prescott.

Odd words from a state newspaper about one of the greatest players to ever represent a Mississippi university on the fields of play.

Under Kellenberger's leadership, *The Clarion-Ledger* experienced a dramatic shift in the direction of their coverage of the Ole Miss NCAA woes. While Blevins chased the story, the paper seemed content to let others break news in his absence.

Rather than write actual news articles with quotes from people involved or close to the story, *The Clarion-Ledger* decided to write articles about articles. Virtual click bait re-runs of other journalists' work became the norm out of Jackson.

Blevins left both the area and the industry, Creglow returned to his native Midwest, and Kellenberger was serving as the shot caller. There was still the matter of hiring an Ole Miss beat writer before the 2015 season began.

Enter Tennessee native, Daniel Paulling. Unlike Blevins before him, Paulling had some experience in the newspaper industry. The Missouri graduate would make the move from Lubbock, Texas, from a position covering the Red Raiders of Texas Tech to Oxford and the Rebels of Ole Miss.

Unbeknownst to Paulling, the football program he was about to cover was one with secrets galore. His predecessor was essentially run out of town for digging to uncover some of those secrets.

Just weeks before the transition was complete on the beat, one major mystery involving Tunsil was already in motion.

Throughout the summer months, speculation surrounding Tunsil's amateur status ran wild. Some suggested he'd played his last down for the Rebels due to NCAA troubles yet to be announced. Supposed and self-proclaimed Ole Miss insiders told the Rebel nation that all was well with the talented left tackle.

"The cat is in the bag and the bag is in the river" narrative was a popular one among Rebel fans and media who were more than happy to whistle past the graveyard in hopes the ghosts of recruiting-violations-past kept their distance.

Giddy Rebel fans had convinced themselves that any claims Tunsil's stepfather made would be easily refuted and in the end Freeze and his reputation as a "good" man with a clean coaching record would be given the benefit of the doubt.

Ole Miss opened the 2015 football season at home against Tennessee-Martin. A blow out was expected, but prior to kick-off Rebel fans were served with a gut punch. The school would announce that Tunsil wouldn't play and the decision was based on potential NCAA issues.

"As a precautionary measure, we are withholding Laremy Tunsil from today's game until the pending process can be completed," the statement read. "We are cooperating fully with the NCAA and feel this is the best way to protect Laremy, our football program and the university."

The Rebels would go on to steam roll the Tennessee-Martin Sky Hawks by a score of 76-3. While there was certainly a lot to enjoy on the field that day, fans grew concerned about what was taking place off of the field, and just how serious the issues were with Tunsil.

Freeze offered no firm time table for Tunsil's return to action during his postgame press conference, but many Rebel media folks citing "sources" felt confident the talented big man would be back in two weeks for sure when Ole Miss played Alabama.

Alabama week came and went without any word on Tunsil. Ole Miss won the game anyway. The Rebels had beaten the Crimson Tide in back to back years for the first time in school history. The 2015 victory was the first Ole Miss win in

Tuscaloosa in the series against the Tide.

Ole Miss started the season with a 4-0 mark before getting shelled in the Swamp by Florida, 38-10.

The Rebels bounced back the next week and beat New Mexico State 52-3 for homecoming. A week later, the Rebels lost on the road against rival Memphis, 37-24.

With their season on the brink, Ole Miss got some good news. After missing seven games, Tunsil was reinstated and deemed eligible to compete for the Rebels down the stretch.

Ole Miss would close out the regular season with a 4-1 record including wins over LSU and Mississippi State earning a berth in the Sugar Bowl.

The contest in the New Orleans Superdome was the first Sugar Bowl for Ole Miss since 1970. The Rebels rolled over Oklahoma State 48-20. New generations of Rebel fans who'd struggled in the proverbial "wilderness" for more than 40 years, now had a Sugar Bowl of their very own.

The celebration ran long into the night as the French Quarter hosted grateful Rebel fans enjoying the spoils of their victory. But, the tab for the ill-gotten gains of Ole Miss football would come soon after.

Chapter 10

Praying for Peace, Readying for War

I'm not sure how other people are wired. What works for me may not work for them and vice versa. I've been an ultra-competitive person my entire life. For as long as I can remember I've been one who is eager to pick teams, and I've been fiercely loyal to whichever side I ended up on.

My brother-in-law, Chad, worked for Pepsi for many years, which meant Coca-Cola was not allowed in our house in support of him and our extended family. When he left that job, we made the switch back to Coke products. It was a tough stretch, but we managed.

In the great music feuds of the early 1990s, it was Pearl Jam versus Nirvana for me, and I picked The Offspring over Green Day. To this day, I've never purchased an album or song by either Green Day or Nirvana. I haven't really shared that with many people until now. Sure, friends and family know I don't care for those bands, but I'm not sure anyone knows how deep it goes with me.

While I maintain a state of indifference about most things that don't directly affect me, the issues I have strong opinions about are things that truly matter to me.

If I'm your friend, then your enemies become my enemies. I'll have your back even when you're wrong, and try to change the subject to something we can both be right about. It's what true friends do.

Call it a character defect if you must, but there's just not much middle ground with me.

When this story hit my radar, I was eager to learn as much as I could about it. I was completely committed very early on in this whole saga. The journalist in me was charged with the notion there could be some major story unfolding few knew about. Additionally, there was an element of a clandestine cover-up at play. I like knowing things that most people don't know. I love learning about things people don't want you to know.

I guess I'm simply nosy.

One of the things that really let me know I had hit a nerve was the response by many in the Ole Miss media. They couldn't beat me on the facts in most cases, so they decided they would make it personal. Their supporters followed suit.

My Twitter feed became a flood of attempted character assassinations, poorly crafted conspiracy theories, and just outright lies about me and what I had to say.

So many people wanted to assign motive and cast aspersions in my direction, rather than aim their angst towards the people responsible for the NCAA issues, and the false narrative to cover it.

On the flip side, the more I talked and told the truth about what I was hearing, support grew, and not just from Mississippi State fans and supporters. Before long, I had members of the national and regional media reaching out to compare notes with me.

Two themes became evident after my discussions with them: First, this story was far reaching; second, outside of a precious few media members friendly to Ole Miss, the national perception of things was changing.

One national personality reached out to me and began the conversation by saying, "When it comes to this Ole Miss NCAA mess, I hear you're the guy to talk to."

I'm not sure if the comment was more flattering or ironic.

As the out-of-state media folks got up to speed, they all seemed to have one question in common, "Why was the in-state media not all over this story?"

Two decades ago, those in the print media looked down on the "internet media" as if putting something on newsstands was the dividing line between the real and make-believe journalists.

As the newspaper industry changed, they have gravitated to more of an online presence. Gone are the one column-a-day jobs. They've been replaced by essentially instant coverage that is featured on websites and social media, much of which never makes the paper.

They used to despise us, and now they've become us. Many of the same writers who looked down their noses at all of us, wondering how we got credentialed, now run websites. By the same token, many newspaper editors today have staffed their sports beat with men and women who got their start working for internet recruiting sites.

Sure, there are still some in this industry who hold on to that same tired, antiquated notion that the website guys are somehow beneath their status, but I am pretty confident most of them would pass on comparing W2s or 1099s at year's end.

It makes for an interesting dynamic when the biggest sports scandal in Mississippi for decades is largely ignored by in-state press, and the one guy—ME—the guy who works for a Mississippi State website, is the guy feeding the masses hungry for real answers.

I have to admit, it does get lonely sometimes. Sure, there are plenty of supportive calls and messages, but those people aren't around when I open the mailbox hoping I don't have a letter from some attorney trying to take what I've worked hard for.

What's ironic about that sort of thing is I've received several letters from attorneys, most Ole Miss educated, wanting to represent me. I never responded to any of them. Honestly, I never just assume anyone's intentions are noble. For all I knew, it could've all been some sort of set-up. I'm always wary of such.

I once got a letter e-mailed from some guy claiming to be friends with some fraternity brothers on the Ole Miss campus. He hemmed and hawed around for days wondering if he could trust me, but he finally relented and sent me the letter.

It was essentially a code of conduct for how to handle things during the big recruiting weekends at Ole Miss. There were inside jokes about previous parties where "Trevor" kept asking some random party goer if he was the five-star and strict instructions to look the other way if brothers saw something going down.

The letter was completely hilarious, but in the back of my mind I was wondering how I got so lucky. How did this document just find its way to me?

I shared the letter privately with several people along with my concerns that it felt like some sort of red herring. Here was this letter typed up on official letterhead and allegedly taped to the backside of a chapter room door.

I spoke with a couple of people in the Greek community who tried to help me authenticate the letter. I was even sent a chapter member list and a composite picture of the Ole Miss chapter in question.

After doing the due diligence, it just didn't feel right to me. I was afraid someone was trying to have a laugh at my expense. I searched the letter looking for some hidden code, but never found anything that made sense.

I elected to just wait it out and see if the "source" of the letter would start pushing me to publish it. In our initial correspondence, he was timid and presented himself as someone who wanted the truth out there without it being linked to him.

As I drug my feet, he began to grow frustrated with me.

He wrote to me if I wasn't going to use the letter, then he was going to share it with some other sites in an effort to get it out there publicly.

I declined. To date, the letter hasn't resurfaced in any media reports, which in some way is a confirmation of sorts that something was up. Perhaps it was a fraternity prank or some attempt to damage my credibility, either way I never took the chance.

If I had to put a number on it, I would say about 75 percent of the tips sent to me about this investigation turned out to be nothing of real value. I appreciated every single one of them, but most weren't solid.

More times than not, the tipster simply didn't understand the rules or the process. Their intentions were good and they wanted the truth to be known, but much of what they alleged either wasn't rooted in fact or wasn't outside of the lines of fair play.

Many others knew something, couldn't prove it or were reluctant to get involved. It's amazing how many people knew of violations, but were content to just let it all go down. Some were eager to see a kid from their town have a chance at doing something amazing, and didn't want to stand in the way of opportunity even if it meant something improper had taken place.

The bulk of tips from people who actually knew something came with the disclaimer, "You didn't hear this from me, but...." Those messages were always intriguing. I never asked people what their motivations where, but many offered them anyway.

There were a lot of people throughout the region who volunteered they just wanted to see Ole Miss go down. The collective sentiment of that group was that they were simply sick of it all; cutting corners, the denials, the spin, and the "catch us if you can" mentality had rubbed many the wrong way.

I appeared on a radio show in Tuscaloosa, Alabama, hosted by Ryan Fowler. He shared my contact information with his listeners. For the greater part of the afternoon I read through a combination of tall tales from the recruiting trail, messages of encouragement and some tips that had some teeth to them.

One person who contacted me was convinced that Ole Miss was responsible for Alabama running back Bo Scarborough being suspended the first four games of his playing career. The former high school All-American was rehabbing from an ACL tear anyway, so chances were Scarborough would've sat out those games regardless.

Crimson Tide coach Nick Saban alluded to some NCAA issues regarding Scarborough's recruitment that didn't involve Alabama as part of a routine press conference.

Rumors began to fly about Ole Miss, which became a popular message board topic of discussion.

I filed an Open Records Request with the University of Alabama inquiring about NCAA correspondence between the University and the NCAA regarding players who'd been suspended and/or reinstated due to potential NCAA violations. The Alabama general counsel office replied they weren't in possession of such documents.

Speculation continued to grow, but I finally learned from multiple parties that Ole Miss wasn't the offending institution involving Scarborough. In fact, I was told no SEC schools were involved in the incident. With his suspension a thing of the past, everybody simply wanted to move on.

The request to Alabama wasn't the first one I'd filed. I filed several with Ole Miss. I actually had my attorney draw up the first one, because I wanted to be taken seriously. I was also unfamiliar with the process at the time and didn't want to make a mistake.

Shortly after I sent the request in, I went public with that bit of news. I made a lengthy post on the topic on our forums at *Genespage.com* that read: "As you are aware, I have been very open about the existence of an ongoing NCAA investigation at the University of Mississippi. While some have been critical of me for my willingness to discuss the matter, I feel it is a matter that impacts the landscape of college football in the state of Mississippi.

"For reasons unknown to me, the in-state media by and large has elected to take a pass on this important news story. Most of them have essentially walked in lock step with the talking points of the Ole Miss narrative without question.

"I was contacted over two years ago about the ACT issues being investigated regarding David Saunders, Ginny Crager and the allegations made regarding the supervision of the testing center there in Wayne County. I am not going to get into all of the specific allegations, but some of them have now surfaced in the Louisiana-Lafayette NCAA file.

"In October of 2014, I was contacted by a friend in Tupelo who caught wind of a neighbor of his being interviewed face to face by the NCAA regarding some potential recruiting violations. Two weeks later, I learned the same NCAA investigator had interviewed folks in and around Jackson.

"It was clear this was more than just a fire drill deal.

"I tried in vain twice to pass this story along to the *Clarion Ledger*, because I felt it was really more in their scope of journalism. They had little interest in the story despite the facts. I was recently told that they simply "had too much on their plate." The state's largest newspaper with all of their resources was too busy.

"Over the course of the past year, I have not run from discussion about this investigation. I have been criticized and told that I should hold quiet. I will not. What I have said, am saying and will continue to say is true. I have had my integrity called into question over this issue and some have essentially dared me to prove my claims. I have taken steps to do that.

"On January 15th, on my direction my attorney prepared a Mississippi Open Records Act Request for the general legal counsel of the University of Mississippi, Lee Tyner. This request was filed on January 16th.

"On January 26th, the University of Mississippi legal counsel responded to my request and agreed to provide some of the documents requested. Many of the documents requested involve the current NCAA investigation. According to the Freedom of Information Act, if anyone on that campus has the documents I have requested, then they are bound by the law to provide them.

"While I suspect most of the sensitive documents will likely be withheld, we are prepared to pursue legal remedy to obtain them.

"The University of Mississippi had 14 business days from the date of my request to supply the documents. Friday the 5th is the final day for the University to comply. I followed up today and found that the person handling my request is out of the office until Monday. I was asked to agree to release those documents next week. I have agreed to that request.

"I sent a second request to the University of Mississippi on January 23rd requesting any NCAA Notice of Allegations received by the University during the calendar year 2016. I have not heard back on that request, so I assume it will be addressed along with the University's release next week.

"Some will ask why I would take these steps. First of all, I will say that I am only going to be called a liar so many times. I knew that I was right and much of the Forde article released last week confirms what I have shared, but there is more to come. Ole Miss AD Ross Bjork has now acknowledged the receipt of the Notice of Allegations, so there is no longer any question about the existence of the probe or that the situation has risen to the level of allegations being levied by the NCAA.

"I am also more than a little tired of people sitting on this story and turning a blind eye to it.

"Finally, I am not Riley Blevins and I will not be run off. How he was treated was absolutely shameful. There is a part of me that feels like somebody needed to finish the deal, so that all he had to endure meant something to somebody beyond himself. The truth is the truth no matter how you slice it and frankly I think it's time we all got the truth rather this bill of goods they keep selling us.

"I am prepared for whatever the next step may be. I am sure this will be a bumpy ride and that there will be people who try to silence me and I am prepared for that. I will not be intimidated or treated less than for wanting the truth to be known.

I will keep you posted."

Those words made the rounds rapidly. I wanted our folks to know I was working to get the truth of the matter, and I also wanted to turn the pressure up on the in-state media.

My hope was those who read about my request would take to social media and ask other media entities if they were following suit and chasing the truth. I wanted to flush the notice out and have it out there for public review.

I was a stranger in a strange land when it came to the Freedom of Information Act. I wasn't even sure if Ole Miss would respond. I thought they may pick and choose who they gave the information to. I thought they might leak it to an Ole Miss friendly media member first, and then send it to the rest of us once it was public. The timing of their disclosure might be after the Rebel talking points had been established.

I actually spoke with David Brandt of the Associated Press, and told him I thought he may actually get it first since he was widely viewed as an objective observer in this state. Brandt explained to me we'd all likely get the same information on the same date to ensure compliance with the law.

Frankly, I didn't care if they sent it to me first or not. I just wanted it out there. For months, Ole Miss fans and media had painted me as a liar who concocted a story about Ole Miss being under investigation, and made claims about a popular coach in Huge Freeze.

I knew I was right and the Ole Miss media folks were either along for the ride voluntarily, or being kept in the dark. I'm not sure many of them cared either way. They just didn't appear to be too keen on the Mississippi State guy being right.

Needless to say, my actions to unearth the truth were met with a lot of criticism and insults from Ole Miss fans. I needed to be shown my place, according to many of them.

One fake Ole Miss insider promised his flock, "Steve will be exposed after signing day."

A few folks weren't willing to wait and elected to take matters into their own hands. E-mails were sent to various people near me, and within our organization in vain attempts to silence me. The e-mails were never provided to me, but the gist of it all is that they wanted me fired. They called me a liar and accused me of making the whole thing up to hurt them in recruiting. They said it was all some pre-signing day plot to tank their recruiting efforts.

There was the usual message board bravado and bluster, but a couple of individuals let their emotions get the better of them and took things a little too far.

My deep sleep was ruined late one morning as my phone simply wouldn't stop ringing. It isn't atypical for the iPhone to get a strong workout on any given day once recruiting efforts reach a fever pitch.

With National Signing Day approaching, there is no shortage of people both giving and requesting information about recruits who're about to close in on a decision. On this particular morning, the messages were of a different sort.

I had double digit texts and missed calls regarding a rather specific threat.

I'm not going to share the individual's identity out of respect for his family and friends who'd certainly be embarrassed by his actions, but I'll share with you the words he wrote on that winter's morning.

The discussions about my records request were widespread and filled with passionate remarks about how this was all unfolding. One man felt the penalty for daring to tell the truth about his beloved Ole Miss football program and its indiscretions should be death to the messenger.

"There are measures going on right now to end him for good," the clown wrote of me. "He will be lucky if he can ever speak again. Trust me when I say he won't be around much longer."

To ensure there were no misunderstandings about his feelings he made another comment to remove all doubt.

"We have been on this for a while," the threat continued. "Your crusade against us will turn out horribly for you. We have our own crusade going on behind the scenes. You will be finished and you are too stupid to see this. So, keep playing the hero. I'm sure this thread gets you off and you can go repost this thread to make you feel important. You will get the letter and whatever else you want. The thing you don't seem to get is that (David) Saunders helped several players get qualified on your team as well as Bama. We've been holding onto shit that will blow your mind. Let's play. You better watch your back. I wouldn't go anywhere if I were you."

I talked with a few friends about the threats that were now everywhere on social media. I called my attorney and shared the developments with him and he simply asked, "What are you doing on the phone with me? Get to the police station!"

As my beautiful wife slept after working overnight, there I was filling out forms, and sharing my personal information with officers who seemed to be taking the matter more seriously than I was.

They made calls to supervisors, set up routine patrols of my house, provided me with tips on keeping myself and my family safe. I wasn't that concerned about it until I met with law enforcement. Seeing them get things moving caused me to elevate emotionally.

I started thinking about my own code of conduct should some idiot with an Egg Bowl grudge show up at my house and come anywhere near my family. How far would I have to go to protect them? How many intruders are too many to handle? Do I need to buy more dogs? Do we need to set up another fence?

How safe is your family if some internet crazy just shows up at your front door unannounced? What do you do when he does?

The possibilities are unnerving.

As I made the drive home, I wondered if I should tell my wife. I didn't want her to worry, but at the same time I wanted her to be aware somebody out there confessed publicly to being part of a larger group, who were planning to prevent me from ever speaking again and advising me not to go anywhere.

No, I had to tell her, but how? What do you say? What are the best words to use to tell someone that our entire family may be at risk, because some guy on the internet got his feelings hurt over college football?

My disgust for the whole situation ran gut level. I felt like puking. I began to ask myself some serious questions. Was this all worth it? At what point is it enough? Do I need to just stop and let somebody else carry the weight of all of this?

As all of those thoughts and possibilities raced through my head, I intuitively made my wife a pot of coffee. I was about to lay some heavy information on her, the least I could do is be sure she'd had a cup o' joe to start the day, or afternoon in her case.

I barely remember what I said after, "Babe, I just got back from the sheriff's office." I do remember detailing the whole thing out to her, and watching her face wash over with worry.

She had been shielded from most of the negativity since this whole thing started and made me live up to a half-hearted promise to only respond to internet trolls if I had something funny to say, but this was different.

Someone we didn't know was making threats of physical harm. She cried as it registered in her mind, and that absolutely wrecked me.

As tears streamed down her face, she reached for me and said, "I don't want anything to happen to you."

I assured her I was fine and everything would be fine. I hoped and believed that I said it with enough confidence to ease her concerns. As I told her we were pressing charges, she dried her eyes and said, "Good, I hope they go to jail."

Those moments in the kitchen with her crying in my arms distressed me. I was fuming, but was determined to channel my anger to getting to the truth. To stop then would've made it all be for nothing. I had to see it through.

In the following days, I'd see deputies pass the house, and it made me feel better. I was never worried for me, but I slept better knowing someone was looking out for my wife and kids if I couldn't.

I cut back on travel and stayed home more. I missed some

work-related things and that bothered me, but I had to be a father first and be home to protect my family.

I kept my eyes open everywhere I went. I checked cars at the gas station for college team regalia and vanity plates. I wanted to know if I was surrounded by friends or foes at all times. I kept my head down, and kept moving in and out of the store. I didn't want trouble.

I didn't want the kids to worry, so I never told them the full details. I just told everybody to be aware of their surroundings, and if anything looked odd to call me. I reminded everybody to check around their cars before driving anywhere. You just can't be too careful.

One afternoon, my oldest daughter Audrey, came home and said. "Hey, my teacher said to tell you that we can handle those crazy Ole Miss fans the old fashioned way if we need to."

Unmoved she went to her room. It was a pretty solid reminder this story was getting bigger, and it was going to be more and more difficult to keep things private. It was now a very public fight.

The next time I was on The Boneyard, I mentioned the threats, and assured everyone I would be reporting all of them to law enforcement. That word made the rounds and a lot of the threats simply went away.

The original coward, who chose to make his threats behind the cloak of anonymity, reached out to me through my colleague David Murray. David forwarded a message he received.

Despite all of the upheaval he'd caused, this guy wanted me to know what a good Christian family man he was and he didn't mean to cause such a fuss. He tried to explain in vain that he really meant he wanted to end my career and not my life. I think one of us has the wrong idea about how Christian family men are supposed to act.

Weeks later I started getting messages and phone calls from people I hadn't seen or talked to in years. Apparently, a lawyer friend of the keyboard cowboy went on Facebook to see which friends we had in common. Several of them contacted me with a similar story about how this attorney was just trying to help his friend stay out of trouble with his family.

What about my family, I wondered.

I had one of my attorneys reach out to the lawyer contacting my friends to let him know we considered it harassment. It stopped shortly thereafter.

They wanted to sit down and talk with me. I thought that was pretty rich. This dude threatens me on a public forum and now he wants to sit down and talk. I passed. What was there to gain? I just wanted to be left alone.

The absurdity of the request still makes me chuckle. If he wanted to apologize, then he could do so in the same way he threatened me—publicly.

I wasn't interested in a meet and greet. I have enough friends and I'm not looking to add any who can't keep their emotions in check.

One person mentioned he didn't really have anything if money was what I was after. As if. It's amazing really. Money always seems to come up when some folks need to get out of trouble.

I didn't need or want any of their money. I just wanted them to leave my family and me alone.

Along those same lines, someone close to me was contacted by someone claiming to represent a group of people hoping to convince me not to write this book. My friend said they wanted to know what it'd take to get me to back off and not go through with publishing the book.

I told them one million dollars. I knew it was a ridiculous amount and they would never pay it, but I felt like they needed to know I was serious about going through with this endeavor.

A week or so later, another friend contacted me and said he heard from an Ole Miss friend I wanted $500,000 to walk away from the story, and just move on with life.

I told him that the Ole Miss "sources" couldn't even get that right, and it was one million dollars.

My integrity was never for sale, at least not for any price they were willing to pay. This is a story that needed to see the light of day and I'm not sure you can put a price on that. People need to know what has gone on, and how so many elected to turn a blind eye to it all.

Chapter 11

One of us was Wrong

February 10, 2016

The Clarion Ledger's headline screamed, "Bjork: NCAA says investigation into Ole Miss is over!" While the usual Rebel lap dogs spread this "news" like the Harry Truman declaration that announced the end of World War II, the failed piece of propaganda read more like a premature rush-to-print "Dewey Defeats Truman" beat-the-deadline gaffe.

The Clarion Ledger's editors and reporters were so woefully behind the curve as this investigation unfolded, I am certain the powers that be at the state's largest newspaper nearly broke their arms patting themselves on their collective backs due to their good fortune. Ole Miss beat writer Daniel Paulling and acting sports editor Hugh Kellenberger were able to get an exclusive interview with Ole Miss athletic director Ross Bjork, who provided a veiled and self-serving update of the University's NCAA troubles.

True or untrue, the story was a coup for *The Ledger*, which had downplayed news of Ole Miss' issues throughout the process. Sure, they'd written articles about other issues, but now the Jackson, Mississippi-based daily was set to generate a lot of "clicks" and sell a lot of papers thanks in large part to getting some comments on the record from Bjork.

With the alleged transgressions of the Jan. 22nd NCAA notice, now brought to the attention of the Ole Miss administration, many fans demanded answers.

Real answers were in short supply in what amounted to an Ole Miss press release with little in the way of substance. Bjork simply hit the highlights:

1. The Investigation is over.
2. There is no second letter coming.
3. Ole Miss wasn't charged with Lack of Institutional Control.
4. Head coach Hugh Freeze wasn't accused of wrong-doing.

In the end, every one of those statements proved to be completely false. At the time, Ole Miss fans were all too eager to believe their athletic director was being honest, and for all intents and purposes he had drawn a line in the sand.

These statements of bravado buoyed the spirits of a fan base that had been beaten down by the realization that all wasn't well within the Rebel football program as their media outlets had suggested. Just a few days before, the University elected to confirm the receipt of the Jan. 22 Notice of Allegations on the very day many star recruits were arriving on the picture-perfect Oxford campus for their official visits.

What was expected to be a weekend filled with food, fun and football, turned into 48 hours of explaining away an inconvenient truth; the signing class of 2016 would spend part of their college football careers on NCAA probation.

Many of the visitors who attended that Jan. 29 weekend event — the last available official visit weekend prior to signing day 2016 — signed on with Ole Miss. Others elected to seek their college football futures elsewhere. But, all told, the Rebel attempts at damage control proved to be mostly effective.

When the ink was finally dry, Ole Miss had signed a strong out-of-state crop led by the nation's top quarterback in five-star Shea Patterson, five-star offensive tackle Greg Little, and four-star safety Deontay Anderson, among others.

The Rebels did well at home signing the state's top

defensive tackle in Benito Jones of Wayne County, Mississippi, wide receiver D.K. Metcalf, the son of former Ole Miss star offensive lineman Terrance Metcalf, and the state's top wide receiver, A.J. Brown, of all places, Starkville High School.

Hugh Freeze's staunchest supporters would suggest the Rebels were simply outworking other programs on the recruiting trail, and the 2016 signing class was evidence of that. Take a look back at the 2013 class that brought in Robert Nkemdiche, Laquan Treadwell and Laremy Tunsil - that was no fluke.

Others outside the Rebel circle of trust declared, "Here we go again."

The fact that Freeze and his staff signed a national-level class under the cloud of suspicion caused by the NCAA probe was both head scratching and noteworthy at the same time.

Fans of rival programs opined that the Rebel coaching staff wasn't being honest with recruits about the severity of the pending NCAA sanctions.

ESPN recruiting insider Gerry Hamilton interviewed blue chipper Deontay Anderson after his official visit to Oxford. The comments from Anderson certainly lead one to believe that evading the truth was a tactical move of the Ole Miss coaching staff during that January weekend.

"It didn't affect me," Anderson told Hamilton when asked about the NCAA investigation. "I talked to Coach Freeze about it. He said it was about things that had happened in the past before he got to Ole Miss. I knew he would be honest with me. When I first heard it, it didn't shake me up."

While Anderson and some of his recruiting class peers were satisfied with Freeze's explanations, a skeptical public wasn't buying it. If anything, the whispers of wrong-doing were now approaching a roar within the Magnolia State.

Rumors of NCAA investigators having boots on the ground

in Mississippi in the weeks leading up to national signing day, and in the days after, apparently had legs. I began to receive tips that NCAA enforcement staff members Chris Howard and Mike Sheridan had spent time interviewing some of the top players in the state of Mississippi about their courtships by college football programs, namely Ole Miss.

I shared some of this information on *The Boneyard* as well as our website forums at *Genespage.com*. While I was reluctant to name names, and cast aspersions at the innocent, I felt it was important my listeners and readers were aware of the fact that the NCAA investigation into Ole Miss was on-going despite their assertions to the contrary.

There was a part of me that was completely shocked when Bjork essentially threw down the gauntlet declaring the investigation over despite the fact some of Ole Miss' priority recruiting targets were face to face with NCAA investigators within days of his interview with *The Clarion Ledger.*

The facts of the matter simply didn't line up with the narrative being spun out of Oxford. The only folks who really believed the probe was over were those who simply wanted it to be over.

My claims that the interview process was still on-going were met by skepticism from Bulldogs and Rebels alike who struggled to wrap their minds around the fact that a sitting Southeastern Conference athletic director would make a deep-water statement publicly unless he had some real facts to support it privately.

I don't know what Bjork knew and when he knew it, but I knew questions were still being asked and they had nothing to do with Laremy Tunsil.

This became a watershed moment in the story. On the one hand, you had a popular administrator, Bjork, making claims in the paper that most Mississippians have turned to for news within their state for decades.

On the other hand, there was this long-haired, tattooed, Mississippi State Bulldog sports writer, riding a wave of popularity, which social media and message boards had provided, who was the lone voice among media outlets calling the whole Ole Miss message into question.

While fans in the middle could find some common ground in the months leading up to this moment about the investigation, now we had a parting of the ways. It was time to get left or get right, because there was no longer any room in the middle. The investigation was over or it wasn't.

Some on the Ole Miss side of things tried to suggest interviews of blue chippers around the state were routine or essentially standard protocol for the enforcement staff.

It was a good try, but once again, part of a false narrative spread by the Ole Miss media.

The fact of the matter, as I learned and later confirmed with the NCAA, is the "Top Prospect" program was essentially abandoned years ago.

That program involved a round of post signing day interviews with some of the nation's most sought after prospects to see what, if anything, could be learned about possible misdeeds during the recruiting process.

These discussions with signees reportedly yielded little if any evidence of real value. While the program was revamped a few times and called various things, it was eventually dropped from the NCAA to-do list long before Ross Bjork set the state ablaze with his line in the sand about his athletics department's woes coming to an end.

I later learned that the NCAA enforcement staff elected to become more proactive in their pursuit of knowledge of wrong-doing. Once a player signs, the hay is essentially in the barn rather than in the field.

As one NCAA staffer told me via conference call, "We would rather prevent a violation than process one."

While it isn't clear what, if any, violations were prevented during the Ole Miss investigation, it's abundantly clear that some were processed while the Rebels were already under NCAA scrutiny.

Long after Bjork was verbally notified by the NCAA that his department was under formal investigation, the Rebels continued to rack up rules infractions. They'd later admit these were violations of NCAA bylaws, many of which occurred during the Hugh Freeze era.

Assistant coaches on the Freeze staff, Maurice Harris, Chris Kiffin and Derrick Nix were named in the Jan. 22 Notice of Allegations, along with former Rebel staffers David Saunders and Chris Vaughn who'd moved on to the University of Louisiana-Lafayette and the University of Texas respectively.

Both were ultimately dismissed from their posts with their new programs amongst rumors pointing back to alleged misdeeds at Ole Miss.

Questions about more Ole Miss coaches and staffers were rising to the surface in early 2016. Meanwhile, the man charged with leading the Rebel athletic programs was declaring the probe over? Now, come on y'all. Somebody's telling a story, here.

One of us was wrong, and even back on that brisk winter day, I knew it wasn't me.

Perhaps Bjork, who was riding the cult of personality, and fighting feelings of frustration over the possible fall of that persona, felt that by declaring the investigation over, he could simply speak its merciful end into existence.

He couldn't.

The noise in the Ole Miss machine didn't go away, nor should it have. It was clear to most caught up in the Rebel culture that claims made surrounding the first batch of allegations, and the arms' length denials made by those in the Freeze camp, which indirectly fingered former Ole Miss coach Houston Nutt, were disingenuous at best and possibly unethical.

Leaks in and around the Rebel football program downplayed the severity of any connections to the current football staff; namely Hugh Freeze himself. Those well-placed information springs played well against the backdrop of a January 30, 2016 press release that Bjork made regarding the reports that the Ole Miss administration had a laundry list of dirty deeds in house.

Outside counsel for the University of Mississippi received a Notice of Allegations from the NCAA – another step in a more than three-year process. Included in the notice are alleged violations of NCAA bylaws in women's basketball in 2012; track and field in 2012-13; and in football, with many of the allegations dating back to the former football staff in 2010 and the withholding and reinstatement process surrounding Laremy Tunsil in fall of 2015.

To be clear, the NCAA has only brought allegations, and as part of the NCAA process, the University and others have 90 days to issue a response. We've been transparent throughout this process, and it is important to note that most of the football allegations are based upon facts that have been publicly disclosed previously in "self-reports" and reinstatement requests or have been reported publicly in connection with another NCAA case.

Out of fairness to the individuals involved and the integrity of the NCAA process, we will not provide further details or comment until everyone has had an opportunity to review the allegations and respond. Once they do so, we will release the official notice and the university's response. In all three sports, I am confident in the leadership of our current head coaches and the manner in which they operate their programs.

While the statement on its face sounded good, as reassuring as one could be with major allegations in three sports under one sitting athletic director, but the fact is, it wasn't completely accurate.

The use of the words "most" and "many" would provide interesting talking points later in the process.

But, here it was in black and white and on official University of Mississippi letterhead. The investigation many said didn't exist had been confirmed by the Ole Miss administration.

The claims on the current staff were summarily dismissed by Bjork, who would only acknowledge that some allegations involved coaches and players that were part of the Ole Miss football program back then.

It was indeed a tough day for "sources" and self-proclaimed Ole Miss insiders. Their claims of football innocence - false narratives and coaching character assassinations - were gone in an instant. What so many had suspected was now a matter of record. The Rebels were in trouble and the allegations of cutting corners on the recruiting trail appeared to have some real substance.

Many dyed-in-the-wool Rebel fans struggled to come to grips with the reality that they were in fact in the cross hairs of the NCAA enforcement staff. Social media was abuzz with accusations that the Ole Miss administration was keeping sports fans in the dark.

I feel certain that the passion and the fear fueling that angst being felt among the Red and Blue faithful was the motivation behind Bjork making a statement like that, hoping to quell the uprising. Looking back on that day, it was clear he was either in the dark about where his programs stood in the process, or he was doing his part in the name of "transparency" to create a false narrative and to ease the anxiety of boosters, donors and season ticket holders.

The vehicle he used to disseminate this information? *The Clarion Ledger;* a former print media giant with a history of spreading the Rebel agenda without much hesitation. It appears they were now complicit in the cover up of perhaps a career-ending indictment and a jaw-dropping story, which they simply elected to ignore.

Ironically, then Ole Miss beat writer for *The Clarion Ledger,* Daniel Paulling, tweeted this gem on January 21, 2016.

To put the tweet in context: Paulling was answering a question on twitter about the Ole Miss investigation. The reader wanted to know what steps *The Clarion Ledger* had taken to gain access to the then rumored Notice of Allegations.

Paulling's response was that he was curious how Ole Miss had received a Notice of Allegations when they didn't have a Notice of Inquiry in hand.

A Notice of Inquiry is issued by the NCAA when a formal investigation of a member institution begins. It's an official declaration that a school is under investigation.

I'd later learn through a Freedom of Information Act request of Ole Miss' general counsel that the University never received a written notice. According to University assistant general counsel Rob Jolly, the University was given a verbal notice of the probe rather than a written one.

I questioned Paulling by direct message on Twitter about his source on the topic. Paulling informed me he had personally questioned Ross Bjork about the Notice of Inquiry and had been told they hadn't received this sort of communication from the NCAA.

Sadly, Paulling later admitted that he asked Bjork if the University of Mississippi had received a Notice of Inquiry in the previous six months, rather than admitting he'd not asked that question as the investigation remained ongoing and further allegations developed.

Bjork's answer to that question would've been factually correct. Ole Miss received their notice much earlier. In fact, according to Jolly, the verbal notification took place back in 2012 when the probe into Ole Miss Women's basketball program was underway.

Word games by a heady athletic director? Maybe, but it was clear to some that Bjork and the totality of the Ole Miss Rebel culture had friends in high places when it came to the media and news outlets of Mississippi.

On Jan. 21, 2016, Paulling essentially said that Ole Miss wasn't even under any NCAA investigation. The initial Notice of Allegations was dated for the following day, January 22.

Does anyone remember journalism?

Chapter 12

Draft Night

April 28, 2016

The campuses of the University of Alabama and Mississippi State University are separated by less than 90 miles along U.S. Highway 82. The Bulldogs and Crimson Tide are the closest neighbors within the Southeastern Conference.

I have made the drive to Tuscaloosa several times. In the final week of April 2016, I made the commute from home to Sewell-Thomas Stadium three times to cover a three-game baseball series between the Bulldogs and Tide.

It was a big series for Mississippi State, which was still in contention for their first SEC Baseball regular season title since 1989. There was tremendous interest from our readership in the Diamond Dawgs, so between David Murray and me, we followed the team home or away down the stretch.

This road weekend was my turn to cover the team and I was grateful it was one that did not require a two-night hotel stay.

At Alabama, the media is given a meal voucher to use at the stadium's concession stand for supper. There is no catered meal for those who cover Alabama baseball.

When covering football games at Bryant-Denny Stadium, you get to see the University pull out all of the stops. Chances are if you get a day game in Tuscaloosa, you can even get a made-to-order egg omelet for breakfast.

I was the first media member for either team to settle into the press box. Mississippi State is a baseball school, so there are several outlets who cover the Diamond Dawgs every single game. There were no members of the Alabama beat on the row when I arrived.

In an attempt to avoid stepping on any Tide toes, I questioned an Alabama staffer before I set up shop, "Do you guys have assigned seats or regular seats for your beat writers?"

He responded, "We won't have anybody here."

I took a seat on the front row, waited for my peers to arrive and prepared for a 6:30 p.m. start.

It was a busy night in sports. State fans had one eye on the game in Tuscaloosa, and one eye on the NFL draft in Chicago. Program-changing and record-setting quarterback Dak Prescott, former five-star defensive tackle Chris Jones, and cornerback Will Redmond were expected to be selected sometime during the three-day event.

Not one of the talented trio were projected as first rounders; but on the other side of the Golden Egg rivalry, Ole Miss was expecting to see three junior players taken on the draft's first night.

Prized left tackle Laremy Tunsil was listed as the top pick in the draft according to some draft experts. Even if Tunsil wasn't the first player taken, he'd certainly be the first offensive lineman selected.

6:32 p.m. – Future SEC batting champ and All-American center fielder Jake Mangum singled to left to get the Bulldogs off on the right foot. A Jack Kruger fielder's choice advanced Mangum to second, a Nathaniel Lowe single to center sent him to third, and a Reid Humphreys' sacrifice fly plated the talented freshman to make it 1-0 State.

As Bulldog starting pitcher, eventual first-round selection of the St. Louis Cardinals, Dakota Hudson toed the rubber for his warm-up tosses, social media was buzzing about Tunsil's stylish shoes, and just who'd go No. 1 in the NFL draft once the St. Louis Rams were on the clock at 7 p.m.

Two weeks prior to the draft, the Tennessee Titans

traded the No. 1 overall pick to the Rams who were talking quarterback. Rumors prior to that change in draft position suggested the Titans needed a blind side protector for former Heisman trophy-winning quarterback and 2015 first-round selection Marcus Mariota.

There was certainly value in the draft and some talented tackles available, so even with a lower pick in the first round, the Titans were on line to fulfill their needs. There were no guarantees Tunsil would be there once the Titans made their pick, but it certainly seemed possible.

6:47 p.m. – A 30-second video of what appeared to be Laremy Tunsil smoking a bong with some sort of gas mask attached to it is tweeted from Tunsil's very own twitter account, @KingTunsil78. Social media exploded.

Courtney Cronin ✔
@CourtneyRCronin   ⌄

What in the hell was just tweeted/deleted from Laremy Tunsil's verified Twitter account?

4/28/16, 7:01 PM

Tunsil and his family were seated in the green room in the Auditorium Theatre on the campus of Roosevelt University as the drama began to unfold. As news of the potential hack spread, Twitter temporarily suspended the Tunsil account.

Meanwhile, the Rams first-round pick was University of California quarterback Jared Goff. North Dakota State signal caller Carson Wentz went No. 2 to the Philadelphia Eagles.

In Tuscaloosa, Hudson is not especially sharp. Alabama scores two runs on an RBI single in the bottom of the first to take a 2-1 lead.

While there was some concern about what was going on in front of us on the baseball diamond, all of the conversation on press row involved what was transpiring in Chicago.

"Why would he tweet that video," one reporter asked. "It makes no sense. He's sitting in the green room waiting to hear his name called. He's probably been hacked."

7:31 p.m. – Ohio State defensive lineman Joey Bosa is on his way to San Diego as the third pick in the draft.

Another Buckeye, running back Ezekiel Elliot, comes off of the board next as the Dallas Cowboys looked to bolster their running attack.

Florida State corner Jalen Ramsey follows at No. 5 as the first selection by the Jacksonville Jaguars.

As Tunsil sweated it out back stage, some of his talented peers were having their big moments and getting their pictures taken with NFL commissioner Roger Goodell.

Just more than 700 miles south, Mississippi State trainers were attending to second baseman Hunter Stovall who looked to have tweaked a hamstring racing down the first base line. Stovall would reach on an error, but would have to leave the game.

Stovall was replaced by John Holland, who tied the game at two as he touched home after a Mangum triple.

The five-run rally ended after a two-run home run from Bulldog third baseman Gavin Collins, which brought the Bulldogs a 6-2 lead.

While the excitement of those moments isn't lost on even

the saltiest of media dogs, discussions about Tunsil's potential free fall in the draft filled the room. Some wondered if he'd even be taken in the first round.

One visiting media member pulled up the live feed of the draft on his laptop, so we wouldn't miss anything. We had a game to cover, but in between innings we were keeping tabs on some surreal moments that were essentially unprecedented.

Millions of dollars were being shifted over a social media posting.

7:50 p.m. – The Baltimore Ravens were on the clock and there was some chatter that general manager Ozzie Newsome planned to take an offensive tackle. It had been more than an hour since the video had made the rounds, but the impact of that visual had not been fully realized just yet.

Yes, some other players had been taken, but most of the teams who selected them weren't expected to take a tackle. The Ravens were in a position to take the top-rated tackle in the draft in Tunsil, but elected to take Notre Dame big man Ronnie Stanley.

Ian Rapoport ✔
@RapSheet

Following ⌄

#OM OT Laremy Tunsil has slipped at least to 7. The video did not help. His agent has been calling teams saying that's not who he is

RETWEETS
1,560

LIKES
1,028

7:53 PM - 28 Apr 2016

This was no longer a matter of conjecture; the video had inflicted some real damage.

The San Francisco 49ers, who targeted a pass rusher, selected 6-feet, 7-inch 291-pound defensive end DeForest Buckner of Oregon.

Tennessee, who'd traded out of the top 10, put together a package to get back in and exchanged selections with Cleveland. Tunsil had taken visits to the Titans' football complex in the weeks leading up to the draft. With the Ole Miss tackle still available, perhaps Tennessee was set to get the guy they were rumored to have wanted all along.

8:05 p.m. – After some first inning wildness, Hudson had settled in for Mississippi State. His pitch count was beginning to escalate, but he had managed to record four strike outs and keep the Alabama offense at bay as the Bulldogs built a lead.

In Chicago, Tunsil sat waiting for Tennessee to end the madness and put an end to what was becoming a nightmare scenario for all involved.

Goodell strode to the podium and announced the Titans had selected an offensive tackle just like many prognosticators had predicted, the problem for Tunsil was it wasn't him.

In the end, Tennessee elected to take Jack Conklin from Michigan State. With eight picks gone in the draft and two tackles taken, there was simply no idea when it would end for Tunsil.

What was expected to be a short stay backstage for Tunsil now creeped beyond an hour and a half with no sure end in sight.

Chicago moved up two spots in a trade with Tampa Bay in order to draft Georgia linebacker Leonard Floyd. A pick later, corner Eli Apple became a New York Giant. Many Rebel fans were hopeful Tunsil would wind up on the roster of the G-Men with Ole Miss favorite son Eli Manning. Those wishes didn't come true.

The Buccaneers, by way of their trade with Chicago, found themselves on the clock and nabbed up Florida Gator corner Vernon Hargreaves, one of the nation's top cover corners.

The New Orleans Saints, who once built a franchise around Ole Miss legend Archie Manning, elected to go defense with their pick, taking Louisville defensive tackle Sheldon Rankins.

Brutal might be the most fitting word of all. The player once forecasted as the number one pick in the 2016 draft had now fallen out of the top 10.

8:40 p.m. – Mississippi State needed three relievers to get out of the Alabama half of the sixth inning. Hudson's night ended after just five innings pitched. The collective effort of Daniel Brown, Keegan James and Blake Smith retired the Crimson Tide side, but not before Alabama had cut the Bulldog lead to 6-5.

Moments later, the Miami Dolphins used their first-round pick, the 13th in the draft, to select Tunsil. At long last, the nightmare was over.

Or was it?

Just as Tunsil was admitting the video was real, screen shots of direct messages appeared on Tunsil's Instagram account.

The messages seemed to indicate Tunsil had asked Ole Miss football staffers to assist in paying his rent, and his mother's utility bill.

The photo was captioned using Tunsil's user name "kingtunsil" with, "Coach freeze and the whole ole miss program are snakes. They cheat!"

It was clear Tunsil was the target of some social media saboteur intent on crushing his reputation. On what should've been one of the happiest nights of his life, the talented tackle was attempting to explain away a situation that wasn't of his doing.

While Tunsil was providing some context to the video he said was years old, the social media assault washed him out of the frying pan and into the fire. Ole Miss looked to be tagging along as these sensitive comments were made public.

9:25 p.m. – Tunsil takes to the dais to answer questions from reporters. It's safe to say the South Beach sun won't be the only topic of discussion.

To his credit, Tunsil was very forthcoming about the social media leaks, and owned up to his part in all of them. He finished multiple answers with gratitude for the Dolphins selecting him. The gifted tackle didn't dodge a single question.

When initially asked about a possible exchange of money between him and his coaches, Tunsil brushed the question aside and said, "No, I wouldn't say all of that."

When another reporter suggested the direct messages may have been altered, Tunsil appears to authenticate the messages saying, "Those are true. I made a mistake of that happening. It happened."

A follow-up question was a bit more direct. When asked again about a potential exchange of money between him and his coach, Tunsil replied, "I would have to say, yeah."

My phone lit up in a blaze of notifications as soon as the words left Tunsil's lips! Folks simply couldn't believe what they'd just heard. That iPhone got a workout; the buzz was so constant and intense, it reminded me of the noise the childhood game Operation made if you were even a little shaky trying to extract that dang old wishbone.

The Ole Miss beat reporter for *Rivals.com*, Neal McCready, asked Tunsil if he had spoken with the NCAA.

Before Tunsil could offer an answer, Amy Milam, an employee of Tunsil's agent, Jimmy Sexton, intervened and told the room, "He has no more comments."

That question proved to be the final one of the night in

a press meeting that lasted just under four minutes. Milam, who also happens to be a Chi-Omega alumna at Ole Miss, shut down the room and ushered Tunsil off stage.

It's rather interesting to note that questions about the bong smoking video, and a possible exchange of money between Tunsil and some of his coaches at Ole Miss, were asked of Tunsil and in return Tunsil patiently answered, but when the subject of a potential NCAA interview was broached, it was time to stop talking.

Tunsil was the subject of rumors throughout the preseason due to claims made by his former stepfather, Miller, about potential NCAA violations during his time at Ole Miss. Tunsil's college eligibility was over. The NCAA could no longer levy any punishment upon him or impact his life in any way. Tunsil could've confessed to anything and the NCAA couldn't have touched him. He was now beyond their reach.

The fact Ole Miss had already received a Notice of Allegations was common knowledge. What was listed in that notice remained a mystery, and now another chapter had just been added.

It was a reasonable question worthy of an answer. Tunsil could've offered a "no comment" or confirmed what everyone already suspected, but instead, the former Ole Miss sorority girl stepped in.

Ole Miss head football coach, Hugh Freeze, is also represented by the same agency that employs Milam and represents Tunsil. To Milam's credit she was protecting the client, and more than likely two, Freeze and Tunsil.

Back on the diamond, Mississippi State had broken it open against Alabama. A five-run ninth, gave State a 12-5 lead, but when Brent Rooker's three-run moon shot settled into the Tuscaloosa night, the eyes of the nation were gazing upon the wildest draft night of all time.

The top story on ESPN's *Sportscenter* wasn't about Goff going No. 1, or what to expect on day two. Instead it was about the bizarre night for Tunsil. Even after a night's rest, most of America had trouble processing what had taken place.

The fact that Ole Miss star wideout LaQuon Treadwell was taken with the 23rd pick by the Minnesota Vikings, and eccentric defensive tackle Robert Nkemdiche was selected 29th overall by the Arizona Cardinals barely registered.

The Rebels had their three first-rounders as expected, but the Rebel's milestone was overrun with allegations of a rule-breaking culture, which had taken root at Ole Miss.

There were accusations leveled at Miller, an obvious suspect, but those were quickly dismissed. Days earlier, Miller had filed a civil suit against Tunsil, so he was a convenient villain for many. The two had history and some recent bad blood.

Rumors of a disgruntled agent made the rounds. One theory suggested a runner for an agent provided Tunsil with a new phone and kept the old one giving him access to the iCloud and sensitive images on Tunsil's phone.

The drop from the top ten and the first projected tackle in the 2016 draft cost Tunsil millions. Message board experts suggested a civil suit was coming and the identity of the hacker would be known soon.

One fan site owner reported the FBI was involved and they had located the individual responsible.

A few crackpots even tried to point a finger in my direction, but I only use my super powers to aid the forces of good. There's a part of me that's a little flattered people would assume I would have the technological know-how to pull off such a caper.

The bitterness and hatred required to attack someone in such a cruel and public way is something I struggle to comprehend. No matter what side of the rivalry folks around the South come down on, I believe we all see the incident with Tunsil's Twitter leaks as absolutely unfortunate at the least, and certainly an invasion of privacy

The draft night Twitter hack cost Tunsil dearly, but in the end, he was still a first-round draft pick expected to earn millions. The more immediate concern for Ole Miss fans was the content of those direct messages, and Tunsil's apparent confession regarding the acceptance of money while a member of the Ole Miss football team.

The spin masters were out early suggesting Tunsil's request for the $305 on his mother's light bill was a proper use of the NCAA's opportunity fund.

The NCAA has financial programs to assist student athletes in times of need. For instance, should an athlete have a death in the family and need to purchase a plane ticket for a flight home to attend the funeral, a request can be made of the opportunity fund to fulfill that need.

There are other instances where a student athlete loses personal property or clothing due to a fire or natural disaster. The fund can be utilized to help them get back on their feet.

Established in 1991 and partially funded by the NCAA Men's basketball tournament television contracts, the opportunity fund is essentially designated to assist student athletes in times of emergency and unexpected personal hardship.

The early spin on that particular Friday morning was that Tunsil's request for funds was simply a routine request of permissible NCAA funds.

Tunsil was set to meet with the Miami media on Friday, April 29, but due to an "allergic reaction" of some sort, he canceled the press briefing for the scheduled time and rescheduled for later that afternoon.

Dressed in a white shirt and blue vest with no tie, Tunsil faced the press with Miami Dolphins Executive Vice President of Football Operations Mike Tannenbaum, Dolphin head coach Adam Gase, and Miami general manager Chris Grier sitting alongside him.

Tunsil was given multiple chances to correct the record from the night before, but he refused and repeatedly stated, "I'm just here to talk about the Miami Dolphins."

Many in Mississippi wanted Tunsil to talk about the Ole Miss Rebels, but he didn't budge. Now far removed from Oxford, and back in his home state of Florida, it was clear Tunsil simply wanted to move on with his life.

In the year since signing a first-round contract with the Miami Dolphins, Tunsil has not publicly clarified, explained, or retracted his statements about an exchange of money between him and his coaches at Ole Miss.

It was difficult to tell if Tunsil's silence was good or bad for Ole Miss and their NCAA woes, but a trying time simply got more difficult with Tunsil's remarks shining an unflattering light on the Ole Reb. They were getting filleted like a Pearl River channel cat.

The Ole Miss administration was scalped by the onslaught of social media commentary. They were already stained with the admission of a lengthy indictment in hand from the NCAA regarding football, track, and women's basketball, but now the Ole Miss administration was being mocked by the national media as a program completely out of control.

Many who wanted to give Freeze the benefit of the doubt, no longer could. The same player Freeze portrayed as a hero who was simply defending his mother, in an incident that happened nearly a year before, had just said on national television that a member of Freeze's football staff gave him money.

Some Ole Miss fans called for Freeze's firing. Tired of the never-ending barrage of body blows, a non-silent minority just wanted to start fresh. There had been whispers in the wind about wrong doing, but now one of their own had essentially removed all doubt. A night that was supposed to be a coronation for Freeze and the Rebels, turned into a public demonstration that something was amiss in a major way with the football program in Oxford, Mississippi.

The prize of Mississippi, the Golden Egg.   (Photo Credit: Gene Swindoll)

Former Ole Miss head football coach Hugh Freeze at the 2015 Egg Bowl
(Photo Credit: Gene Swindoll)

Auburn offensive lineman Austin Golson   (Photo Credit: Jason Caldwell)

Ole Miss offensive tackle Laremy Tunsil
(Photo Credit: Michael Campbell)

Ole Miss defensive tackle Robert Nkemdiche
(Photo Credit: Michael Campbell)

MSU QB Nick Fitzgerald post game Egg Bowl 2016
(Photo credit: David Murray)

Steve Robertson covering a Mississippi State practice
(Photo Credit: Gene Swindoll)

Mississippi State linebacker Leo Lewis vs LSU 2016
(Photo Credit: Steve Robertson)

Mississippi State defensive end Kobe Jones at the St. Petersburg Bowl
(Photo Credit: Steve Robertson)

Ole Miss wide receiver LaQuon Treadwell (Photo Credit: Michael Campbell)

Mississippi State defensive tackle Chris Jones rushes Ole Miss QB Bo Wallace (Photo Credit: Gene Swindoll)

Mississippi State QB Dak Prescott shares a post-game moment with Hugh Freeze following the 2015 Egg Bowl (Photo Credit: Michael Campbell)

Mississippi State defensive end Kobe Jones during 2017 spring practice. (Photo Credit: Gene Swindoll)

Mississippi State linebacker Leo Lewis post game Egg Bowl 2016
(Photo credit: David Murray)

Bully gets the best of Colonel Reb at the 1991 Egg Bowl
(Photo Credit: David Murray)

Chapter 13

A New Day and a New Worry

April 29, 2016

Ole Miss has historically been considered a huge party school. Hangover medications and home remedies abound after long nights spent on Oxford Square. The collective fog and headache the Rebel fanbase woke up with on this particular Friday morning had grown immune to aspirin and hair-of-the-dog concoctions. It was time Ole Miss fans felt the pain of truth.

The night before, an absolute nightmare had played out for Tunsil on the sports stage for the entire world to see.

While there will be other memorable moments when the NFL franchises pick players, the evening's first-round pick, left tackle Laremy Tunsil, had been held hostage by a social media terrorist. The evening would forever be known by college football fans in Mississippi as simply "Draft Night."

As if the victimization of Tunsil wasn't enough, Ole Miss fans who'd bought into the Rebels' public relations push that positioned Tunsil as their star player, were now coming to grips with the fact that he admitted on air that he'd taken money from his coaches while on the active roster at Ole Miss.

The shocking nature of it all was hard for them to digest. Ole Miss fans were essentially a listless cork riding the waves of an angry sea of sports.

Before the infamous Draft Night, the Red and Blue powers were able to keep control of the narrative. Most of the NCAA talk coming out of Oxford was that football was not a major part of their NCAA investigation, and that whatever serious charges there were involving the pigskin, largely involved the football staff before Hugh Freeze came along.

A trusting fanbase, hungry for winning seasons, wanted to believe the best about their administrators and coaches, and simply turned a blind eye and went along with the spin. In many Rebel minds, this was all some grand conspiracy to derail their rising football program. Their most popular narrative was that Ole Miss had stepped on the wrong toes and had forgotten their place as a modern-day SEC also-ran.

Consequently, on *The Boneyard*, I once compared Ole Miss winning the Sugar Bowl to Milli Vanilli winning the Grammy for best new artist in 1990. The German-based hip-hop group received national acclaim for their album, "Girl, You Know It's True."

The album spawned four hit singles selling more than six million copies in the U.S. alone, but Rob Pilatus and Fab Morvan, the group's front men, were lip syncing frauds. After the duo won the Grammy, reports of the group faking live performances began to surface.

Finally, under a mountain of media pressure, the agent for the group, Sergio Vendero, came clean. The scam was finally over. Not only were the live performances glorified pantomimes, but neither Rob nor Fab had sung a single note on the award-winning album.

All that glittered in the dread-locked, high-cheekbone world of Milli Vanilli certainly wasn't gold, or platinum for that matter. Many fans of the band felt betrayed, but others said they still liked the songs, no matter who sang them.

A similar sentiment was, and still is, prevalent in a certain segment of the Ole Miss fanbase. It might not have all been above board, but they had a Sugar Bowl trophy to show for it. The end justified the means. Right?

As Rebel fans did their best to face each day in the aftermath of Tunsil's Draft Night admissions, there was plenty of blame to go around. There would be no "Blame-it-on-the-Rain" moment, though. People wanted answers and they wanted them now. Patience with the Ole Miss administration was wearing thin.

While much of the media coverage regarding the Ole Miss NCAA investigation was of the single serving variety, the draft night debacle breathed new life into the case and the coverage of it.

Tunsil's comments weren't just a story on ESPN's *Sportscenter*, it was THE story.

Privately, I began to get reports about people who were once reluctant to talk with NCAA investigators, were now reconsidering their position. It was now clear in a very, very public way that there was more going on with the Ole Miss football program and the NCAA, and it wasn't "secondary" or "minimal" as the Rebel-friendly media had communicated earlier in the year.

In the wake of the newfound drama, Ole Miss officials worked to authenticate the direct messages that were allegedly between Tunsil and Ole Miss director of football operations John Miller and the referenced "Barney," assumed to be then football recruiting specialist Barney Farrar.

The school released a statement that read, "Like we do whenever an allegation is brought to our attention or a potential violation is self-discovered, we will aggressively investigate and fully cooperate with the NCAA and the SEC."

Even if the Rebels could quickly put these new issues to bed, this was trouble Ole Miss simply didn't need. Bjork's thin denials worked on Rebel fans for a while, even when he admitted the program had been put on notice by the NCAA. Now with new trouble on the horizon, the misery continued to grow.

Just over a month after the draft night drama, Bjork

and Freeze took part in the annual SEC spring meetings in Sandestin, Florida. With spring football long over, there hadn't been a lot of media access to Freeze since Draft Night.

On Friday, May 27, Ole Miss released a summary of the Notice of Allegations as well as their response to those charges. We will soon get more in depth about the contents of those documents, but with the spring meetings looming the Rebel woes would be a topic of conversation.

The Destin meetings would provide the Ole Miss athletic director and coach chances to share some things about their current predicament and their plans going forward. With the beautiful Gulf of Mexico surf behind them, Ole Miss had their turn on the SEC Network.

Anyone expecting Paul Finebaum, host of the SEC Network show *Finebaum*, to give the pair a solid, on-air grilling were disappointed. Freeze and Bjork looked the part of professional grifters acting out various fashions of flim-flammery. Finebaum lobbed a few softballs Freeze and Bjork's way that allowed them to get their talking points out and call it a day.

"In terms of compliance, in terms of running a program the right way, we have the utmost faith in Coach Freeze and his staff, and how they do things and why they're here at the University of Mississippi," Bjork said. "Being a Mississippian, this guy (Freeze) has got more pride in the program than anybody who walks on our campus,"

Mind you, neither Bjork nor Freeze could speak publicly about the specific details of the NCAA investigation due to the bylaws that prohibit such dialogue, but a few self-serving comments to appease angry and uneasy Ole Miss fans were offered.

"The narrative that we're out, our staff is out, purchasing players, to my knowledge, there is zero allegations to that and zero truth to that," Freeze said. "But that continues to be the narrative. Wherever I get a commitment, that's the narrative that comes out. I want to point out, we've lost a lot of battles in recruiting, too, against some good schools. Again, I want to be careful to say, yeah, I do feel like that some, and I'm biased, of course. There were mistakes made."

Mistakes were made. Yeah, what an understatement.

That one-liner became a huge part of the vernacular when fans from opposing schools discussed the Ole Miss case. The definition of what a mistake was began to evolve.

There was talk of "owning it," but that the duo did anything but own anything. While the Notice of Allegations was not yet public, Bjork mentioned there were allegations back to 2010, there were some things in the 2013 recruiting class, and some booster involvement they were dealing with.

It became a lovefest for Bjork to talk about his coach and what he stood for rather than talk of culpability regarding his own athletics department with multiple programs under fire on his watch.

Instead, the story was about what good guys they were, and how they wanted to be treated fairly. Apparently, their feelings were hurt at being labeled cheaters despite rising evidence that the tasseled loafer of wrongdoing appeared to fit.

The next time Freeze came face to face with the extended media would be at SEC Media Days. Ole Miss was the last team of the 2016 event making their appearance, third behind South Carolina and LSU, on Thursday, July 14. It was a bit of a break for the Rebel contingent as most of the SEC press corps had already headed for home.

Making the trip to the Wynfrey Hotel in Hoover, Alabama alongside Freeze, were quarterback Chad Kelly, tight end Evan Engram, and defensive tackle D.J. Jones.

Following SEC Commissioner Greg Sankey's introduction,

Freeze touched on his relationship with Sankey, and about the great coverage dedicated to SEC football. It didn't take long for Freeze to go to the mic about the NCAA probe.

"Before I get into football, I would love to address our NCAA case right now, and as I've said, with the limited amount that I can discuss, I remain very confident in who we are and our core values and how we do things," Freeze said from the podium. "We have fully cooperated with the NCAA throughout the entire process, which has been a long process.

"We discovered most of the facts that led to self-reports, and that's how a good compliance office works. You know, with them already being on our campus, we had to report many things that are a part of the Notice of Allegations that maybe typically just get reported and handled with self-imposed penalties.

"We believe our response to the Notice of Allegations stands on its own. As a head coach, I understand that I'm held accountable for the things that happened within our building and even outside the walls of our building.

"Our compliance team is working extremely hard to seek a resolution to this case, and also into the events from NFL draft night and we look forward to the conclusion of this entire process. No one looks forward to that more than I do."

Good words for sure, but there was one item mentioned that I took issue with. The statement about self-discovery of violations doesn't really match up with the documents released regarding the January 2016 Notice of Allegations.

Of the 13 football allegations levied in the first round of charges, the overwhelming majority of infractions were uncovered during NCAA enforcement interviews rather than during the "good compliance" work of the University.

In Ole Miss's answer to the initial NOA, talk of responsibility for the charges takes a backseat to blaming several people who show up to work each and every morning somewhere other than the Ole Miss football complex at 1810 Manning Way.

"The fact that all but one of the 16 Level I violations arose from intentional misconduct committed by rogue former employees or boosters outside the University's direct control acting in contravention of rules education provided to them by the University," was the University's response.

Everybody can't be rogue. There's a better case here for a wide spread conspiracy of non-compliance than of some rogue booster who's run off the road of his own volition.

Boosters allegedly working in concert with Ole Miss coaches were now being painted in a negative light. It's funny how friends of the program are treated once the heat comes down. Not that I'd expect them to be defended, but their burden of responsibility is considerably less than the coaches who make a living working for an NCAA-member institution.

Also of note, the Ole Miss legal team contradicts itself in its own response to the allegations regarding three sports. Complete with a nifty pie graph, the Rebels suggest they uncovered 20 of the 28 allegations in the 2016 notice.

According to the University's response, the probe into the women's basketball issues was prompted by a "request" from the SEC office rather than any internal action by the Ole Miss compliance staff. The women's hoops issues comprise seven of the 28 allegations.

Of the 13 football allegations, the Ole Miss answer to the Notice suggest they had uncovered three of the violations, two of those being the least severe of the allegations and classified at Level III.

The University elected to "self-report" another violation that was uncovered during joint interviews with NCAA enforcement staff, but they should hardly get credit for any after-the-fact piling on.

At this point, not a single member of Hugh Freeze's staff at Ole Miss has been relieved of his coaching duties despite the fact a handful were already named in formal allegations, and others were facing a similar fate.

"I obviously believe that I am responsible for things that happen in our program and some that are outside, and you have to be able to prove that you've set a tone of compliance, which I'm confident that I have done that," Freeze stated. "But ultimately that's not my say. I can't comment on anything that's ongoing with the NCAA.

"Look. Everybody has – everybody's got a narrative. You have one, I have one, our rivals have one. All of us have one in regards to us going on in the world, and in our world with the NCAA. It's obvious that the allegations have come. We've got our notice. I would encourage you to read our response, and we look forward to that day.

"But with everybody's narrative going on, the truth is probably somewhere in the middle and the facts are this, there will come a day where we get to stand before the committee on infractions, which are the ones that matter, and we will be held accountable for any wrongdoing that is found, and that's the way it should be. We don't want it to be.

"I have zero interest, zero interest, in cutting corners to be successful, and our staff knows that very well. I have a lot of things that I'm not very good at, but that is not a temptation. But we will be responsible and held accountable for anything that happened on that day, but until that day, we're going to stay focused on being the best football team we can and continue to be relevant and having confidence in who we are. Because I see it every day, I see the impact it has. Recruiting is still going really well, because people know us for who we are."

Freeze's media circuit wouldn't be complete without an appearance on the *Finebaum* show. Needless to say, those moments before the SEC *Nation* cameras went much different than the first-date show a few weeks earlier in Sandestin.

While Freeze had done his part to play the victor on the big stage, faced with tougher questions by the television crew made up of Finebaum, former LSU defensive lineman Booger McFarland, and ESPN anchor Dari Nowhah, the embattled coach took on the role of the victim.

Defending his program, Freeze made comments about how no one complained when Ole Miss was losing, but now that they were winning, people had issues with the Rebel way of doing things.

Finebaum referred to a *Sports Illustrated* article where an SEC coach was quoted anonymously about the Ole Miss program. Due to the anonymous nature of the report, Freeze appeared miffed, and sarcastically dismissed any talk of alleged indiscretions cloaked by anonymous sources.

Following the awkward and argumentative discussion before a live television audience, Finebaum and Freeze were caught in a testy exchange by sports reporter Tom Annino of WVTM Channel 13 in Birmingham, Alabama.

From the gist of the report, Freeze didn't care for the line of questioning from Finebaum. While the encounter ends with Freeze smiling before he drank from his bottle of water, it was clear that the coach was unhappy with what had transpired on air.

Within days of those interesting moments, another storm was building. The NCAA enforcement staff had petitioned the Committee on Infractions to provide grants of immunity to certain players who possibly had information about Ole Miss and potential violations that may have occurred during the Rebels' recruitment of them.

NCAA Bylaw 32.3.8.2 reads as follows:

At the request of the enforcement staff, the Committee on Infractions may grant limited immunity to a student-athlete or prospective student-athlete when such individual otherwise might be declared ineligible for intercollegiate competition based on information reported to the enforcement staff by the individual or a third party associated with the individual. Such immunity shall not apply to the individual's involvement in violations of NCAA legislation not reported or to future involvement in violations of NCAA legislation by the individual or to any action taken by an institution. In any case, such immunity shall not be granted unless the relevant information would not otherwise be available to the enforcement staff.

Now, a grant of immunity is not a "Get out of Jail Free" card for life, but it's a rather significant development.

Essentially, the NCAA guarantees a student athlete their eligibility won't be negatively impacted no matter what benefits they may have taken as long as they're honest about what has occurred.

Immunity interviews aren't necessarily a common practice, but they aren't what most would consider rare either.

In recent years, testimony obtained from individuals with limited immunity have been used in cases against Southern Mississippi (basketball), Miami (football), and Southeastern Missouri State (basketball).

Contrary to popular belief, the decision to grant immunity isn't an easy one to make. The NCAA enforcement staff petitions the Committee on Infractions chairman for permission to extend the security blanket to student athletes in order to get the truth about potential violations.

It isn't a fishing expedition.

The enforcement staff must already have reasonable proof a

violation has occurred before the process moves forward.

The news of these interviews didn't make the newspaper until August 25, 2016, despite having taken place a few weeks earlier. The reaction to the news was immediate.

Many who'd become punch-drunk on the Ole Miss Kool-Aid suggesting the investigation was over, and the NCAA would likely just give the Rebels little more than a hand slap, now realized the enforcement staff was playing hard ball.

The NCAA was essentially willing to allow players who'd taken impermissible benefits the opportunity to retain their amateur status without any personal penalty, provided they tell the truth.

It was clear now to all, Ole Miss was in a heap of trouble, and the future of the football program would likely be a dreadfully bumpy one.

Reports out of Oxford suggested the Rebel administration was completely blindsided by the news and they were unaware those immunity interviews had taken place.

It wasn't a good day for anyone involved with Ole Miss athletics. For nearly seven months, the talking points were, for the most part, reassuring. Yeah, they had some problems, but they sold their fans on the notion they had it all contained.

Ole Miss wasn't in control, and in fact, out of the loop. The public perception of the Rebel administration was not positive. They looked inept at a very crucial moment in the investigation.

No, the case against Ole Miss wasn't winding down. The talk of more allegations brushed aside by Bjork in February now began to ring true.

Players at SEC programs were talking with investigators about the Rebels with no fear of reprisal. Just as Ole Miss fans were recovering from the anxiety associated with Tunsil's draft night comments, a fresh, new misery had arrived.

Freeze supporters had to come to grips with the fact that their football program was facing 13 allegations from the NCAA, and that number was expected to climb in the coming months. Gone was the notion the remaining issues facing Ole Miss were draft night related. There was no joy in Oxford.

Six weeks after the news broke, more trouble was on the way. The NCAA announced it was separating football from the women's basketball and track issues in an attempt to allow those programs to move forward. The investigation into Rebel football kept hanging around like a bad penny.

In the NCAA release announcing the sanctions that Friday, Greg Christopher, the Xavier athletic director, spoke for the Committee on Infractions, "No football-related materials were part of our record, and we will only take up the football allegations once the investigation has concluded."

Some fans suggested enough was enough and it was simply time to sanction the Rebels, and consider the matter done with. The problem for all involved was more evidence of recruiting malfeasance kept sprouting like mushrooms after a warm rain.

How could the investigation end when new evidence trickled in unceasingly? It made for an interesting conundrum. Perhaps, if the Rebels just kept breaking the rules, the investigation would continue indefinitely without any penalties being assessed.

Chapter 14

Tunsil-itis

May 27, 2016

At long last, Ole Miss planned to shed some light on the Notice of Allegations (NOA) received Jan. 22, 2016. The Rebels had been "eager to tell their story," according to Ross Bjork. On this fine Friday, it was time to get a look behind the curtain and see what the Rebels were being charged with and how they planned to defend themselves against those allegations.

Par for the course, the website Ole Miss officials directed interested parties to, www.athleticsworking.wp2.olemiss.edu, and it crashed just as the release was made available. It was the icing on the "commitment to transparency" cake.

If one was looking for a microcosm of the Rebels' handling of the entire process this was it. Not only were the powers that be shooting themselves in the public relations foot, they kept reloading the gun.

The fact that the website wouldn't load at that moment seems like a small thing now, but it was downright hysterical on the big day. I'm not sure a Mississippi State Bulldog could've written a better script.

The site was restored without a long delay, but jokes at the Rebels' expense wrote themselves. The snickering stopped rather quickly as the scope of the current charges were now known.

Of course, the Ole Miss outside legal team had done their best to compartmentalize the allegations in what appeared to be an attempt to downplay the severity of the pending allegations.

It was almost as if they were saying, "I know it looks bad, but hear me out."

The football allegations were grouped into four categories:

The David Saunders Allegations

The 2012-13 Recruiting Allegations

The Level III Allegations

The Booster Allegations

If your allegations can be divided into sub-families of infractions, then you have an awful lot of explaining to do. Let's get into what was being alleged.

The Saunders allegations were made up of the ACT testing concerns at Wayne County, as well as the out-of-state Ole Miss signees who attended The Education Center School (Ed Center) in Jackson, Mississippi.

Saunders was sanctioned for his part in the University of Louisiana at Lafayette (ULL) case. An eight-year show-cause penalty was his assigned penance by the NCAA, which served as a harbinger of things to come for the Rebels. The personal sanction for Saunders was one of the longest in NCAA enforcement history.

The fact that Saunders' name appeared in the Ole Miss NOA came as a surprise to no one. ULL had let the cat out of the proverbial bag in their own NCAA response that Saunders' actions at Ole Miss were the focus of questioning of investigators when they showed up in Cajun Country for a sit-down with Saunders.

Saunders' alleged misdeeds on behalf of Ole Miss dated back to 2010.

Charged with Saunders was former Ole Miss assistant coach Chris Vaughn. Hired to coach safeties as a member of Houston Nutt's staff on December 12, 2007, Vaughn served as the Rebels' recruiting coordinator through 2011 before taking a position at the University of Texas.

Saunders was cited for allegedly arranging fraudulent ACT scores for Ole Miss signees.

Both Saunders and Vaughn were charged with allegedly arranging lodging, meals, and transportation for six football prospects who attended the Ed Center in Jackson. To add even more insult to offensive injury, the pair were reportedly enlisting the services of a church leader in the Jackson metro area to facilitate the improper benefits.

The dynamic duo was also accused of unethical behavior during the course of the investigation. Getting down to the brass tacks of the whole matter, Saunders and Vaughn were cited for being dishonest during interviews with NCAA staffers. Vaughn took it to the next level by being dishonest, and then reportedly encouraging others to follow his lead and attempting to mislead investigators.

If a man is a cheater, he will be a liar, too. It's part of the job description.

By the time the notice was made public, Saunders and Vaughn had long been terminated from their positions at ULL and Texas respectively.

The 2012-13 allegations comprised the indiscretions attributed to Walter Hughes, the FCA Huddle Leader from Memphis, Tennessee.

It turns out his "work" with athletes from East High School in Memphis didn't pass muster with the NCAA enforcement staff. To be fair, his activities weren't deemed acceptable by the Ole Miss administration, which took some steps to curtail his activities, but failed.

One wonders what the outcome would've been had they been more proactive about Hughes prior to signing day, February 6, 2013. The compliance got much cleaner once baseball season rolled around. Bringing those players to football games did little to change the landscape of things, but showing up at a baseball game had all of the buzzers and whistles going off.

The three level III allegations were uncontested, and all appeared to be rather minor in nature.

Former defensive line coach, Chris Kiffin was charged with allowing Laremy Tunsil to stay at his residence during the summer of 2013, months after Tunsil had signed with the Rebels.

Kiffin was also part of an allegation involving impermissible contact with prospects on May 8, 2014, during the spring evaluation period.

Finally, the University was charged for using personalized recruiting videos reportedly created at the direction of Hugh Freeze during two official visit weekends during the 2013 recruiting cycle, Jan. 18, and 25.

The meat and potatoes of the January 2016 notice involved Tunsil and several charges of benefits provided to both him and his family during his recruitment, after he enrolled at Ole Miss as a member of the Rebels active roster.

It's been stated many times, had Tunsil and his former step-father Lindsey Miller, avoided their dust up in the family's Oxford home, the investigation would've gone in a much different direction, and the penalties would've likely proven to be less severe.

Oddly, the Ole Miss NCAA response to the Notice of Allegations nearly paints the domestic incident as a stroke of luck for investigators.

"Had it not been for this altercation, which resulted in (Miller's) decision to disclose his secret dealings in an effort to harm (Tunsil), it is unlikely that the University or enforcement staff (or Tunsil) would have discovered (Miller's) connection to the two boosters," the response reads.

So just who are these boosters and what did they allegedly provide Miller?

Ole Miss worked very hard to conceal the names of these gentlemen throughout the NCAA probe despite multiple Freedom of Information Act (FOIA) requests to learn their identities.

My first request for the names was dated Jan. 23, 2016. Despite being on the wrong side of the Mississippi Open Records Law, Ole Miss didn't express any interest in sharing the names of the third parties accused of wrong doing until May 12, 2017, when they were on the business end of a state ethics complaint.

The two boosters mentioned prominently in the allegations involving benefits provided to Miller were Biloxi businessman Michael Strojny, and Oxford hotel owner Chan Patel.

Strojny, a 1968 graduate of Ole Miss, has been an avid supporter of the Rebels on and off of the field, establishing an endowment for faculty members of the Ole Miss Business School.

Patel, a native of Zimbabwe, has carved out a successful niche in the Oxford hotel scene. While not an alumnus of the University of Mississippi, Patel is very much a supporter of the Rebel athletics programs.

Strojny is alleged to have provided Miller with $800 in cash on Aug. 22, 2014, during a meeting at the Oxford-University Airport. Strojny owns his own plane, and flies it himself from Biloxi to Oxford regularly, so a meeting at the airfield in Oxford appears to be reasonable.

In Ole Miss' answer to this charge, they agree the violation occurred, and reference text messages between Miller and Strojny that seem to show the interaction and delivery of a "package" actually took place.

During his joint interview with the NCAA and the

University, Strojny denied ever providing any funds to Miller, but couldn't provide any other explanation for the "package" he reportedly delivered.

Patel is accused of providing Miller and his family free lodging at businesses he owned in the Oxford area at least a dozen times between June 7, 2013 and May 27, 2014. The value of those benefits has been assessed at $2,253 by the NCAA.

To put a nice bow on it, Miller alleges some of the times he stayed in Patel's hotels the rooms were in Strojny's name, and he and Patel discussed the arrangements through direct messages on Facebook.

Screenshots are forever. – Apple 3:16

Faced with the mounting evidence, Patel admitted to providing rooms to Miller a "couple of times," but didn't implicate Strojny in his statement to investigators. In the end, the NCAA clearly sided with Miller's version of events. There are no heroes in this story. Everybody involved knew better, but acted otherwise.

Both Patel and Strojny were disassociated by the University for an indefinite amount of time.

In a letter dated May 6, 2016, Ole Miss Athletics Director Ross Bjork notified Patel that the University of Mississippi was formally disassociating him.

"We concluded, based on the totality of the evidence gathered, that cost-free lodging was provided on more occasions than you admitted during your interviews," Bjork wrote.

Strojny received a similar letter signed by Bjork the same day. As was the case with Patel, Strojny's May 4, 2016, letter was a written notice to formally document a phone conversation that had taken place on April 28, 2016.

"As we discussed, that based on the totality of the evidence gathered, the University of Mississippi has acknowledge[d] that on or around August 22, 2014, you provided at least $500 to [Lindsey Miller] and understood that such action was contrary to NCAA rules.

"Your conduct has violated NCAA bylaws prohibiting representatives of the University's athletics interests (i.e., boosters) from providing benefits to student-athletes, their families and friends."

While Tunsil didn't receive any personal benefit from the lodging provided to his family, the talented tackle was found to have been taken care of in other ways during his time as an Ole Miss Rebel.

One of the allegations naming Tunsil in the Notice of Allegations involved loaner cars provided by Cannon Motors. The CEO of Cannon Motors is Michael Joe Cannon, a lifelong Ole Miss fan.

Cannon, a Calhoun City, Mississippi native, played football beyond the high school level at Northwest Community College (1978-80), and eventually for the University of Memphis, where he was voted as a team captain and earned All-Metro Conference honors as a senior defensive end.

Once his playing days were done, Cannon got into coaching and returned to Northwest Conference College, where he served two years before taking a graduate assistant position at Ole Miss under Coach Billy Brewer.

Following the death of his father, Cannon elected to leave the Rebel coaching staff and enter the family business as an auto dealer. Cannon Motors was born from that decision. With more than a dozen locations between Arkansas and Mississippi, the business appears to have done well.

In the summer of 2014, it's reported Tunsil took his 2002 Chevy Impala to Cannon Motors for repairs. While his vehicle was being serviced, Tunsil was provided with a 2012 Nissan

Titan as a loaner.

On or around Aug. 11, Tunsil elected not to follow through with the repairs on his Impala. He also elected not to return the Titan until Oct. 28, 2014.

What prompted Tunsil to return the Titan is rather interesting. The Ole Miss Compliance Department had learned Tunsil had use of the cost-free vehicle and instructed him to return it.

According to the documents provided by Ole Miss, despite bragging about their "robust" vehicle monitoring program, the University didn't become aware of Tunsil's use of the Titan until after it was booted on Oct. 1, 2014, because of eight parking tickets.

Once aware of the vehicle, the University set up a meeting with Tunsil to discuss his use of the loaner from Cannon. After this meeting, Tunsil was instructed to return the Titan despite the fact the University didn't believe an actual violation had taken place. They wanted to avoid the "appearance of impropriety"

Apparently, that message was not received by Tunsil.

Three and a half months later, Tunsil returned to the dealership looking to buy a Dodge Challenger. February 16, 2014, saw Tunsil drive away with another loaner vehicle, a 2004 Chevy Tahoe. This vehicle was kept as a loaner until May 11, 2015, nearly 15 months later!

The Tahoe had been sold, so Tunsil was then provided with his third free loaner car, a 2008 Nissan Armada that he kept until June 10, 2015, when the global search for a used Dodge Challenger apparently succeeded. It took nearly four months from the day Tunsil walked in looking to buy a car until the day his new vehicle was located.

Kingdoms have been bought and sold in less time.

In their answer to the January 2016 Notice of Allegations,

Ole Miss references their "high profile" vehicle program that's in place to protect potential draft picks from driving vehicles provided by agents, or others that may negatively impact their status as amateur athletes.

Despite their best "efforts" to stop him, the one-time projected top pick in the NFL draft procured the services of not one, but two additional loaner vehicles after Ole Miss told him not to in a face-to-face meeting.

With the 2010 Challenger now on the lot, Tunsil put pen to paper on a financing agreement that reflected he had put up a $3,000 cash down payment towards the purchase of this apparently rare and hard to find vehicle.

I'm not sure if it would've been damning to source the down payment of three grand or what actually happened.

The dealership elected to give Tunsil an interest-free, deferred payment loan for the 3K. Now, you and I can't get that sort of deal, but we don't play offensive tackle for the Ole Miss Rebels.

An unemployed college student with no down payment was provided multiple loaner cars free of charge, given a deferred interest-free loan and provided, essentially, in-house financing to purchase a car. It's good work if you can get it.

In a letter from Bjork dated June 22, 2016 documenting an April 14, 2016 meeting, Cannon Motors and its owner were both disassociated for a period of three years.

"The University genuinely appreciates the cooperation exhibited by you and your employees throughout the inquiry. Unfortunately, given the involvement of you and your dealership in violations of NCAA legislation, the University must formally disassociate you and (Cannon Motors) from its athletics programs for a three-year period of time."

While talk of cars and money move the needle, the compliance missteps as they pertain to Tunsil date all the way back to his status as an unsigned recruit in the final stages of his recruitment in 2013.

Tunsil's family at the time was a blended one. Both his father and mother had moved on with life and began new relationships. In the final stages of his college recruitment, the entire group lined up behind the five-star tackle with one goal in mind—Tunsil's future.

The NCAA allows college prospects the opportunity to take five official visits, one per school, as part of the recruiting process. The opportunity to officially visit is extended by invitation only.

NCAA bylaws allow a member institution to pay expenses for food, lodging, and travel for the prospect and their parents or guardians. This became an issue when Tunsil visited Ole Miss.

While the motivation is unclear, Tunsil had more than just his parents visit with him, he had an entourage like you'd see with presidents and foreign diplomats when he took his all-expense paid trip to Oxford, Mississippi. Staffers and boosters laid out the red carpet for his entire crew on their visits.

The NCAA alleges former Ole Miss defensive line coach Chris Kiffin, who served as Tunsil's area recruiter, arranged for additional family members of Tunsil's to receive more than $700 in meals, and two nights lodging at The Inn at Ole Miss.

Ole Miss blames the whole thing on "miscommunication," but the rooms were booked and paid for anyway. Perhaps the embarrassment of the moment could have negatively impacted the Rebels' pursuit of Tunsil. They didn't take that chance.

One wonders if the same steps, regardless of the rules in place, would've been taken for a three-star safety rather than a five-star future first-round left tackle.

The Freeze phrase that pays, "Mistakes were made."

The football allegations were serious, and ones that

threaten the sanctity of the game. Academic fraud, booster involvement with multiple players, cash, gifts, and more drove the headlines. Many of the charges involved current and previous coaches and took place with their knowledge.

While member institutions provide continuing education for their coaches and support staff to ensure proper compliance with best recruiting practices and new NCAA rules regarding the courtship of college bound athletes, sometimes it doesn't matter. Most of the charges leveled at Ole Miss could've been avoided with basic common sense.

Don't cut corners with academics or standardized testing.

Don't use boosters to assist in recruiting efforts.

To fully illustrate the trouble Ole Miss was in as an athletics department, it's important to understand that football was just part of the puzzle. Multiple violations were charged across multiple sports, under the direction of multiple coaches, supervised by multiple athletic directors, and during the tenure of multiple university chancellors.

The Rebel problems weren't isolated to a rogue booster, coach or program. The issues looked to be both systemic and systematic.

There were more than enough football charges to justify a serious set of sanctions, but with allegations of major violations in multiple sports the dreaded "lack of institutional control" charge loomed in the distance.

When it came to women's basketball, Michael Landers, the former Ole Miss director of women's basketball operations, and his wife, Kenya Landers, a former Ole Miss assistant women's basketball coach, allegedly committed academic fraud, and then worked hard to conceal their actions.

The Landers husband and wife team had won National Championships at Trinity Valley Community College in Athens, Texas.

Not long after arriving in Oxford to join newly hired women's basketball coach Adrian Wiggins, the Landers duo went to work in more ways than one.

Soon after, the Southeastern Conference contacted Ole Miss in regards to some reports of potential academic fraud involving the new women's basketball staff.

The University's investigation would later prove a pair of Rebel signees had some of their online coursework completed by both Kenya and Michael Landers. Some of those online courses were reportedly paid for by the Landers family.

Initially, Coach Landers and director of operations Landers denied the allegations. Faced with e-mails he had attempted to delete, Michael admitted he was, in fact, responsible for committing academic fraud, and attempting to cover his tracks. Like most husbands would, he tried to protect his wife by saying she was unaware of his activities.

Kenya later came clean and admitted to completing coursework for recruits in hopes of helping them become eligible for participation at Ole Miss. Eventually, the entire sordid tale was detailed in recovered e-mails and text messages.

Ole Miss women's basketball signees Sha'Kayla Caples, a former junior college National Player of the Year, and Brandy Broome wouldn't enroll in Oxford or ever suit up to play a game for the Rebels.

Caples, a Vicksburg, Mississippi native, played two years for the Landers coaching duo and won a National Championship in 2012.

Broome, a transfer from Pensacola State college, was also expected to provide some lift to a women's basketball program in Oxford that had fallen on hard times.

The scandal would cost Adrian Wiggins his job at Ole Miss. His former boss, Bjork, said, "Although there is no current evidence that Coach Wiggins was complicit in or had direct knowledge of this misconduct, as head coach, he is accountable for the actions of those who report to him."

The laundry list of misdeeds continued as the alleged rules infractions reached into the Rebel track program.

Former assistant track coach Erin Dawson was cited with charges that involved impermissible contact with prospects in what amounted to tryouts for prospective track athletes.

Former Coach Lena Bettis was also named in the allegations, as was head track Coach Brian O'Neal. Perhaps O'Neal's greatest misdeed was not properly supervising his staff, or promoting an atmosphere of compliance.

No matter how you slice it, Ole Miss had charges of academic fraud, impermissible benefits, failure to monitor staff members, and a failure to promote good compliance in multiple sports.

These charges were serious and far reaching. It was abundantly clear the NCAA had a lot of things to consider and there was much more on the way.

With many of the blanks now filled in, the reaction to the allegations was severe. The talk of "minor and secondary" for football proved to be outright lies. The leaks to Ole Miss friendly media looked to be complete fabrications.

The fingers once pointed at Houston Nutt seemed to disappear. While Nutt wasn't named in a single allegation, Freeze was mentioned in two, and several members of his current staff were now under scrutiny.

The national media was now setting the curve on an all-out blitz on the Ole Miss tall tales. In January, people were willing to take the Rebels at their word, but with the oppression of truth and confessions, and the oppression of the summer heat, and the Mississippi humidity on the way, Ole Miss had worn out their welcome with many. It was getting hot in the Magnolia State in more ways than one.

OLE MISS REBELS
ATHLETICS

June 22, 2016

Dear ▮▮▮▮▮▮▮:

I am writing to document our meeting on April 14, 2016. As we discussed, based on the totality of the situation and information gathered, the University of Mississippi has acknowledged that during periods between late August 2014 and early August 2015 ▮▮▮▮▮▮▮▮▮▮▮▮▮▮ allowed two University student-athletes to retain loaner vehicles for a time period extending beyond what was necessitated through normal business arrangements. Additionally, you approved a $3,000 interest free promissory note to be executed as part of a vehicle purchase arrangement for one of the aforementioned student-athletes. The conduct described above has been determined by the NCAA to be a violation of the bylaws prohibiting representatives of the University's athletics interests (i.e., boosters) from providing benefits to student-athletes, their families and their friends.

The University genuinely appreciates the cooperation exhibited by you and your employees throughout the inquiry. Unfortunately, given the involvement of you and your dealership in violations of NCAA legislation, the University must formally disassociate you and ▮▮▮▮▮▮▮▮ from its athletics program for a three-year period of time. The conditions of the University's disassociation are set forth below in accordance with procedures adopted by the NCAA for disassociation of representatives of its athletics interest.

Under NCAA legislation, disassociation is defined as set forth below in the 2015-2016 NCAA Manual under Bylaw 19.9.7-(i):

19.9.7 **Additional Penalties for Level I and Level II Violations.** In addition to the core penalties for Level I and Level II violations, the panel may prescribe one or more of the following penalties: *(Adopted: 10/30/12 effective 8/1/13)*

(i) Pursuant to a show-cause order, disassociation of relations with a representative of an institution's athletics interests, including:

(1) Not accepting any assistance from the individual that would aid in the recruitment of prospective student-athletes or the support of enrolled student-athletes;

(2) Not accepting financial assistance for the institution's athletics program from the individual;

(3) Ensuring that no athletics benefit or privilege is provided to the individual that is not generally available to the public at large; and

(4) Taking such other actions against the individual that the institution determines to be within its authority to eliminate the involvement of the individual in the institution's athletics program.

You and ▮▮▮▮▮ are expected to adhere to the restrictions and limitations set forth in NCAA Bylaw 19.9.7-(i) as well as other applicable NCAA rules. The length of this disassociation is three years. You must have no contact or involvement with any prospective student-athletes (or their families) whom the University might recruit or with current student-athletes (or their families), and any conduct to the contrary will be given great weight in any decision whether to extend or make permanent your disassociation. Please be advised that your level of cooperation with the terms of your disassociation and the instructions I have provided you will be an important factor when re-evaluating your status with the University after three years. If you have any specific questions about the terms or details, please contact Lee Tyner at (662) 915-7014.

The University and our athletics program have appreciated your support so this action is regrettable and an unfortunate circumstance. Thank you for your cooperation and for your understanding of the overall situation.

Sincerely,

Ross Bjork
Director of Intercollegiate Athletics

Chapter 15

Red Flags and the Memphis Blues

February 6, 2013

National Signing Day is a holiday to those who follow college football closely. As prospects put pen to paper, their written declarations are sent by facsimile to college campuses all over the country. It's the one day a year the fax machine actually means something.

Once a university compliance officer has the documents in hand, they're reviewed to ensure all proper protocols are followed, and then the signing is announced by the school, usually by way of an administrative assistant tweeting as a head football coach.

Social media has become a huge part of the recruiting process. On the first Wednesday in February, National Signing Day, schools share their best graphics and visual aids used on social media to announce the inkings of their latest crop of reinforcements.

As the 2013 signings were officially announced by the Ole Miss football staff, Rebel fans around the country were downright gleeful as they imagined trips to an SEC title game that they'd never take. The jubilation over the day's events was wide spread, but the Rebels had bigger fish to fry. One helpful Rebel fan found himself in hot grease.

Memphis, Tennessee businessman Walter Hughes spent a portion of Ole Miss' big day answering questions about his involvement with a handful of Memphis high school prospects the Rebels had recruited during the 2013 recruiting cycle.

At issue was Hughes' relationship with Ole Miss targets Bobby Billingsley, Christian Morris, Herbert Moore and

Marcus Robinson. The talented quartet all attended Memphis-East High School where Hughes volunteered as a Huddle Leader for the Fellowship of Christian Athletes (FCA).

The FCA is very involved on both college and high school campuses in a major way. Based out of Kansas City, Missouri, the FCA is a Christian organization that promotes a relationship with Jesus Christ through sports.

The FCA mission statement reads: "To present to coaches and athletes, and all whom they influence, the challenge and adventure of receiving Jesus Christ as Savior and Lord, serving Him in their relationships and in the fellowship of the church."

Schools may elect to have "Team Huddles," which are essentially Bible studies, team chapels, or devotionals led by volunteers who serve as "Huddle Leaders." A huddle leader can be a coach, player, or volunteer from within the community.

Moore and Robinson, two of the four prospects at the center of the inquiry, signed with Ole Miss earlier that Wednesday.

The Memphian met the definition of an Ole Miss booster in more ways than one. Hughes, the owner of his own landscaping business, previously attended classes at Ole Miss, purchased season tickets for Ole Miss baseball and clearly identified himself as a fan of the Rebel athletic programs.

As his fellow Rebs celebrated what looked to be their coming out party, Hughes sat across from Ole Miss General Counsel Lee Tyner and the Rebels outside counsel William King of Lightfoot, Franklin, and White trying to explain himself. Hughes was interviewed on both the Ole Miss campus and later in his home. There were also some phone calls in between to shore up some details of just what had taken place.

Hughes had hit the Ole Miss NCAA Compliance Office radar over the course of the previous months and it was time to clear the air.

Allegations of impermissible benefits soon followed.

The narrative followed by Ole Miss media painted Hughes as a Good Samaritan. Hughes was only trying to do right by some under-privileged kids whom he'd built relationships with through his work in inner city Memphis as an FCA leader.

It appears whatever explanations Hughes offered to the Ole Miss compliance and legal team weren't satisfactory.

"They said, 'You can't do this.' It made me mad. I said, 'That's not right. It's discriminating. You are accusing me of doing this for different reasons,'" Hughes told Parrish Alford of the *Northeast Mississippi Daily Journal*.

Hughes went on to say that if any rules were broken, they were done so unintentionally.

"Not coach Harris, (Ole Miss assistant coach Maurice Harris, the Rebels' area recruiter for Memphis) or anyone, ever asked me to do anything. That's what hacks me off. They're trying to tie in my relationship with Coach Harris and these kids as a recruiting scandal. That's the furthest thing from the truth there is," Hughes told the *Daily Journal*.

Ole Miss fans took to message boards and social media platforms to defend Hughes, and to call the NCAA heavy-handed for their position regarding their fellow Rebel.

Of course, they were only getting part of the story.

The NCAA has strict rules regarding third parties and prospective student athletes. In an attempt to limit the number of hangers-on who seem to come out of the woodwork once a high school athlete shows college football promise, the NCAA passed by-laws that consider any "new" relationship stemming from the athlete's newfound status as a prospect as improper.

Essentially any "mentor" outside of a player's high school coaches who elect to involve themselves in the recruiting process after the prospect enrolls in high school is classified as impermissible.

For highly recruited athletes there's no shortage of new "friends" who just want to help. Who they're trying to help is often a difficult question to answer. Those who genuinely want to help will do so within the framework of the NCAA by-laws and will abide by the wishes of the family.

There are others who're looking to exploit student athletes for their own personal gain. These "street agents" approach college prospects with promises of better offers, or possibly cash, and gifts under the table, all outside the lines of recruiting regulations.

They're out to help their favorite teams recruit student athletes, as if their own coaching staff is incapable of handling the chore. There're some college coaches who enlist the help of friends of the programs to give them an advantage as they attempt to woo players to their commitment list.

Some fans simply cannot help themselves, and assume their involvement in the courtship is the one thing that will put their team over the recruiting hump.

It could be something as simple as a free T-Shirt, a ride to a ball game, or a $100 handshake. All are against NCAA rules and have been for decades. When it came to Hughes, just about all of the boxes on the NCAA's what-not-to-do checklist were filled in.

While the public perception about Hughes' involvement was light hearted, the actual allegations were incredibly damning. A laundry list of charges was lobbed at Hughes, some alleged to have taken place with the full knowledge of Ole Miss assistant coach Maurice Harris, the Rebels' area recruiter for Memphis.

Ole Miss officials were concerned about Hughes' actions and rightfully so.

When the Rebels won their first SEC game in more than two years, a 41-20 spanking of Auburn during the 2012 season, Hughes was on hand with Moore and some of his Memphis-East teammates in tow.

Moore and Hughes both tweeted about the unofficial visit later in the weekend.

The same group returned to Oxford at the University's next home game, a 27-26 loss to Vanderbilt.

Billingsley, Moore and Robinson were all present when Rebel fans rushed the field following the team's win over Mississippi State.

Over the course of the next few weeks, it was alleged that Hughes was part of the Rebels' recruiting efforts to sign some of the recruits with whom he'd forged relationships.

Hughes was allegedly working with Harris to set up an in-person visit between Morris and Ole Miss offensive line coach, Matt Luke.

A few days later, Hughes reportedly took an even bigger step by attending and providing food for an in-home visit at the home of Moore, where Coach Hugh Freeze and Harris both attended.

It was alleged by the NCAA enforcement staff that Hughes paid phone bills for Moore and the mother of Robinson during the month of December 2012, mere weeks away from National Signing Day.

A month after the in-home visit with Freeze and Harris, Hughes elected to take Billingsley and Moore to Birmingham, Alabama, to see Ole Miss take on Pittsburgh in the BBVA Compass Bowl game. Since prospects aren't allowed complimentary entry to bowl games, the prospects were provided meals, tickets, and transportation to and from the bowl site. The NCAA estimated the weekend trip to the Bowl site and back cost around $350

Hughes was apparently not done. For the final three weekends of the 2013 recruiting calendar, his helping hands found the steering wheel yet again and drove prospects to Oxford, each time reportedly, with advance notice given to Harris.

Just before signing day, Hughes hosted Harris as part of an in-home visit that Billingsley, Moore, and Robinson all apparently attended along with some family members

In addition to all of the all-expense trips from Memphis to Oxford, and in one case Birmingham, Hughes was alleged to have set up academic and ACT tutoring for multiple prospects, and provided three of those recruits with more than $500 worth of Ole Miss clothing.

I was able to obtain some documents from Ole Miss in regards to these matters, and it appears the Rebel compliance team was having a difficult time getting Hughes to comply with the wishes of the University.

After the signing day interview between Hughes and the Ole Miss legal team, Hughes was directed on multiple occasions not to interact with the prospects any longer, nor provide them with any benefits.

These directives were reportedly communicated to Hughes once again by Ole Miss counsel during face-to-face conversations on both Feb. 13 and 21, 2013.

Despite the pleas of his university, Hughes elected to continue his inappropriate conduct placing both the prospects and the football program at risk. His next feast of generosity was when he allegedly provided meals, tickets, and transportation to the football prospects to watch the Rebels play Texas A&M in a baseball game in Oxford the weekend of March 24, 2013.

In a strange twist of fate, the person who notified the Ole Miss compliance office about that visit to campus was the very coach whom Hughes communicated with in the months leading up to signing day. The one and only Maurice Harris.

This final indiscretion drew the ire of Ole Miss Athletics Director, Ross Bjork.

Left with no choice, Bjork informed Hughes of his disassociation from Ole Miss athletics in writing and revoked his remaining season tickets for Rebel baseball. In a scathing communication, Bjork pulled no punches and outlined in great detail the reasons why the University would no longer associate with Hughes, accept donations from him, or sell him season tickets.

While Hughes' motives can certainly be questioned, it's abundantly clear in the end he was no friend to the program to which he professed his allegiance. Despite repeated requests to cease his activities, he simply wouldn't.

In the final tally, Hughes' actions didn't yield much, as far as on the field success for Ole Miss, despite the fact that three of the four 2013 Ole Miss prospects associated with Hughes signed a national letter of intent with Freeze's Rebels.

Entering his senior season in Oxford, defensive tackle Moore has recorded just three career tackles. The Memphis-East High School product missed all of 2015 with an ACL tear and spent last season working himself back into good health.

Offensive tackle Morris initially signed with UCLA, but never made the move out West. The former four-star enrolled at Ole Miss in January of 2014, but injuries limited his playing time in Oxford. Following a scary play against Texas A&M, Morris collapsed coming off of the field at the end of the first half due to a neck injury, his Rebel career ended. It was believed he'd never play football again, but in December 2016, Morris announced he was joining the Grambling football program.

Robinson signed with Ole Miss, but enrolled at Northeast Mississippi Community College. Once his time in Booneville, Mississippi, was done, the talented linebacker signed on with the University of North Alabama. Robinson never made a tackle in an Ole Miss uniform.

Billingsley initially planned to walk on at Ole Miss in hopes of later earning a scholarship. He is now out of football.

While the on-the-field contributions of this Memphis quartet are minor in the grand scheme of things, the method in which they were recruited will certainly leave a mark on Ole Miss football.

Hughes wasn't the only Ole Miss booster to be chastised for their involvement with the Memphis East prospects. DeSoto County school teacher Carla Belk also found herself in hot water after providing Moore with a ride to Oxford. Small potatoes? Maybe so, but this incident shows that sanctions aren't limited to the Daddy Warbucks variety of boosters.

Even though Hughes was officially disassociated from the Rebel program in less than two months after his 2013 meeting with Ole Miss lawyers, it'd take over three more years before this news was made public.

THREE YEARS!

How's that possible in a *"Wikileaks"* world? We live in a time where major motion pictures and music from national recording artists get leaked online on a regular basis. Despite the loose lips culture of today's social media, where anonymous hubris abounds, one of the biggest sports stories in recent Southeastern Conference history was successfully kept under wraps... for the most part.

One of the key components in a cover-up of this magnitude is having friends in the media—writers, editors, publishers, and owners—and Ole Miss has plenty of those.

As I began to get tips about NCAA investigators spending time in Mississippi asking questions about Ole Miss, I took it all with a grain of salt. I started getting a lot of phone calls that began with "You didn't hear this from me...." And some of it began to match up.

To be blunt, we'd been here before with rumors of an Ole Miss investigation running rampant only to see nothing materialize. There was always talk and always somebody with a story to tell, but this time things were different. The reports from independent sources were very specific and very consistent.

I decided to fly a few things up the flagpole to see who else in the in-state media would salute it. While most were interested in talking, they didn't have much else to share other than their own intrigue.

Many others were skeptical, encouraging me to just simply leave it alone. Mostly, their tone struck me as odd. How could any in-state sports reporter be disinterested in an NCAA scandal involving one of the major universities of Mississippi? It simply made no sense.

Looking back, I'm sure some simply wanted to stay out of it, write their daily stories and continue the regular work-a-day life journalism often becomes. Others may have had more of an interest in the positive outcome of things and didn't want some Mississippi State guy kicking up dust.

I had one salty veteran reporter tell me, "This is trouble you don't want."

There was a small part of me then that felt like some were simply scared of the Ole Miss machine. That part of me has grown exponentially in the past few years. Some were merely happy with the order of things, while others just didn't want to see the boat rocked. That reporter's comment fanned the flames burning within me to push forward with more gusto than ever.

I've wondered many times if the greater sin is in the misdeed of the many participants, or in the decision of those charged with reporting on it, simply deciding to ignore it. Either way, I'm not sure the common good is served.

In my mind, one of the biggest parts of this story is the fact Ole Miss has benefited from people in the media being complicit in the cover-up, by either their own willful decisions, or woeful ineptitude.

Outside of my own commentary on *The Boneyard, Genespage. com*, or social media, not much was said about the ongoing probe into Ole Miss football. I was painted as a Maroon malcontent who was not to be believed.

Even some of my own friends were reluctant to get on board. It was hard not to take a lot of that personal, but at the same time, I knew I was holding all of the Aces. I joked, "hide and watch" to those who doubted me.

I went it alone for a long time, but the bandwagon got

pretty crowded after Pat Forde of *Yahoo Sports* published the article, "Sources: Mississippi under investigation for rules violations in multiple sports" on Oct. 2, 2014. It just so happened to be Alabama week for Ole Miss and many in the Rebel fan base expressed some skepticism. Some accused Forde of writing the article as a well-timed favor to friends in Tuscaloosa.

Forde clearly had a good source on the matter and even reached out to Ross Bjork for comment. Bjork confirmed the existence of the NCAA inquiry, but didn't offer much other than the standard "We are cooperating... and can't comment further."

As well sourced as Forde was, his informant clearly didn't have the full story. The story read as though it was believed that "much" of the football inquiry involved the previous staff, and no new allegations had emerged, that interviews were over, and Ole Miss was simply waiting for their day before the infractions committee.

"*Yahoo Sports* filed a Freedom of Information request with Mississippi on Sept. 2 requesting all correspondence between the school and the NCAA Department of Enforcement between Sept. 1, 2013, and Sept. 1, 2014," Forde wrote. "The request was returned Sept. 26 showing 19 secondary or Level III violations in that time period, with names and affected sports redacted."

Forde's article, and much of the juicy details, were attributed to anonymous sources. Ole Miss football and women's hoops were both rumored to be the subject of the probe, but Freeze and his staff weren't expected to be wrapped up in the major football violations. Former Coach Houston Nutt's staff was allegedly responsible for those, but more on that later.

There wasn't much in the way of outright allegations or any specific charges. Supposedly, there was simply a fly in the

Rebel ointment, quality piece to let the world know, on a more national level, that there was some fire associated with the smoke billowing up from Oxford.

Those comments were routinely used as Rebel talking points, but wound up being completely false. It would be a while before anybody really paid attention, though.

Ole Miss beat Alabama the following Saturday, and any talk about an NCAA investigation faded like yesterday's news. The new narrative centered around ESPN performance indexes, national rankings, and where the Rebels would be in the first ever FBS playoff poll.

No one reading or writing newspapers in the state of Mississippi focused on the Forde report for very long. Mississippi State and Ole Miss were both undefeated and highly ranked. This was a good news year in the Magnolia State and that is where the focus shifted both regionally and nationally. The college football "Mayhem" in 2014 was Mississippi made.

OLE MISS REBELS
ATHLETICS

 **COPY**

Dear

  I am writing to follow up on a telephone conversation you had with Lee Tyner and our outside counsel ███████ on March 26, 2013. As they told you, the University of Mississippi learned that you brought three student-athletes to Oxford to attend a baseball game during the weekend of March 23-24, 2013. In addition to transportation to and from ███████, the information we received indicated that you also provided them with tickets to the game, food and beverages at the game and perhaps a meal after the game. You confirmed all of this with the possible exception of the provision of food and beverages. Your conduct appears to have violated NCAA bylaws prohibiting representatives of the University's athletics interests (i.e., boosters) from providing benefits to prospects.

  My understanding is that Mr. Tyner and ███████ have told you several times over the past two months that as a booster, you must refrain from providing benefits to any prospects. Those discussions focused in particular on the three prospects listed above and other prospects at ███████. We specifically told you that you should refrain from having contact with these prospects and under no circumstances should you bring them to campus or provide them with any benefits. These directions were repeated during your interviews on February 13 and February 21, and based upon your commitment to follow them, we were confident you would in fact do that. It is now clear that you instead disregarded these directions, potentially causing problems for these young men and the University in the process.

  Effective immediately, your season ticket privileges for the remainder of the 2012-13 baseball season are suspended. You should return your tickets to Matt Ball in the compliance office immediately. You will not be allowed to attend any games using your season tickets, and you should not attempt to purchase tickets from the University. We will refund the cost of your season tickets on a prorated basis.

  Given your failure to follow the University's clear instructions, and your involvement in violations of NCAA legislation, the University must formally disassociate you from its athletics program for an indefinite period. The conditions of the disassociation are set forth below in accordance with procedures adopted by the NCAA for disassociation of representatives of its athletics interest.

  Under NCAA legislation, disassociation is defined as set forth below in the 2012-13 NCAA Manual:

Page 2

19.5.2.6 Disassociation of Representatives of Athletics Interests. The disassociation of relations with a representative of an institution's athletics interests may be imposed on a permanent basis, for the duration of the applicable probationary period or for another specified period of time. When an institution is required to show cause why a representative of the institution's athletics interests should not be disassociated from its athletics program, such disassociation shall require that the institution:

(a)   Refrain from accepting any assistance from the individual that would aid in the recruitment of prospective student-athletes or the support of enrolled student-athletes;

(b)   Not accept financial assistance for the institution's athletics program from the individual;

(c)   Ensure that no athletics benefit or privilege be provided to the individual that is not generally available to the public at large; and

(d)   Take such other actions against the individual that the institution determines to be within its authority to eliminate the involvement of the individual in the institution's athletics program.

You are expected to adhere to the restrictions and limitations set forth in NCAA Bylaw 19.5.2.6. The length of your disassociation is indefinite. You must have no contact or involvement with any prospective student-athletes (or their families) whom the University might recruit, and any conduct to the contrary will be given great weight in any decision whether to extend or make permanent your disassociation. Please be advised that your level of cooperation with the terms of your disassociation and the instructions Mr. Tyner and previously provided you will be an important factor in determining the length of the disassociation period. If you have any specific questions about the terms or details, please contact Lee Tyner at (662) 915-7014.

We have not had a chance to meet face to face so this action is regrettable and an unfortunate circumstance. However, the University intends to take every step necessary to comply with NCAA rules and regulations and not to jeopardize our rich athletic tradition.

Sincerely,

Ross Bjork

Ross Bjork
Director of Intercollegiate Athletics

Chapter 16

Hacked

October 13, 2016

Those of us who cover sports get to do a lot of cool things. Make no mistake, it's a great job, but it's still a job. As much as I love doing what I do, I would much rather be able to travel, see the world, sleep 'til noon every day, and live off of room service. Who wouldn't?

All of that said, I feel like I was built with this career in mind. I love the job. I'm confident my wife would agree that I never complain about working. There are some days it's tough leaving the driveway knowing I'm not going to see my family for a couple of nights, but I'm crazy about the work.

I love the feeling of walking up towards a packed football stadium. Hearing the roar of the crowd, seeing everyone in their school colors, and smelling overcooked popcorn. Buckle your chinstrap, and tee it up! It doesn't matter to me if it's high school or college. The pigskin pageant is a national treasure full of pomp and circumstance native to America. It's our sport.

In my line of work, I attend a lot of ball games of which I don't really care about the outcome. Sure, a winning player or coach provides better postgame comments, so there's that. By and large, the final score is of really no consequence to me.

To truly cover college football recruiting, you have to go see the players in person as best you can. I've joked many times that some of the people ranking prospects in the state of Mississippi must be much smarter than me. They've figured out a way to evaluate guys they've never seen play.

See... smart!

I take a lot of pride in the windshield time I've racked up in the past decade going to see college bound prospects play football. I once watched the first half of the battle for Chattanooga, Tennessee, between rivals Baylor and McCallie, and then raced across the state line at halftime to Ringgold, Georgia, to catch the second half of Notre Dame and Signal Mountain High School.

While I take pleasure in the work, that sort of stuff is just plain fun for me.

Over the years, I've also learned what it means to those players and their families. Yes, the subscriber owns my loyalty, but I hope I never forget what it means to those young people to have someone from a national company come watch them play.

The game pictures will slide down the wall of Instagram over time, but these student athletes appreciate people making the effort. They don't forget it.

On the other side of things, there are fans who're hoping their favorite team signs those players. They want to know what we saw, what we thought and what we learned. There's so much you can learn in person, while attending a game you could never learn otherwise.

The aunts, uncles, cousins, Pop Warner coaches, classmates, and many others often know the score much more than guys who stay home all day combing social media for a story. You do the real work, the leg work, and you get rewarded. It's how life works.

On this night, I made the drive down to Goodman, Mississippi, to the campus of Holmes Community College to see the HCC Bulldogs take on the Wolfpack of Copiah-Lincoln. It was a big game for both teams, to say the least. Both squads were battling for spots in the post season.

Leading the charge for Co-Lin was a group of players

Mississippi State was expected to sign. Long-time commitment Tommy Champion of Callaway High School in Jackson, Mississippi, anchored the offensive line former Michigan State Spartan Montez Sweat provided the pass rush, Collins, Mississippi, native Deion Pope proved to be the drain plug in the middle of the Wolfpack defense, safety Jaquarius Landrews handled the deep third in pass defense, and freshman Nero Nelson gave Holmes fits from the slot receiver position.

As I made my way to the far sideline to set up to shoot pictures and video of the night's action, I ran into former Mississippi State defensive line coach David Turner.

Turner had left Starkville for College Station, Texas, and as a result had had the chance to coach Myles Garrett, the future No. 1 overall pick in the 2017 NFL draft.

One of the candidates to replace Garrett in the Aggie rotation at defensive line was on display that night in Goodman. Then Texas A&M commitment Tyree Owens was having an up and down year, but looked to be locked in with Coach Kevin Sumlin's program. Perhaps the former West Virginia Mountaineer would receive a favorable in-person evaluation from his prospective position coach.

Many Mississippi State fans were hopeful Turner wasn't there to get a better look at Sweat, an MSU Bulldog verbal. That's how life is in major college football. Once a player is uncovered by one team, he's essentially in the spotlight for competing programs as well. It's not about who's offered then; it's who you have to beat.

The game also allowed me the chance to catch up with a newfound friend I've made over the last few years, David Culpepper, during our free football combine series in the state of Mississippi.

I first began doing football combines in 2008 in an effort to help our state's football players have a real chance at getting on a recruiting list somewhere out there.

Many kids in Mississippi don't have the money to drive to a college campus for a one-day camp much less the funds needed to pay the registration fee. It gets expensive.

One year, *Scout.com* partnered with Under Armour to hold a high school football combine in Mobile, Alabama, the week of the senior bowl. It was 18 degrees that day, but we still had a great turnout.

Future Alabama quarterback A.J. McCarron, future Mississippi State all-time receptions leader Chad Bumphis, and other SEC notables were in attendance.

I was approached after that event about bringing an event just like that one to Tupelo, Mississippi. I had never managed anything of that sort before. Sure, I had covered combines before, but what do you do when everybody's looking at you to know what to do?

We were able to arrange sponsorship, and everybody got to work. We had just about all of the top players in the state show up, including future first round pick of the Philadelphia Eagles, and future MSU star, Fletcher Cox.

Nobody got hurt and everybody appeared to have fun.

As the Tupelo event grew, so did the demand for more events around the Magnolia State. Growing up in south Mississippi, I always felt a lot of talented players got overlooked in some under-recruited areas. I really wanted to find a home for an event in the south, and Culpepper made that happen in Brookhaven.

I didn't know Culpepper before our first planning meetings for the event that would become the "Miss-Lou All-American Combine" sponsored by King's Daughter Medical Center (KDMC).

While the event serves as a marketing vehicle for KDMC, Culpepper has a deeper understanding. He wants to see those kids from south Mississippi have a real chance to play college football and get an education.

Culpepper is an Ole Miss fan, but there's never been any talk of the Egg Bowl at these events from either of us. These free camps are a chance for all of us to come together under the banner of community, and help our young people earn some real opportunity.

While Culpepper and I visited during that game between Co-Lin and Holmes, his daughter cheered the Wolfpack on as a cheerleader. It was a nice evening to catch up, and just talk some football.

Co-Lin built a 28-6 halftime lead, and then hung on to secure a 35-21 victory. Pope led the Wolfpack with nine personal stops, Sweat, and Landrews notched five each, Nelson had a 28-yard touchdown catch, and Champion helped pave the way to 473 yards of offense.

It was a good game from my perspective, because the players I went to see shined. I was able to get solid pictures and videos of all involved. I was also able to gain some better insight into the quality of their play, so I could share more credible information with our subscribers.

I made the 90-plus-mile drive home without incident. Shortly after I got home, I elected to post a few observations on our message boards at *Genespage.com* about the Co-Lin players Mississippi State was recruiting.

As I finished up and prepared to declare the work day done, I got a text from my pal Brandon Walker who works for *SECCountry.com*.

"Did you mean to tweet that," he asked.

My immediate thought was perhaps I had shared a direct message openly, and it seemed out of place in the Twittersphere.

Before I could even get my Twitter account open, another message was in. This time it was Brian Hadad of

BulldogSportsRadio.com.

"Have you been hacked?" The message read.

Once into my Twitter account, I saw a handful of tweets I never sent. They were either derogatory comments about Mississippi State, or over the top positive about Huge Freeze and Ole Miss.

They were written with the wit and intelligence of a middle schooler, and not consistent with anything I've ever tweeted. My followers knew right away it wasn't me making those comments.

I deleted the tweets, and changed my password, and thought the incident was over. Boy, was I wrong.

Minutes later the tweets started up again, and one of them included a link to a third-party image site where several of my direct messages were now posted for the world to see.

Thankfully, I didn't have much in there that was especially embarrassing to me. Sure, there was some language I wish I had back, but my more immediate concern was for the other people in those conversations.

Some very candid messages from some sources for this book were now exposed. One especially detailed story, which I'd never made public, was now available for public consumption.

I'd been contacted by the father of a recruit I covered for a couple of years who signed with an out-of-state program. According to this father his son had been approached by Ole Miss boosters about being a Rebel.

The father shared some rather sordid details about promises of trips and other benefits should his son sign with Ole Miss.

I was certainly intrigued by his story, but the truth of the matter was I couldn't confirm any of it. I had no reason to doubt him, but without something else to support his word I couldn't really build a story around it.

As a result, I never went public with any of that

information. Why the hacker elected to share that was beyond me. The social media bullies were on the father immediately. He eventually recanted his claims, but I believe he did so in an attempt to just end the flare up.

I never intended for him or his family to be impacted by any of that. He had a story to share, and I was willing to hear it. His story fingered some major players within the Ole Miss family—a tobacco lawyer, a prominent businessman and a local home builder. Some of the parties mentioned would be considered in the who's who of Ole Miss fans.

The father was the first person I contacted about the hack. I wanted him to know the things he had shared with me in private were now public in a very major way. His response completely blew me away. He never batted an eye.

"No problem, Steve," was his message to me.

Not everyone was as charitable, but I am happy to say I made apologies to everyone involved, and did my best to make amends. In the end, everyone stayed in my corner.

Many of them who'd been pretty neutral about Ole Miss, and the direction of the NCAA probe, became raving fans of the enforcement process. I cannot count how many messages of support I received from people I'd never met who wanted me to know they were pulling for me.

One of the reasons you are reading this book today is because of this hack. Any second thoughts I had about going through with this process ended the night those clowns hacked me, and hurt people I care about.

The world has taught me that screen shots are forever. The worst part of losing control over my social media account was that people began making comments immediately.

Before I was able to put an end to my online hostage situation, I was completely locked out. The hacker had changed my password as well as the e-mail account on file with Twitter. As a result, I couldn't even request a reset code.

I just had to report the account as hacked, and encourage others to do the same. Several friends tweeted that I had been hacked, and asked their followers to report my account to Twitter.

Just as I'd made my peace with the fact I'd done all I could do, it was over. Twitter had suspended my account, and contacted me with questions to reclaim control. It was a relief, but the damage had been done.

It was a powerless position to be in, but in the grand scheme of things it changed nothing. If anything, it gave me a greater resolve to finish the deal.

The next day, I was sitting at my desktop working through changing passwords when I got a notification from Apple that there was a login to one of my old Apple accounts. I logged in, got the phone number attached to the device, and called it.

No answer.

I elected to text to see what response I'd get. The guy finally responded, and tried to play dumb. He said he wasn't much of a sports fan, but understood rivalries ran deep. He said he didn't have social media accounts, because he didn't see the point.

He turned out to be an Ole Miss fan from Tupelo, Mississippi, complete with Facebook, and other social media profiles.

Rumors spread that several other accounts of mine had been hacked, and direct messages copied. The issue with that is, outside of Twitter and Facebook, I didn't have any messages to copy.

Some "insiders" said my Scout mailbox had been compromised as well as my personal e-mail. None of that was true. Some even insisted my accounts on other Mississippi State sites had been hacked. The problem with that is I don't have accounts on other sites, Mississippi State or otherwise.

It was all false.

One of the craziest things about it all is that I kept almost all of the credible tips and sensitive information on an external hard drive. If someone really knew what they were doing, they could have found it all, and found more than a little trash talk on Twitter.

The reaction to the whole thing was about what you'd expect. People who didn't like me, cheered. Those who were supportive of me, stood with me.

Brandon Walker called me and told me, "I have your back no matter what."

Several members of the national and regional media contacted me to offer their support, and encouraged me to stay the course. Not that I needed it, but it helped.

Having an account hacked is sort of like losing your wallet. It's a big hassle getting everything secured again. I didn't use the same password for everything, but I changed them all.

I sprang awake one night at 2 a.m. realizing I forgot to change the password on PayPal. I ran downstairs to ensure the account hadn't been cleaned out. Thankfully it was still secure. I changed it anyway just to be certain.

We've become a password-protected society in every way, but we're as much prisoners to it as we are protected by it. Everything requires a password to access it, but there is no guarantee our privacy is being protected. No matter how confident we are about it, we shouldn't be.

Words to the wise: Never settle into a comfort zone where you feel protected from prying eyes. Nothing is completely private. It never has been, and likely never will be.

As the technology to protect us evolves, so does the means to circumvent it. If you use social media platforms, be sure to use their advanced security measures to protect your accounts. You never know when some crazy person will buy some hacking software, and go to work trying to find out what you're talking about privately.

I saw the hacking of my Twitter account as an act of war. For months, Ole Miss fans said I was making the whole thing up.

While they took cheap shots at my credibility publicly, they tried to get me fired privately. Under the cloak of conspiracy, they worked to have my combine sponsors pull out on me; one did. Some had threatened to kill me, and now this hacking business.

That seems like an awful lot of time and trouble to invest in a guy who was allegedly telling a tall tale about Ole Miss football.

If they were looking to intimidate me, scare me or just simply show me "my place," they failed miserably. If anything, they added fuel to the fire. Their actions to silence me only made me more confident I was right about it all.

If I was wrong, why would they have cared?

Chapter 17

Scapegoat Herding

From the outset of the public declarations regarding the Ole Miss NCAA investigation, many Rebels have spent a lot of time and energy figuring out just who to blame.

Bjork? Freeze? Rogue assistants and rogue boosters?

Again, they can't all be rogue. It's a contradiction in terms to say the least, but it appears to be much easier to cast aspersions at nameless and faceless villains.

As Ole Miss' pop music mirror, Milli Vanilli once sang in their smash hit "Blame it on the Rain," the Rebs were chiming right on in, "Whatever you do, don't put the blame on you."

Once the news media let the cat out of the bag about the University's extensive list of alleged NCAA sins, a few spin masters began working their magic.

As the phone records suggest, the Rebels' "story" may have been shared privately, but it's reasonable to assume their side of things came from those who served in an official capacity.

Dating back to the infancy of this story, recall that the women's basketball and track programs were convenient sacrificial lambs on the altar of public relations. Perhaps that tall tale was fueled by the growing fear and realization that the "aw, shucks" football coach from Tate County, Mississippi, wasn't quite what he'd been billed to be.

Faced with the reality check that an NCAA Notice of Allegations often brings, it appears steps were taken to keep those who gleefully followed down the yellow brick road from looking behind the curtain to see they really weren't in Kansas anymore.

Once the truth was out there for everyone to see, the Rebels and their supporters struggled mightily to come to grips with where they were. Many had spent months denying the existence of an investigation into Ole Miss football, and now they were being forced to admit that they were either grossly misinformed, or asleep at the wheel.

It might be both, but it can't be neither.

A growing problem for all involved was they were having a very difficult time returning a 'true bill of indictment' against a patsy outside of the current football staff.

Women's basketball coach Adrian Wiggins had been fired on what Bjork called "a sad day for the University of Mississippi, our profession and most importantly our student athletes."

Bjork went on to say that Wiggins was ultimately responsible for the actions that went on during his tenure despite his lack of involvement with wrong doing.

"Although there is no current evidence that Coach Wiggins was complicit in, or had direct knowledge of this misconduct, as head coach, he is accountable for the actions of those who report to him."

As the clock ran out on Wiggins' tenure as an Ole Miss head coach, Freeze remained entrenched as the head man for Rebel football despite similar circumstances.

So, if Freeze's reputation was to be salvaged, someone else would have to shoulder the blame.

The end around to drop the whole mess in Houston Nutt's lap was tackled for about a 10-yard loss, and a monetary penalty is likely to come later.

It still amazes me that recruits, their families and members of the media were led to believe the current staff wasn't a subject of the probe. There was plenty of bravado about the buck stopping here, but the childish gossip appeared to start there as well.

When the first Notice of Allegations was made public,

Nutt's name wasn't mentioned. Not once. The red and blue herring the spin masters had been floating around in the days before signing day 2016, where they were calling into question the integrity of their former head coach Houston Nutt, turned into a real stinker.

Some national pundits cried foul, and reminded their readers that the fantasy of "sourced" reports of January 2016 didn't match up with the fact findings of May. With the revelations of reality now fully realized, most no longer gave the Ole Miss administration the benefit of the doubt.

Even many longtime Rebel fans had trouble accepting anything just based on the words of their leadership. With Nutt absolved of any personal involvement in the allegations, the court of public opinion rendered a stinging verdict against Bjork and Freeze. Many were waking up to the fact that if they didn't know, then they should've known. They're paid quite handsomely to know.

After the Tunsil draft night fiasco, some suggested that Freeze and his staff should be terminated immediately. Of course, that didn't happen, but changes were on the way.

One of the names mentioned as part of the Tunsil hack was Rebel staffer Barney Farrar. Ole Miss Director of Football Operations, John Miller had apparently instructed Tunsil to "get with Barney next week" about some funds required to pay his mother's light bill.

Before we get into what happened to Farrar, it's important to know who he is and where he came from.

Farrar's home town of Kossuth, Mississippi, is in extreme northeast Mississippi. The tiny hamlet boasts a population of just more than 200 residents. The entire town covers roughly one square mile of Magnolia State real estate.

While many towns in Mississippi are named for families or local heroes, Kossuth is named for Hungarian freedom fighter

Lajos Kossuth. Perhaps the most famous resident of Kossuth is famed Mississippi writer Thomas Hal Phillips, who made a career as a novelist and Hollywood writer contributing such works as "Huckleberry Finn," and "Thieves Like Us."

Farrar found his way to hometown notoriety as a football hero. As a senior in 1978, Farrar was wildly popular. He was elected class president by his classmates and voted football team captain by his teammates.

Once his time at Kossuth High School was done, Farrar earned a football scholarship at Northeast Mississippi Community College where he went on to play with future Mississippi State University president Mark Keenum, and attorney Bruse Lloyd.

After his two years in Booneville were complete, Farrar joined the football program at Delta State University in Cleveland, Mississippi, where once again he served as a senior team captain.

With his two seasons of on-the-field service exhausted, Farrar went to work at Delta State University as a graduate assistant for three years for the Statesmen. He then left for a position at Clemson University working for Coach Danny Ford.

After Ford resigned as the Tiger's head coach following the 1989 season, Coach Ken Hatfield was hired away from Arkansas to replace him. Ironically, Ford filled the vacancy in Fayetteville.

With that game of musical chairs completed, Farrar was retained by Hatfield at Clemson as a strength coach.

Hatfield left Clemson three seasons later over a contract dispute with the Tiger administration. Weeks later, Hatfield accepted the head coaching position at Rice University.

Farrar made the move to Texas with Hatfield where they served together for 12 seasons. After a 1-10 campaign in 2005,

Hatfield resigned, and Farrar took an off-the-field position at Ole Miss on Coach Ed Orgeron's staff as Assistant AD for External Affairs.

During his time as a football staffer under Orgeron, Farrar developed a deep and personal friendship with then fellow assistant coach Hugh Freeze, a former assistant AD himself had transitioned into an on-the-field assistant coach.

As the Orgeron era began winding down, his staff scattered. Farrar joined Gene Chizik's staff at Iowa State as the director of football operations.

Freeze was retained as a transition coach who helped Houston Nutt's newly hired staff get settled and acclimated at Ole Miss. Freeze later interviewed for the offensive coordinator position, but Nutt elected to hire former Rebel quarterback Kent Austin who'd found success as both a coach and player in the Canadian Football League.

With no room left in the Rebel Inn, Freeze accepted the head coaching position at Lambeth College of the NAIA.

While Freeze was making the move from Mississippi to Jackson, Tennessee, Farrar was headed home to join Coach Larry Fedora's staff at Southern Mississippi (USM). Freeze turned Lambuth's program around, going 20-5 for his two-season record, and a 12-1 final-season finish and a sixth ranking in the NAIA. In 2010, Freeze used San Jose State like a pinball bumper and bounced from there to Arkansas as offensive coordinator. His offensive savvy worked improved the Red Wolves' offensive proficiency that season, and quickly led to a promotion to head coach.

Farrar spent three seasons coaching tight ends for the Golden Eagles and receiving national acclaim for his proficiency as a recruiter. *Rivals.com* named Farrar one of the top non-power five recruiters in the country for the 2010 recruiting cycle.

In 2011, Farrar, who'd won a battle with cancer, took an

off-the-field position at USM as the director of High School Relations and Player Development. The Golden Eagles went on to win the Conference-USA Championship that fall.

Across the state line and into the state of Arkansas, Freeze was winning the Sunbelt Conference Championship at Arkansas State.

The Red Wolves were headed to their first bowl game since 2005, but Freeze wouldn't be there to take part.

On Dec. 5, 2011, Danny Hugh Freeze Jr. was named the 37th head football coach at Ole Miss.

Within days, Freeze reached out to Farrar and extended an offer to rejoin the Ole Miss coaching staff. Sources told me that Farrar was one of the first people Freeze called when assembling his staff in Oxford.

Farrar jumped at the chance to reconnect with his old friend. The University made the news official Dec. 12, but the deal was done days before.

Back in the Rebel saddle, and sporting a red polo shirt, Farrar went to work buttressing the Ole Miss recruiting efforts.

Due to a unique circumstance involving a family issue with offensive coordinator Dan Werner, a request was made of the NCAA to allow Werner to handle the on-the-field coaching responsibilities and for Farrar to carry the recruiting weight.

Essentially, Farrar and Werner were one person. Now, Farrar didn't have the burdens of game planning, managing a personnel group or the basic duties of coaching. No matter how you slice it, Farrar had it good.

He was free to recruit, recruit, and recruit.

Farrar made a big splash in the class of 2014 when he was credited with orchestrating the flip of Holmes Community College four-star cornerback Tee Shepard. The talented defensive back defected from rival Mississippi State to Ole

Miss on National Signing Day. Shepard hadn't mentioned the Rebels after committing to the Bulldogs, but signed with Freeze and Farrar before even taking an official visit to the Ole Miss campus.

The following recruiting cycle, Farrar led the charge in the Rebels' pursuit of prized linebacker Leo Lewis of Brookhaven High School. The details of the alleged tactics used became a central focus of the Amended Notice of Allegations delivered to the Rebels in February 2017.

For the 2016 signing class, Farrar was named one of the nation's top recruiters for his labors to land prized recruits A.J. Brown, Shea Patterson and others. In fact, Farrar likely had more signing day skins on the wall than any other Rebel assistant coach when the fax machine stopped squealing.

To be fair, the longtime coach had some big misses in the final tally as well. Talented target Kobe Jones and the state's top prospect, five-star Jeffery Simmons had inked with rival Mississippi State.

Prior to his bio being removed from the Ole Miss official website, Farrar was praised for his successes on the recruiting trail.

"(Farrar) plays a vital role in recruiting, which has helped Ole Miss land four straight top-15 signing classes, including the 2013 and 2016 hauls that ranked top five in the nation," Ole Miss' website said at one time.

Before Farrar could aid in the final efforts to bring another solid recruiting class to Oxford, his major college coaching future was called into question as the NCAA began to finalize its investigation.

In November 2016, it was learned that Farrar had been placed on administrative leave by the Ole Miss Athletics Department. While no official explanation was provided, the popular belief was the admissions of Laremy Tunsil on draft night likely had a connection to Farrar's unexplained absence.

As freshman star, Shea Patterson took over under center in the Rebels final three games of the 2016 season, Farrar was forced to watch from somewhere other than the Ole Miss sideline.

After a loss on the road to Vanderbilt, the sixth for the Rebels in their last 10 against the Commodores, rumors began to circulate that Farrar's leave from the Ole Miss football program involved potential indiscretions that had nothing to do with Tunsil.

Some well-place leaks revealed that Mississippi State linebacker Leo Lewis had given testimony to the NCAA enforcement staff, and had been given a grant of immunity to do so.

Smoke began to rise signifying that questions about Farrar's recruitment of Lewis was the reason behind the coach's suspension. Needless to say, friends of Farrar were unhappy about the accusations, and took to social media to share their frustration.

Yancy Porter
@YancyPorter

Replying to @Smokey__420

no, Leo Lewis snitched on Barney and claimed he called him on a phone that was not the universities. Pretty pathetic.

11/21/16, 9:54 AM from Oxford, MS

Once the truth was known, burner phones were likely the very least of the Rebel worries. It was now public knowledge that allegations involving Lewis were on the way. The fact that a coach was suspended signaled something more sinister than pre-paid cell phones were at issue.

The timing of the leak made for some interesting internet fodder. Mississippi State and Ole Miss both entered the Battle for the Golden Egg needing a win to keep their bowl hopes alive. Some suggested that painting Lewis as public enemy number one was a cheap motivational tool to distract the Bulldogs and fire up the Rebels.

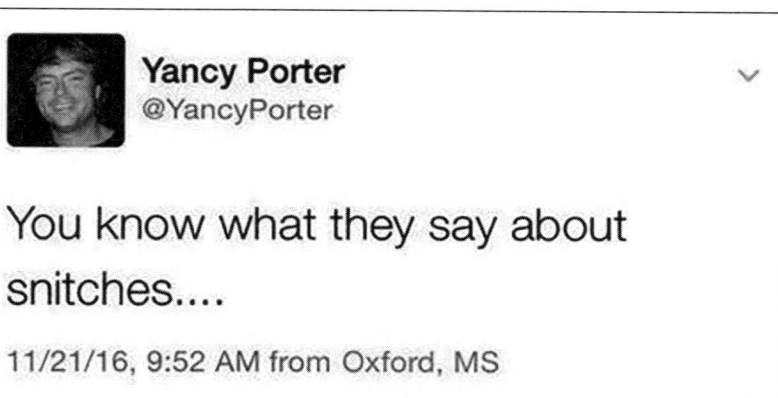

Yancy Porter
@YancyPorter

You know what they say about snitches....

11/21/16, 9:52 AM from Oxford, MS

In this case, "snitches" got six tackles, a sack, and a five-touchdown blow-out win on the road in a rivalry game. Lewis helped lead a defensive effort that shut out Ole Miss in the second half as the Bulldogs cruised to a 55-20 cakewalk win.

While the Bulldogs made postseason plans for south Florida, Ole Miss made coaching changes.

I was in Montgomery, Alabama, covering the Mississippi/Alabama All-Star game practices when the news broke that Farrar and Werner were not returning to the Ole Miss staff.

The news surprised many in the Rebel fanbase in large part due to reports from Yancy Porter of the *OMSpirit.com* and David Johnson of *Rebels247.com* that suggested Farrar would be reinstated.

Instead, Farrar was terminated and required to turn in his University-issued cell phone and laptop. The man labeled by many as Ole Miss' top recruiter was no longer a member of the Rebel coaching staff.

While some with sources attempted in vain to suggest Farrar was fired over a burner phone, many others took a more measured approach. Perhaps one of the factors behind a vote of no confidence from the "insiders" (i.e., Ole Miss beat reporters) was the fact that those expected to provide information were surprised by the news of Farrar's departure.

As Christmas Day approached, the only thing known for certain, at least publicly, was that Farrar was gone. Fans would have to wait two more months to get a real sense of the trouble.

A last place finish in the SEC West and now this....

Just when it appeared things couldn't get worse, they did. Due to some attrition on the Ole Miss coaching staff, Freeze had to interview several applicants to fill those vacated positions with the cloud of pending NCAA sanctions looming in the background.

College football veteran Dave Wommack resigned his post as the Rebel defensive coordinator just before Ole Miss took the field in what would prove to be the final game of their 2016 season.

The Rebels finished the campaign 111 out of 128 FBS schools in total defense. Ole Miss allowed 34 points per game, which ranked 100th nationally, and dead last in the Southeastern Conference.

Longtime Defensive line coach Chris Kiffin elected to leave Oxford and join his brother, Lane, at Florida Atlantic

University (FAU). Kiffin was named the nation's top recruiter by Scout.com after the Rebels landed a top-five class in 2013.

Now, some of the methods Kiffin used to secure those signing day signatures came under scrutiny.

Kiffin was mentioned prominently in the original notice of allegations, so much so that Ole Miss compliance officials elected to take the long-time assistant off the road as a recruiter for a period of 30 days.

Safeties coach Corey Batoon had been reassigned to an off-the-field position by Freeze as part of the post season reshuffling. Once Kiffin made the move to Boca Raton, Florida, as the FAU defensive coordinator, Batoon joined him.

The lone Rebel defensive assistant to survive the carnage was cornerback coach Jason Jones.

On the offensive side of the ball, some changes were also in order. Wide receiver coach Grant Heard, a former Rebel wideout himself, left his alma mater for the same position at the University of Indiana.

Offensive coordinator and quarterbacks coach Dan Werner was reportedly terminated, but managed to land on his feet as an offensive quality control analyst for Coach Nick Saban and the University of Alabama.

All told, five of nine on-the-field assistant coaches, and one major off-the-field staffer, Farrar, were no longer on the University payroll when the dust settled.

Despite being cited in connection with major allegations in the first NOA, tight ends coach Maurice Harris was retained.

Freeze eventually filled those vacancies, but the Rebels limped towards signing day needing to finish with a flurry.

Despite chasing some highly ranked players who had some work to do in order to qualify, Ole Miss finished outside of the *Scout.com* top 25 for the first time since 2012, Freeze's first class.

The Rebel signing class of 2016 finished No. 5 nationally, and second to only Alabama in the SEC. In 2017 Ole Miss reeled in the No. 29 class, which was good for 11th overall in the 14-team SEC, and dead last in the SEC Western division.

There was a dark cloud hanging over Ole Miss football and it was seriously impacting their ability to sign quality football players. Perhaps the investigation also had Rebel coaches making more of an effort to color inside the lines.

With the signing class now put to bed, and the coaching staff now working towards spring football practice, there remained the matter of the long awaited second Notice of Allegations.

The allegations naming Farrar were among the most serious. While Rebel fans mocked many of the charges leveled in the first Notice of Allegations, the second round of indictments were no laughing matter.

The talking points of old that comforted the tenderhearted were smashed in an instant as allegations of cash payments, free clothing, food and lodging, as well as the dreaded "lack of institutional control" charges wrecked the Rebel requiem.

Chapter 18

A Funeral Procession

February 22, 2017

The day began like any other, but as the morning raced towards high noon, it was clear to me that this day would be one closely followed by college football fans in the state of Mississippi, and one they wouldn't soon forget.

In recent days, rumors began circulating that the long-awaited amended Notice of Allegations had arrived in Oxford, or would be there shortly.

One popular message from a supposed Ole Miss insider began making the rounds: "Prepare for Armageddon!" signaling both the arrival of more allegations and the severity of their collective sting.

With a back drop of Rebel blue bloods bracing for NCAA investigative impact, the social media sites were buzzing with activity.

Of course, many claimed to have a "source." All had an interest.

Some Ole Miss fans had bought into the false hope that the NCAA would simply accept their self-imposed penalties and call it a day. It was becoming clear that those "tidbits" from supposed insiders were coming up snake eyes.

As the day wore on, a sense of optimism swelled on the Mississippi State websites and a dueling sense of panic emerged among the Ole Miss faithful. Something was happening. We weren't sure what just yet, but something was brewing.

Suddenly, like an angry wave crashing onto a tranquil sandy beach, there it was. Word began to spread that the Ole Miss administration had received important correspondence from the NCAA enforcement staff, and they were preparing a press conference to discuss the matter publicly.

So, there I sat in that shrine to *Dawgs' Bite Magazine* in Starkville's Lost Pizza. I guess I could've been anywhere, but I found it almost poetic that I chose that location for lunch to discuss sports coverage with two young aspiring sports journalists unaware that the bomb was about to drop.

As we did our best to discuss building a brand, podcasting and writing for an audience, my phone nearly melted from the surge of calls, texts, tweets, and well wishes. The moment that so many had been waiting for had now arrived.

You can't always pick your traveling companions as you dive down the rabbit hole, but there I was with two people I barely knew about to witness one of the biggest moments in Mississippi college football history.

I did my best to scroll through the messages as more came in on top of each other. The crux of the matter was that Ole Miss had news to share, and they were about to do it on YouTube, of all mediums.

The video service provided a place to essentially have a press conference minus the press, a dog and pony show to the very end. It was another attempt to put a calculated spin on their story with a veiled attempt at being transparent.

I pulled up the link, grabbed another piece of finely prepared Italian cuisine and pressed play.

The video, all 20 minutes and 52 second of it, seemed rather surreal. Ole Miss Chancellor Jeff Vitter wished us all a "good afternoon" and away we went.

There they sat, Vitter, Bjork, and Freeze, dressed in their Sunday best, wearing their Ole Miss-faithful lapel pins, and ready to preach to the choir.

Vitter let the Ole Miss family know that more trouble was on the way. The good news, if there was any in the prepared statements, was that the NCAA investigation into the Ole Miss football program had concluded.

As Vitter turned the program over to Bjork to summarize the new allegations, Freeze, wearing a dark red tie, sat at the end of the row looking unsure what to do with his hands.

It was clear that the Rebel football coach had been "rode hard and put up wet," and the process had worn him out.

In almost robotic form, Bjork placed both hands on the table and began to read.

While I'm sure we'll never know what was going through Bjork's mind at the time, I suspect it wasn't pleasant.

Just more than a year earlier, Bjork had essentially drawn a line in the sand and stated that the NCAA had informed him that the investigation was over. But, some 12 months later, Bjork sat there in front of a camera, thanking the Ole Miss Chancellor and began to read the summary of a document he'd said wasn't coming.

"As you know, the 2016 notice contained 13 football-related charges," Bjork shared. "There are now 21 football allegations—eight of which are new, and one allegation from the prior Notice has been expanded."

The Ole Miss athletic director went on to admit there was credible evidence to support some of the new allegations, but there were other elements of the notice the University planned to contest.

While there were more than enough allegations in the original notice to justify a very lengthy and crippling probation, the new charges removed all doubt.

As the video presentation went forward, Bjork detailed allegations of impermissible benefits that involved hunting trips that were allegedly arranged by the football program itself.

That misdeed barely raised an eyebrow, but the alleged

indiscretions to come sent shock waves throughout the Southeastern Conference.

Former football staffer "A" (Barney Farrar) was accused of arranging thousands of dollars in benefits regarding visits to Ole Miss for prospects and then lying about those benefits to the NCAA enforcement staff.

Farrar was also alleged to have "initiated and facilitated two boosters having impermissible contact" with Mississippi State linebacker Leo Lewis during his recruitment by Ole Miss as part of the 2015 recruiting cycle.

The alleged benefits are reported to have exceeded $13,000 and could possibly have reached more than $15,000.

Ole Miss agreed there was credible evidence to support the charge regarding improper booster contact, but wasn't completely sure there was enough evidence to support the amount of the cash payments.

The hits kept coming.

The NCAA alleged that a former Ole Miss staffer arranged for multiple recruits to receive thousands of dollars in free clothing from an Oxford clothing store that specializes in Ole Miss related sportswear.

More improper contact was alleged, a budding Rebel tradition, along with more free meals. Ole Miss contested these issues, but in the end the severity of these pale in comparison to what the program has already admitted to, but, seemingly in a show of forthrightness, and for all intents and purposes, had fired people for.

Just as the Ole Miss fan base wobbled on their collective feet against the ropes, Bjork delivered the coup de gras' with a two-punch combo that sent them to the canvas and rival fans to a neutral corner with arms out stretched screaming, "We told you so!"

Coach Hugh Freeze was charged with violating head coach

responsibility legislation and the University was cited with the dreaded "lack of institutional control" charge.

"The additional allegations announced today are serious," Bjork continued. "But, we will vigorously defend the university against those allegations we believe are not appropriately supported, including that we lacked institutional control and that our head football coach did not promote an atmosphere of compliance or monitor staff in our football program."

As a matter of general principle, Ole Miss has no choice other than to contest those two charges. That said, the abundance of charges makes that attempt look rather futile.

Currently, Ole Miss has three athletics programs, (football, track and women's basketball), on or about to be on, major probation after being charged with multiple Level 1 violations. It is difficult to defend any claims of institutional control with that fact established.

Freeze saw multiple staff members involved with multiple prospects, in multiple recruiting classes, named in wrong doing, while under his direct supervision. One would have a hard time arguing against the fact that Ole Miss football has been part of a culture of non-compliance, and a complicit obedience to the Rebel culture's groupthink and Southern identity.

The Ole Miss football team, despite being picked by many to contend for an SEC title in 2016, finished the year 5-7 and then was out of the bowl picture. The nail in the coffin on that season was delivered by Mississippi State in a 55-20 shelling in Oxford.

Rebel fans spent the holidays at home for the first time since 2011. Barely more than a week after Valentines' Day in 2017, Ole Miss folks learned that their team wouldn't be part of the post season again as the program had elected to self-impose a one-year bowl ban for 2017.

"I feel terrible for our players and staff who have to handle the consequences for the actions of a very few," Freeze said. "Unfortunately, these penalties are necessary for our program to be responsible and move forward.

"While it is extremely difficult to ask current players to suffer penalties based on the actions of others, I agree with the decision to self-impose a one-year bowl ban by our University."

It's absolutely amazing how far we've come. The ever-changing Rebel talking points had just revealed the Ole Miss administration now planned to remove the possibility of a post season berth before they ever set foot before the NCAA Committee on Infractions.

A far cry from the early days of this story when the mere suggestion of any indiscretions during the Freeze tenure was essentially a declaration of war for Ole Miss fans.

Those fans so ready to defend their coach and football program, despite the mounting evidence of wrongdoing, would have to prepare themselves for another holiday season with the Rebs tucked away in their beds with visions of vacated bowl games dancing in their heads.

The entire house of cards was built on a foundation of "faith based recruiting" as Freeze called it in the early days of his time as the head coach in Oxford. The Mississippi native mentioned several times how much he resented the accusations against his character.

True or untrue, Freeze was now branded as a coach who cut corners, a football CEO who failed to hold his assistants accountable, and the poster boy for a program looking to get rich from their ill-gotten gains.

While some would argue for probable deniability, the facts of the matter suggest that if Freeze didn't know he should have known. Men he hired, worked alongside every day, and broke bread with, were accused of violating just about every one of the tenets held dear in college athletics.

Over the full scope of the probe into Ole Miss football recruiting, there were allegations of academic fraud, impermissible benefits, booster involvement, and the kicker was that most of them implicated Rebel staff members.

When it came to NCAA enforcement bingo, Ole Miss filled in all of the boxes.

The claims of "doing it the right way" quickly turned to "well, everybody does it." The spin of the moment never really connected with the early declarations that the Ole Miss staff simply outworked their SEC peers. All of that chatter was now silent.

You can't pick the defining moments in your life. They're simply left to fate and circumstance. For Hugh Freeze, one of the most lasting images of his professional life will be the scene that played out on his self-serving, half-hearted video presentation on YouTube. He just sat there like a whore in church as his boss read aloud the sins the Ole Miss football program stood accused of committing.

Chapter 19

A Probation for a New Rebel Generation

In the earliest days of this story, an Ole Miss old timer shared his concerns with me about the "younger" generation of Rebel boosters and fans, and by younger he meant guys who were middle-aged; they were the guys who wanted access to players, and sustained on-the-field success.

His line of thinking was that going to back-to-back Cotton Bowls in 2009 and 2010 had breathed new life into the Ole Miss program. New shareholders in that collective success became increasingly frustrated as Rebel football bottomed out over the course of the next two seasons, winning just one SEC game and losing to FCS program Jacksonville State in the process.

As the Freeze era began, Ole Miss had been to just two bowl games since Eli Manning rode off into the sunset with the Cotton Bowl trophy in tow after the 2003 season.

Having suffered through the Ed Orgeron era that yielded just 10 wins over the course of three seasons, and the four-year roller coaster ride under Houston Nutt, Rebel fans were ready for some stability, and at the very least a football program that routinely earned bowl bids.

As the old timer suggested, a new generation of Ole Miss boosters had been birthed feeling the ends justified the means no matter what corners had to be cut. His fear was the win-at-all-costs mentality would ultimately cost the Rebels, and set the program back.

He was confident the new regime simply wouldn't know where to stop.

It's amazing how far things have come since the early days of the Freeze tenure. Talk of doing things the right way resonated with many in the Bible belt. Faith-based recruiting according to Freeze involved reaching young people on a personal and spiritual level.

The desire to connect with families and identify the "champion" in the lives of recruits were top priorities.

If Freeze was to be believed, the recruiting tactics used in the jungle that is the SEC would mirror his personal value system.

With a 21-count indictment in hand from the NCAA enforcement staff, it was clear that many at Ole Miss charged with upholding those values missed the message.

As Bjork shared some of the contents of the amended Notice of Allegations in February 2017, it was clear those who were mere teenagers the last time Ole Miss got the NCAA haircut now had a pending probation all of their very own.

It would take some doing to identify those responsible for the charges and to reward them with the credit they so richly deserved for their indiscretions. Unlike other Universities in the SEC, Ole Miss did their best to protect the names of the guilty all in the name of privacy.

One has to wonder if the cloak of secrecy was to protect these individuals or to ensure their future cooperation. A repentant program serious about compliance and fair play, would do everything within their power to deter friends of the program from coloring outside the lines. Ole Miss wasn't of that sort without some encouragement.

One of the things I've said from the outset about this story was that I would finish the deal. I learned a lot about myself and about journalism through all of this. I learned more about the Mississippi Open Records Act than I ever cared to know. The law is in place to ensure the people of Mississippi have an idea of what's going on behind the scenes.

Ole Miss talked about having a commitment to

transparency, but that was all window dressing. They spent a lot of time and effort trying to deflect and delay at every turn. Talk of being open and available sounded good in a press release, but there was simply no action behind any of it.

I've lost count of the number of Freedom of Information requests I've filed over the course of this book. I've been in contact with attorneys and compliance officers at several college programs. Many of them played word games and dodged requests as best they could. Ole Miss takes the crown though.

Perhaps one of the requests that drew the most attention was the one I filed in January of 2016 in an attempt to flush out a copy of the original Notice of Allegations. Ole Miss' response to the request was to send me a copy of their self -reports, which was a list of minor violations the University sent into the NCAA enforcement staff.

Not only did Ole Miss not send the NOA, they essentially thumbed their noses at all requests for the document. When the University finally released a summary of the allegations along with their response, they redacted many of the names alleged of impropriety.

It was clear after repeated requests that the Rebels were not going to comply, and would delay and deflect as much as possible. Ole Miss was going to do things their way, and the rest of us were going to have to deal with it.

Despite their best efforts, the names of the boosters involved with the first notice leaked out. Of course, all involved had the most noble of intentions, and would never do anything outside the lines, right? Right, so sayeth the spin doctors, who were saying that it was all purely coincidental and circumstantial.

It's funny how it all works in a house of cards.

While the names in the first NOA were essentially a matter of public record within days of the notice being made public, the names charged in the amended notice were a little tougher to obtain. Apparently, the second round of boosters weren't in a huge hurry to explain themselves.

My father, Freddie Robertson, told me more than once that explanations were often a waste of time. He said your friends don't need it, and your enemies wouldn't believe it anyway.

I believe those principles were at play with those alleged of wrong doing in the final NCAA charges against Ole Miss.

Eight new allegations faced Rebel football to go along with the baker's dozen delivered exactly 13 months earlier, so 21 indictments of the Ole Miss football program in all.

The first freshly minted allegation involved multiple hunting trips for Auburn offensive lineman Austin Golson who signed with Ole Miss as part of the 2013 signing class. The NCAA alleges that Golson took a hunting trip arranged by the Ole Miss football staff on a booster's land during his official visit, and then took subsequent trips after he enrolled in Oxford.

After playing 12 games as a true freshman at Ole Miss, Golson elected to leave the Rebel program for Auburn, a program closer to his home in Prattville, Alabama.

The charges involving Golson were Level III violations.

Some of the most serious allegations involved former Ole Miss recruiting specialist Barney Farrar, and a pair of Ole Miss boosters from the Jackson, Mississippi metro area.

The NCAA alleges that Farrar "initiated and facilitated" improper contact between the boosters and Mississippi State linebacker Leo Lewis. The boosters in question are currently listed as "John Doe" and his employee. These names will come to light sooner rather than later. It's also alleged that the two boosters provided cash payments to Lewis, with Farrar's knowledge, totaling as much as $15,600.

Farrar is also alleged to have arranged improper lodging

and transportation for multiple prospects including Lewis and Mississippi State defensive lineman Kobe Jones in excess of $2,200 as well as $235 worth of meals. The alleged wheel man in the Rebel's operation to land Lewis was 25-year-old Raleigh, Mississippi native Arya Keyes. Charged with providing improper transportation to and from the Ole Miss campus, Keyes was later disassociated by the Ole Miss administration.

In addition to the charges of arranging impermissible benefits, Farrar is charged with another level 1 violation for providing "false and misleading information" to both Ole Miss and the NCAA enforcement staff.

Ole Miss acknowledges that their boosters had improper contact with Lewis, but wasn't sure if the payments were made. I think it's safe to say they didn't reach out to a four-star linebacker to discuss the latest stock price, or tee times at their favorite country clubs.

In addition to those allegations, the amended notice went on to suggest various Ole Miss recruiting targets were able to obtain clothing at Oxford business Rebel Rags at no cost. The NCAA claims two Ole Miss staff members arranged for three prospects to receive the complimentary clothing for nearly three years.

The value of the clothing is set at $2,800. That's a lot of Ole Miss t-shirts and sweatshirts.

As if cash, clothing, lodging and transportation weren't enough, the enforcement staff claimed Lewis and others were provided food and drinks at Funky's Restaurant, an Oxford bar and grill owned by Clarksdale, Mississippi, native Lee Harris.

Funky's claims to "Put the Fun in Funky's," and there was plenty of fun to be had back in 2014 when the Rebels beat Alabama in Oxford. Adopted alum Katy Perry shared some post game libations with Rebel fans right there on the square.

Some fans claimed to have paid a $100 cover charge just to

be in the same room as the pop star who was filmed draining a Bud Light longneck, and diving off the roof of Funky's bar into the crowd.

The event was even mentioned in the *New York Times*, which thrilled the souls of those caught up in an image-first mentality.

One of the eatery's most famous moments in recent memory was hosting an announcement party for Ole Miss fans who watched Mississippi's top 2017 prospect Cam Akers commit to Florida State.

It was quite the show.

Just about everybody outside of the Ole Miss red and blue cotton candy bubble projected Akers leaving the Magnolia State. Rebel insiders deluded themselves into believing they had their man.

Despite the fact Freeze had only produced one 1,000-yard rusher as a head coach, the Red and Blue propagandists were doing their best to convince their followers that Akers could win a Heisman trophy at Ole Miss.

Many of those true believers were able to watch live from Funky's as Akers broke their hearts. Sadly, there were no pop divas there on that night to mend their spirits.

Akers admitted the black cloud surrounding the Ole Miss football program played a small part in his decision. Looking to enroll at the school of his choosing in January, 2017, the five-star standout simply couldn't gamble on the Rebels.

With talk of bowl bans, and crippling sanctions coupled with an anemic running game in the Freeze pedigree, Akers elected to sign on with the Seminoles.

The gut punch wasn't just felt by Ole Miss fans desperate for some good news, some members of the Rebel media saw what was left of their credibility torn up and set on fire by supporters looking to blame someone.

Rebel supporters wanted so badly to believe it was business

as usual when it came to the procurement of prospects. After all, recruiting was the Rebels' favorite sport. Akers' decision sent a strong message to all involved that perceptions about Ole Miss and their ability to "recruit" were changing.

With the state's top prospect electing to pass on an Ole Miss football future, the first real casualty of the pending NCAA case was felt in a major way. There was no one to call, no appeals to be made, and no second chances.

Fans who were able to bury their heads in the sand and tell each other it would all be okay could no longer pretend it was all just a bad dream.

The kicker for Rebel supporters was that these violations were alleged to have taken place during the Freeze era with coaches he personally hired.

While the early 2016 talking points falsely implicated Houston Nutt, the reality of the Rebel case was that those who'd been trying to get the truth out there about what was really going on, many anonymously, in the Ole Miss staff under Freeze's direction, were suddenly vindicated.

Mistakes were made. A lot of them were made, and by a lot of people.

As a result of the new charges, the Rebel football head coach was charged with violating head coach responsibility legislation.

Years ago, coaches could argue plausible deniability. They could blame a "rogue" coach or a booster, and protect their head man.

The NCAA changed the accountability of actions within a college football program with by-law 11.1.1.

11.1.1.1 Responsibility of Head Coach. An institution's head coach is presumed to be responsible for the actions of all institutional staff members who report, directly or indirectly, to the head coach. An institution's head coach shall promote an atmosphere of compliance within his or her program and shall monitor the activities of all institutional staff members involved with the program who report, directly or indirectly, to the coach.

In layman's terms, if it happens on your watch, it's your fault. This rule was adopted in 2004, but revised in 2014 as part of the new NCAA penalty matrix. Coaches can no longer plead ignorance.

Ole Miss had been charged with failure to monitor in the 2016 NOA, but that charge was upgraded to the dreaded Lack of Institutional Control charge in 2017. The University was essentially charged for a failure to monitor the activities going on within its football programs.

Of course, the Rebel administration planned to contest the more serious charges, and rightfully so. While the evidence suggests Freeze, as well as the Ole Miss administration, are at best, derelict in their duties as overseers, and at the worst, of promoting an atmosphere of compliance. They will argue in their own defense. Admitting to those charges would be foolhardy. Ole Miss simply has to contest those on principle.

If there was ever an institution that lacked institutional control, this was it. Over the scope of this probe, Ole Miss coaches and staffers in multiple sports, officially stood accused by the NCAA of fixing the ACT scores of students, making arrangements for out-of-state players to attend the Ed Center in Jackson, a facility without residence halls, and in some cases doing the on-line course work on behalf of Rebel signees.

I've been told by multiple sources that Bjork was troubled by Mississippi State's marketing campaign that featured the slogan "Our State." The Bulldog administration had purchased contracts for billboards around the state of Mississippi staking their claim to the Magnolia State as their territory.

Motorists entering the state saw pictures of Dan Mullen waving to them welcoming them to Bulldog country. Over the course of the campaign, a collection of current and former Mississippi State athletes, as well as a trio of Miss Mississippi winners, graced the billboards.

While Mississippi State's attempts to market their brand was pleasing to Bulldog fans, the campaign got under the skin of Ole Miss fans in a major way.

I was told that Bjork voiced his concerns about the billboards to some within the Mississippi State family. Apparently, the rivalry was getting out of hand.

Billboards? Yes, billboards.

A sitting athletic director at an SEC school was concerned about another school's billboards.

Bjork was reportedly asking for both schools to dial the rhetoric back a bit, meanwhile he had multiple coaches on his watch who were cheating their asses off. While the billboards were labeled as "bad" for the rivalry, I submit cheating in multiple sports involving Rebel coaches was far worse.

Talk about majoring in minor things. The Mississippi State marketing efforts hurt Rebel feelings, but the Ole Miss systemic efforts to cut corners on the recruiting trail was billed as the cost of doing business in the rugged SEC.

It's laughable.

The "Our State" campaign ended, as all marketing efforts do. I'm not sure if Bjork's feelings on the issue had much impact, but they are noteworthy. It makes for an interesting juxtaposition.

Mississippi State publicly, and proudly celebrated their successes on the state's highway system, while Ole Miss fought tooth and nail privately to conceal the names of the boosters who colored outside of the lines.

In what was surely an inside joke among Ole Miss administrators, as the Rebels referenced a commitment to "transparency" in just about every communication about the NCAA probe and those involved.

It took the involvement of the Mississippi State Ethics Commission to really make any strides towards true transparency. After yet another half-measured response from Ole Miss for an open records request, I filed a complaint with the commission seeking some relief.

It's been my argument from the outset, that Ole Miss has worked to circumvent state law by directing the delivery of NCAA correspondence to an out-of-state attorney.

The very idea a state-funded entity would take steps to conceal documents of wrong doing by a governing body is intrinsically unethical. The law is the law even when it's inconvenient.

In the advisory staff report to the Mississippi Ethics Commission, Ole Miss was found to have violated the Mississippi Open Records Act by not providing me with the Notice of Allegations of January 2016, and the Amended Notice of Allegations from February 2017.

Perhaps of greater importance, the report states Ole Miss violated state law by redacting the names of the third parties who involved themselves in the recruiting process, and that they no longer had an expectation of privacy.

This was an important finding for several reasons, because despite their best efforts, the University cannot protect the names of third parties who are charged with wrong doing in NCAA investigations.

My hope is this ruling will serve as deterrent to all those who believe they can conceal their activities under the cloak of secrecy like that provided for staffers and boosters at the

University of Mississippi in recent years. The time for hiding the truth about NCAA allegations is over.

Chapter 20

Robertson vs. The University of Mississippi

June 2, 2017

It was a Friday, but it was a Friday like none I had ever known. The Mississippi State Ethics Commission (MEC) was set to hear my complaint against Ole Miss for essentially thumbing their noses at my open records requests.

I had filed several over the course of the last 18 months with limited success through Ole Miss, but they were throwing me crumbs rather than providing me with what I was legally entitled.

At issue were three items: The 2016 Notice of Allegations; the Amended Notice of Allegations of 2017; and the names of the boosters who the University had redacted in their public releases involving both sets of allegations.

Ole Miss had provided some information about their NCAA investigation, but they hadn't released the names of the parties accused of wrongdoing in their probe. Many of the parties named in the allegations had already been disassociated by the University.

To the Rebels' credit they had elected to decline contributions from these individuals, and in some cases, ban them from home athletic events. I'm not sure how enforceable the second punishment is, but it looks good on paper.

No matter what the personal penalties were for those individuals they were still able to enjoy anonymity by Ole Miss essentially providing them cover.

Other institutions within the state of Mississippi had, as a matter of practice, revealed the names of boosters who'd run afoul of NCAA guidelines for "representatives of the

University's athletics interest."

Ironically, the names of the boosters were protected, but as fate would have it, some of the student athletes who'd given testimony against Ole Miss over the course of the investigation were "leaked" to some Rebel-friendly media.

The firestorm on social media was intense. Well before the Ole Miss fanbase knew the content of the testimony against them, the student athletes were painted as liars and villains.

On the other hand, some saw the boosters all too eager to assist in Ole Miss football recruiting as heroes, or means to an end in the war for Saturday supremacy in the Southeastern Conference.

Frankly, I have issues with that. It takes two to tango. If any names should be made public, it should be the adults in the situation who should've known better. That was part of my motivation for filing my complaint with the Ethics Commission.

Perhaps the biggest part of it all, is I felt it was high time all state institutions played by the same set of rules. My hope was by making these names public it would serve as a deterrent to boosters of all institutions.

It's funny how it all works. Some Ole Miss boosters were full of bravado, and school spirit when they had access to Rebel coaches, facilities, and in some cases recruits. When the rubber met the road and it was time for their identities to be known, they no longer wanted credit for being insiders.

Now at least one person who claimed to be mentioned in the amended NOA was concerned with having his name made public. As the cloak of secrecy was now being snatched away, concerns about a loss of business, or personal harassment were of paramount importance.

The price of fame is high.

My argument then, and now, is individuals who want to

enjoy the privacy afforded the average citizen should refrain from involving themselves in matters of public interest.

I filed my complaint with the state Ethics Commission on March 10, 2017. Just a matter of days after Ole Miss sent out a mass denial to all requesters of the Feb. 22 Amended Notice of Allegations, I decided it was time to challenge the University's flawed position as it related to public records.

For years, Ole Miss has basically done things the Ole Miss way rather than following the guidelines set forth in the Mississippi Open Records Act. It was time for someone to call them on it. That someone was me.

I felt confident in my argument as well as the central points of my complaint. After doing my own research, I discovered that the case law appeared to support my position.

It's been the practice of the University to direct correspondence from the NCAA to their out of state law firm in Birmingham, Alabama, Lightfoot, Franklin and White. By having those documents delivered out of state the thinking was it would be beyond the jurisdiction of the state of Mississippi.

Part of my argument was the University's attorney is an extension of the University and his or her possession is their possession.

The fact the documents were addressed to the Chancellor of the University from the NCAA meant attorney/client privilege didn't apply, and those communications weren't protected.

The fact a state-funded entity would elect to direct potentially embarrassing documents out of state in an attempt to circumvent state law was about as unethical as it gets. If this was about campaign finance rather than college football, there would probably be a march on the state capital, and possibly a criminal trial.

The bottom line was Ole Miss had no legal standing to

withhold those documents, or to protect those names. I believe they knew it, and were content to sit back and do things their way until someone forced the issue.

Who was going to do it? *The Clarion-Ledger?*

Ole Miss's response to my complaint was due March 24. That day came and went without any word from the University lawyers or the ethics commission.

Had I won by default? Had my complaint been dismissed?

I wasn't sure what had transpired. Who should I e-mail? I spent the weekend with my wheels spinning, and wondering how to handle things.

Monday came and went, and there was still no word. Tuesday became Wednesday, and then Thursday arrived with no developments. I began to think that somehow the rules didn't apply.

On Friday, March 31, the Ole Miss response arrived. It was a week late, and filled with legalese and case citations related to public privacy rights. For a lay person dipping his toe into unfamiliar waters, it was a great deal to absorb.

I hadn't done my research or reached out to anyone else yet, but I knew they were tardy with their response. I e-mailed all parties involved and raised my concern about the leisurely pace in which Ole Miss handled things.

I was informed the Rebel legal team had requested a one-week extension unbeknownst to me. Apparently, one of their lawyers was out of the country, and they needed more time to respond to my complaint.

I was both flattered and frustrated. Ole Miss has a campus full of lawyers, yet they needed a full three weeks to respond to a very straight forward complaint about an open records case.

Due to the delay, it was next to impossible for the necessary research to be completed in time to get my complaint on the April agenda. How fortunate for the University.

I will never believe that it was all happenstance. Because one lawyer was on vacation, Ole Miss had an additional 30 days before there would be any action from the Ethics Commission.

In Mississippi, the Ethics Commission meets just once a month. The meeting for the month was scheduled for Friday, May 12.

As that date approached, I received calls, e-mails, and texts from people who were interested in the case. I had a couple of conversations with people who specialize in Freedom of Information requests who offered their expertise if I needed it.

Every person, and I mean every person, I spoke to about my complaint was in agreement that Ole Miss didn't have a leg to stand on. While their comments were great to hear, we still needed a formal ruling from the folks who mattered.

I went to record my show, *The Boneyard*, that Friday just like any other Friday. As I sat down to begin, I got a text from a friend who had a screen shot of the report from the staff that advises the MEC.

It appeared the ruling was set to go my way.

I checked my e-mail and there were a couple of messages from Ole Miss assistant counsel Rob Jolly, and Tom Hood of the MEC.

Around 9:15 that morning, 45 minutes before the MEC was set to consider my complaint, Ole Miss had changed their position. The Rebels were now ready to comply and negotiate the release of the documents with me.

As a result, the MEC tabled my complaint. While it appeared the Rebels were crying "uncle," it felt like another stall tactic. Looking back, I'm pretty sure that was the plan all along.

It took nearly a week for the University to contact me, and begin to talk about the legal release of the documents that had been wrongfully denied in the first place.

As the talks moved forward, Ole Miss wanted me to pay the hefty sum of $2,145 for a document they were about to release for free to the general public. Even when I discussed possibly paying that ridiculous sum, they couldn't guarantee delivery of the documents before their own release the week of June 5. The whole thing was a sham.

I contacted the MEC and informed them of the discussions, and my feelings that the University hadn't negotiated in good faith. I was even willing to hold the names in confidence until the official release, and expressed that openly to both the MEC and Ole Miss, but they never followed through.

So now, we had two delays, because Ole Miss was tardy in their response, and then changed their position on the complaint. I tip my cap to them. It was a disingenuous act, but they were able to essentially delay the release of the booster names for months.

The MEC June meeting was set for June 2, 2017. My alarm clock went off at 6:30. I showered, pulled my hair back, put on a shirt and tie and made the drive to Jackson, Mississippi, to ensure that I would be on site should Ole Miss try to play any other wild cards.

That Friday morning didn't get off to a great start to say the least. I rarely wear dress shoes, so I had trouble finding them in the closet. Although scuffed and flattened, I laced 'em up.

My anxiety swelled.

I couldn't find a good tie, I didn't have time to eat, and I had to stop for a gas. I was already going to be pressed for time and these time-stealing issues weren't helping my mood.

In the car and down the driveway, I discovered my satellite radio wasn't working. Apparently, they upgraded the channels overnight, and nothing synced.

I'm not a person who rides in silence. I want my XM! And

now it's raining.

I kept turning the radio on and off hoping it would finally link up with the great trash can in orbit beaming out the great sounds of 1980s metal.

As I eagerly awaited the voice of Dangerous Darren on Hair Nation, I noticed my ETA was 9:39 a.m. That was cutting it close, but without any delays I'd get there on time. Within 30 seconds, the ETA changed to 9:50.

Even the GPS was working against me.

Somewhere south of Louisville, Mississippi, the radio started working. When I passed through Carthage, Mississippi, the sun was shining. By the time I hit the Hinds County line, my on-air pal Darren was spinning "Smooth Up in Ya" from the Bulletboys. I was ready to run through a wall by then.

I even listened to it twice.

I was the first person in the conference room where the Ethics Commission was set to meet that morning. A small victory, but an important one in my eyes. I wanted everybody who walked into that room to know I was there to hear the discussion of my complaint.

I took a mental inventory of the room as I took a seat. While it wasn't a huge room, it was an impressive one. On the far wall was the seal of the great state of Mississippi. On either side of the seal were the American and Mississippi state flags. This venue may be the only place you can fly them both without a march forming outside.

The Commission members filed in and took their seats around an impressive, and substantial table—big enough to seat King Arthur's court. A few of them walked up and said hello before the proceedings began.

I felt completely out of place, but I didn't let that show. I knew I had a compelling argument, and I was merely exercising my rights as a Mississippian. I wanted those documents, and I had a right to those documents.

At some point you have to ask yourself how long you're willing to take "no" for an answer. I hit my limit long before I showed up in the capital city in a room where I was the only person with visible tattoos.

Just down the street from that North Street address is the Federal Building for the state of Mississippi. My father, Freddie Robertson, worked in that building for many years. I thought about him a lot that morning.

My dad was a person who loved accountability, and responsibility. He was the kind of man who believed a person's value was based on what they did rather than what they said.

He worked hard for the American taxpayer, and expected others to follow suit. He hated government waste, and the red tape that often accompanied it.

He taught me how to work, and how to take joy in working. He also taught me how to stand up for myself, and not simply let people tell me "how the cow ate the cabbage."

I think of him often, and I hope he is proud of me and my efforts. There have been many times in this process where I wished I could've called him, and asked for advice or used him as a sounding board.

He passed away in October, 2005. I was able to be with him in his final moments on Earth, which is one of the greatest gifts God has given me.

Even though it was hard for me, I was able to tell him that it was okay to let go. I told him we would all be just fine. He didn't have to fight anymore.

My daddy was my best friend. I miss him every day, especially when the Bulldogs are playing.

My moments to reminisce were broken by a staff member who was passing out the day's agenda. I saw that I was down the page, so I took some time to read the staff's preliminary report about my case.

Nine pages in all and incredibly thorough. I skimmed through most of it and got to the staff recommendations, which were all in my favor. Now I simply had to wait to see if the Commission would vote to accept those recommendations.

I patiently waited through talk of the ethical dilemma that may arise by a county sheriff electing to hire the son of a bail bondsmen.

There was discussion about another open records case that essentially asked the City of Meridian, Mississippi, to create a document to satisfy a newspaper request for a list of city employees.

It may sound boring, but it was interesting to see our government at work, forming official positions on matters that impact hometown Mississippi.

With those issues addressed, the matter of Steve Robertson vs. The University of Mississippi was next on the agenda. Before the matter could be heard, one member of the commission recused herself. I was never given a reason why.

Staff attorney Chris Graham detailed out the complaint to the remaining members of the Commission. As he spoke, I got a little concerned even though I had already read his report. As he spoke about public privacy and the civil torts that go along with it, I wondered if anyone would vote my way.

Just as I was about ready to vomit, the tide turned and Graham began explaining the merits of my complaint and how the citizens of Mississippi had a right to know who was responsible for causing Ole Miss to self-impose a bowl ban costing the University millions of dollars.

Graham went on to discuss the Ole Miss answer to the complaint and share that some of the cases cited in their response weren't applicable to this situation. As he began his closing remarks, Graham said, "Frankly, this wasn't even a close call."

Now the Commission just needed to vote, but there was plenty of discussion. The entire meeting took right at two hours. There were more than a dozen items on the agenda, but it took nearly 30 minutes to handle my case.

Complicating matters was a motion to intervene in the proceedings by a "John Doe" whose attorney claimed he was named in the amended notice of allegations. Doe had sought a protective order from the Hinds County Chancery Court prior to the MEC meeting, but wasn't granted any relief.

Running out of options, Doe petitioned the MEC for the opportunity to intervene and provide arguments why his name shouldn't be made public. The MEC agreed to allow him the chance to make his argument, but the news wasn't nearly as good for Ole Miss.

After a motion and a second, the commission was set to vote, and one member wanted to continue the discussion. "Do we really want to get out here in the deep water?"

The gentleman was concerned about setting a precedent where citizens could attempt to intervene in matters before the MEC. In the end, the measure passed as well as all of the recommendations by the staff.

The most important ones being that Ole Miss violated the Mississippi Open Records Act by not providing the 2016 NOA, the amended NOA of 2017, and by redacting the names of the boosters from those documents.

I felt I was right all along, but it was awfully rewarding to hear someone in state government agree officially.

In addition to the more immediate concern of the NOA documents, the MEC closed the loophole Ole Miss looked to exploit by sending their NCAA-related communications to an out of state attorney.

No longer can Ole Miss on-campus attorneys claim that

these documents are "not in possession." The precedent has been set that those documents are in fact public records and required to be made available for public inspection.

In the days that followed, I began to get phone calls and messages from people concerned about friends and relatives who were expected to be named in the NCAA documents.

One gentleman offered information in exchange for keeping his loved one's name out of this book. As I explained to him, the names are going to be a matter of public record no matter what I choose to write in this book.

Many Ole Miss fans scoffed at the ruling claiming that the Rebels had always planned to release the names of the boosters. When that opportunity came, Ole Miss didn't come through.

They even referenced my ethics commission complaint in the cover letter of their June 6 update to their NCAA case. When we get down to the brass tacks, they would've protected those names until the end of time.

I don't believe anyone would've ever seen a public declaration of those names without the involvement of the state Ethics Commission. I was the only non-lawyer involved in the process, but this case shows that a determined citizen armed with the truth can get a win every once in a while.

There is no way to make the wrong argument right without the benefit of the law. I'm thankful the Commission took up my complaint and offered an official position.

Before I left Jackson, I thanked all of the Commission members except for the lady who recused herself. As I addressed the room, she recused herself again.

I wanted the record to reflect that I was present. While John Doe and Ole Miss all had a part in the proceedings, I was the only one who made the effort to show up, and show the process the respect it deserved.

I'm not sure how much that mattered in the grand scheme of things, but it mattered to me. I don't have a law degree, nor the ability to cite case law from memory, but I had the right legal position.

This ol' boy from Marion County, Mississippi, stepped into unfamiliar territory armed with conviction and the truth, and came out the other side a victor. It felt good to see the system work.

The final order from the MEC came down on July 14 along with the Commission's ruling that John Doe did not make a compelling argument to preserve his privacy. Appeals have been filed, but I am prepared to go all the way to the Supreme Court if necessary. There needs to be transparency for all involved.

Chapter 21

Hot in the Shade

Legendary college basketball coach John Wooden of UCLA once said, "A true test of a man's character is what he does when no one's watching."

Wise words from a winning coach, this is sage counsel for all of us who fall short of being the people we hope to be.

Coach Hugh Freeze has made several comments over the years about the value of good character and making good decisions.

On Sept. 10, 2014, days before leading his team to a 56-15 win over Louisiana-Lafayette, Freeze shared some words of encouragement with his Twitter followers.

"Character is not hereditary, it's the product of people we follow, habits we form and choices we make" Freeze shared.

Given the chance to personify those words of wisdom in the early hours of the University's acknowledgment that a Notice of Allegations from the NCAA enforcement staff had been received by Ole Miss' outside counsel, the Rebels appear to have come up short with the choices THEY made.

While there hadn't been official denials on the public record from the Ole Miss administration about the on-going NCAA probe, the Red and Blue attack dogs of misinformation had ferociously defended the program against any talk of pending sanctions.

On Jan. 29, 2016, Yahoo's Pat Forde dropped a bombshell at an incredibly inconvenient time for both Freeze and Ole Miss. Forde's story hit the worldwide web at 1:40 Friday afternoon

Just as Freeze and his staff were set to welcome official visitors to Oxford, the cat was out of the bag. This wasn't just any official visit weekend. This was THE official visit weekend.

Ole Miss was set to host 20-plus potential signees that weekend. Seventeen of those expected guests were rated four-stars or better by scout.com, including All-American five-star talents Greg Little and Jeffery Simmons.

It was perhaps the most important recruiting weekend of Hugh Freeze's coaching career.

Needless to say, the weekend didn't get off to a roaring start. Just as many of the prospects set to spend the next two nights in Oxford were loading the car or boarding planes to embark on their all-expense paid excursion, the headlines screamed that the Rebels were in big trouble... "Ole Miss Charged by NCAA for Rules Violations" – Sports Illustrated.

Athletics Director Ross Bjork was quoted in the first of two statements on the matter.

"As has been the case for the past three years, we are bound by confidentiality and cannot comment publicly on the matter," Bjork said in a statement. "However, I can say that I'm confident in how our coaches and staff operate our program, and we take compliance, NCAA and SEC rules very seriously. We are working hard to seek a resolution to this matter."

While the Rebels weren't commenting publicly, according to documents provided by Ole Miss in response to a Freedom of Information Act (FOIA) request, it appears that those in charge of the Ole Miss message had plenty to say privately.

Within minutes of the story breaking, Thayer Evans then of Sports Illustrated, reached out to Freeze and Ole Miss associate Athletics Director Kyle Campbell.

At 2:40 p.m. Central time, Jackson, Mississippi, based writer David Brandt of the Associated Press is listed as having called Freeze for a four-minute conversation.

Phone records indicate that Freeze called Bjork moments after his call with Brandt ended. The chain of calls continued with Bjork then calling Campbell.

What happens next is incredibly important in more ways than one. The University-issued cell phone assigned to Bjork appears in the records as having called Brandt of the Associated Press at 3 p.m., and then called noted Ole Miss friendly, Ed Aschoff of ESPN at 3:06 p.m.

Aschoff, a graduate of the University of Florida, is the son of a former Ole Miss professor of Anthropology and African-American Studies.

Later that afternoon, Brandt published an online article recapping the day's events, and sharing some of what he had learned from "anonymous" sources.

"Some of the allegations regarding the football program date back to previous coach, Houston Nutt, but others involve current coach Hugh Freeze's tenure, a person familiar with the investigation told the Associated Press on Friday," Brant wrote.

"The person spoke on the condition of anonymity, because the investigation is on-going. The person said the Ole Miss football program has already taken some steps – like reducing recruiting official visits – to try to mitigate any punishment from the NCAA," Brandt continued.

Some fairly specific information to say the least.

That same afternoon, ESPN's Chris Low, who actually appears to have spoken with Campbell earlier that morning, penned an article about the Ole Miss admission. Unlike Brandt, Low placed the blame solely at the feet of Nutt.

Low wrote, "Sources told ESPN.com that the announcement was expected. Allegations connected to Mississippi's football team (are) largely derived from the 2008-11 tenure of Houston Nutt, sources said. Freeze was named the Rebel's coach in

December of 2011."

While we can all take a somewhat educated guess at who the "sources" may have been, it was clear they had an interest in deflecting blame from Freeze and onto Nutt.

Low went on to quote Aschoff, who also referenced a well-placed, yet clandestine source. Just under two hours after Bjork's phone call to Aschoff, ESPN published this:

"(There) is an infraction involving our current football staff," a source told ESPN's Ed Aschoff. "Some of those things, we've already self-imposed some penalties around and already dealt with. This just happens to be part of a broader process."

Edward Aschoff ✓
@AschoffESPN

Ole Miss charged with NCAA violations in three sports but this was expected. Football not affected much

Sources: Most Ole Miss charges predate Freeze
Ole Miss faces charges of violations connected t...
espn.com

Shortly after the call to Aschoff, Freeze's records indicate that he received a call from FOXSports college football writer Bruce Feldman. The two became acquainted during Feldman's work on the book Meat Market that highlighted Coach Ed Orgeron's tenure in Oxford.

It's evident in Feldman's writings, and social media postings, that he still has a soft spot for Ole Miss. That sensibility continued in his Friday afternoon article for FoxSports.

"Multiple sources tell FOXSports that the majority of the allegations stem from women's basketball and track as well as from incidents occurring with the previous Rebels staff from the Houston Nutt era, and that the Notice of Allegations does not contain anything that surprises the program," Feldman wrote.

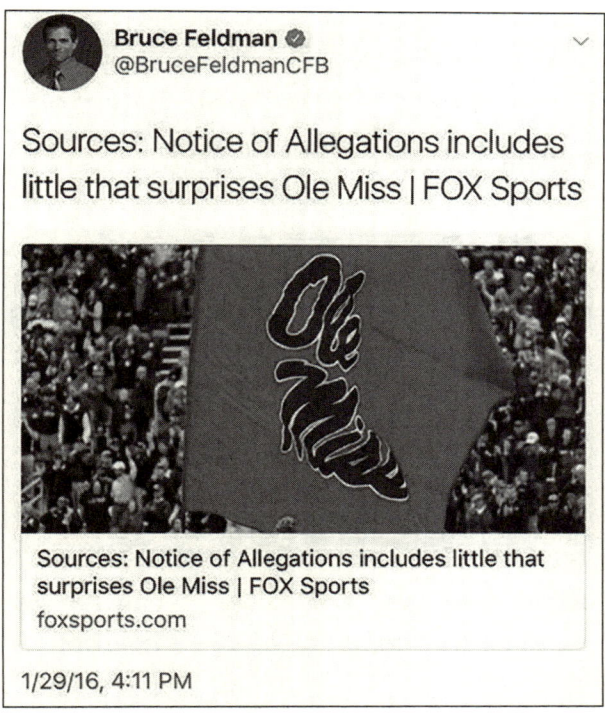

In what appears to be more than an odd coincidence, multiple national sports writers all had contact with Ole Miss staffers that eventful Friday, and all wrote stories casting aspersions at Nutt, and minimizing the talk of trouble for Freeze and his staff.

Everybody was singing from the same sheet of music.

Interestingly enough, a wild and rambling narrative written for SB Nation by Ole Miss alum Steven Godfrey featured a picture of Houston Nutt and the cut line, "The Rebels aren't all that worried about the potential of major violations impacting the football program."

While the phone records provided show evidence of contact between Ole Miss staffers and the Associated Press, ESPN, FOXSports, and Sports Illustrated, there is no record of any Mississippi beat reporters connecting with Rebel decision makers by phone. But, hell, the water had already been carried.

Let me summarize it like this. Ole Miss released a statement saying they were bound by confidentiality. But, then at least three staffers' phone records suggest they had conversations with national sports writers, who in turn wrote articles throwing Nutt under the bus, and all but absolved Freeze and his staff from any major violations.

Of course, that wasn't true.

When the Notice of Allegations was finally made public, Nutt's name wasn't even mentioned. Needless to say, the longtime college football coach was upset about what had transpired.

"I have never been more devastated in my life," Nutt said in an exclusive interview. "It's very disappointing, especially when you're sitting up there in a room [and] I'm fortunate enough to be up there with a good group of people, and they were suddenly asking me, 'What's going on? What are the allegations about, Coach Nutt? Your name is going across the ticker,' so it's devastating, man!

"While the conversations with friends and colleagues were difficult, one of the most challenging moments of the whole ordeal was having to deal with the first call from home.

"The straw that basically broke the camel's back is when I called my mother one week later and she was like, 'Son, I know you didn't do this, but you have the majority of the violations at Ole Miss? You don't have one major violation in thirty years of coaching,'" Nutt shared.

"I said, 'Right mom, there is no truth to it.'"

"You're sitting there on three or four years of your name being out there, first. It's devastating. I'm in uncharted waters," Nutt explained "I don't know how to defend myself in this situation. You're not talking about previous staff members of other sports. You're talking about me and my name is going across the ticker. That's what was upsetting."

There were media outlets painting Nutt as the villain, and suggesting that Freeze was not complicit in any wrong doing.

Freeze compared his experience with the NCAA enforcement staff to a "colonoscopy," While Nutt said his interaction with investigators was extremely limited. A rather interesting juxtaposition considering that the talk perpetuating around the investigation on Jan. 29, 2016, was that Nutt was the cause of the Rebel discontent.

"I talked to them on the phone for fifteen minutes, and once they knew that there was nothing there, that was it," Nutt explained. "I asked them if I was going to be interviewed again and they said no.

"I didn't get the Notice of Allegations, and my research has taught me that was the key. There is no connection there. They told me clear as can be, that there was no connection, and that I had no responsibility."

Despite his limited involvement with the NCAA inquiry, Nutt has had to deal with the consequences of being labeled a scapegoat. While it's difficult to win one's name back after being associated with a scandal, the former Ole Miss head coach is struggling to do just that.

"Number one, the NCAA says that I didn't have anything to do with it," Nutt clarified. "Number two is, I had no responsibility for it if it did happen.

"I never got one Notice of Allegations, and that is the biggest thing that I can stand on, not one Notice of Allegations in this whole four or five years. I am going on my sixth year without a team, so all of those years, those main three or four years, and I haven't received any Notices of Allegations from the NCAA, not one."

Despite a stellar record of compliance, a pair of appearances in the SEC title game, a National Coach of the Year award and a handful of bowl wins, Nutt has had a tough time getting his foot in the door with other college football programs.

The 30-year coaching veteran believes the fingers pointed in his direction have hurt his ability to get interviews with programs looking for a new head coach. While Nutt enjoys his time as a television football analyst, the competitive fire still burns.

"I am very appreciative of CBS first and foremost," Nutt said. "It's hard to believe I am getting ready to go into my sixth year without coaching, but I love the group I work with, the co-workers, they've been awesome," Nutt said. "It's been good to watch college football. That's awesome.

"Before [Ole Miss] threw me up under the bus, I really felt like there were going to be some [coaching] opportunities. I always had this hope that there was going to be this one team. I know they're hiring a lot of young [coaches] right now. I know I'm 59, but I feel like I'm 30.

"I just felt like there was going to be one opportunity out there for a coach to come help a team where there's a fit. I am happy doing what I am doing, but you miss it."

Nutt shares that the ability to impact young men's lives is a key component of coaching. Drifting off to melancholy, Nutt reflected on a former Ole Miss player who stays in touch.

"Here is what you miss; it's the relationships. It's the e-mails and the texts you get," Nutt said. "I got one last night from (running back) Enrique Davis. I had to bench him, because Dexter McCluster was better. It was very difficult.

"This guy was highly recruited, highly sought after, and he sends me a text. It was so good that I had to call him. I said, 'Enrique, I can't tell you how proud I am of you. I know you're a man now.'

"He told me, 'When you put me on the bench, I was so bitter and so mad at you, but now I get it. I understand. I'm a father, I got a great job. I got a great work ethic and a great attitude. [Because] of the things I learned in college and the things y'all taught us, I am a better husband and father.'

"That's what you miss. That and the celebrating in the locker room when you beat your big rival, or when you beat Texas Tech in the Cotton Bowl. You miss that. Something like that, you can't put a price on it."

While Nutt was explaining himself to people over and over, Ole Miss took their time releasing the Notice of Allegations. The personable coach was eventually vindicated.

Anyone expecting a ticker tape parade was disappointed. Nutt recounts there may have been some feelings of relief once the truth was known publicly, but there was no cause to truly celebrate.

"To see it all come out finally, it's like, 'Yes!' But it's not like I'm doing flips and I'm really happy now. I don't have that kind of feeling," Nutt disclosed.

"It goes back to that first time. Research shows that there is this window of opportunity that once you get past 55 (years of age) that window of opportunity begins to close. I was thinking that there were some really promising things getting ready to happen. That one year there was over 32 jobs that were open. Then you get that deal where the first time your name is mentioned going across that ticker on the TV."

While Nutt stopped short of saying it, there is some history between him and Freeze. Recall that when Nutt took over at Ole Miss, Freeze had been retained for a short time as the transition coach.

Once signing day came and went, Freeze was informed that he wouldn't be part of the new staff going forward. Despite some emotional pleas from Freeze, he would not be a member of Houston Nutt's staff at Ole Miss.

Only Freeze knows if that bitter disappointment played a role in this campaign to cast aspersions at Nutt once the news of the first Notice of Allegations hit the national sports wire.

"There wasn't a mix up," Nutt said. "This was deliberate. It was calculated to really protect a recruiting class. I know how it is in recruiting. I know how it is in those times, especially when you're in the battle of it. To me, there is just no doubt in my mind. It was a deliberate and calculated deal."

Nutt reports that during his tenure at Ole Miss, he worked hard to recruit players without involving the assistance of third parties. In both the Billy Brewer and Hugh Freeze cases, there are serious allegations of booster misconduct. Not so with Nutt.

"I didn't concern myself with that," he said "I always tried to sell the fact that it's a good time to be a student athlete. Most of you get a Pell grant. You get a chance to get a summer job, if you want one. But it's difficult to do that. You would probably have to go part time.

"The other thing we have is the SEC opportunity fund. If there was an emergency, and a young man needed to go home, or a guy needed a winter coat or needed something like a lap top, there was an avenue.

"The things we sold the parents was that we were going to do things the right way, but there are avenues for us to be able to help you. With the scholarship, you are going to have all you want to eat. You got tutors and you got good education, so let's not get hung up on trying to do things under the table and all of this other stuff, when we have avenues to get it done the right way."

Nutt suggests that coaches simply shouldn't feel the need to cut corners to gain a recruiting advantage.

"The first thing is that the campus of Ole Miss is beautiful. It's a beautiful place," Nutt said. "It's an excellent education. You have a good support staff as far as academically. The FedEx Center, Fred Smith has done a tremendous job with that building.

"All of that is awesome, but when an 18-year-old comes to campus, they're pretty much interested in one thing most of the time - they want to know how (they're) going to get to the next level.

"If you look at the SEC, you're in the best conference in America. Bar none, you're in the best conference, and it's proven every time the draft rolls around. Most of the players are from the SEC. The majority of the numbers are going to come from the SEC most of the time.

"That was a real easy sell. If you look back at the history of the players that have been drafted out of Ole Miss, it's very good, and then the thing you could sell is, you start with mom and academics, but it's that SEC. The stadiums are full. The tailgating, the Grove, it's full. They're going to be there. It's ESPN. It's CBS. You're on TV and there's a lot of recognition the SEC Network. All of that was easy.

"It was just a good place, and everybody talked about the beauty of the campus. The people were friendly, and all of those things add up. It makes it a good place to recruit (to), but the main thing is that you're in the SEC."

The lure of the SEC is a major part of the recruiting pitch, but it appears that the previous administration at Ole Miss was not totally committed to keeping the Rebels competitive in the football facilities arms race.

"You know, we would have Archie Manning and Eli Manning that spent their summers there, and they would ask about working out and I'd say, 'Great!'" Nutt explained. "We wanted our quarterbacks around Eli and that would be awesome.

"After the second year that we won the Cotton Bowl, Diana (Nutt) and I decided to give back to the school, because they had been so good to us. We gave $100,000, and asked Archie and Eli, and I really spoke to Archie first about maybe contributing to Ole Miss.

"Let's get a weight room, and I would love to put your name on it with Eli's. The bottom line was, he wouldn't do it, because of the leadership (at Ole Miss) at the time. As long as Pete Boone was there, he wasn't going to do it.

"One of the things that was sort of funny was that, Eli was so religious about working out in our weight room, and all of the throwing, and all of that that day, the music wasn't working. I made a joke in front of Archie (Manning) and Don Decker about how here we have an NFL MVP, and we can't get the music going for him, so he can lift weights."

Nutt reveals there was a real sense of apathy from some of the Rebel fans despite the fact that the team had won back to back Cotton Bowls. With confidence in the leadership eroding, fundraising was difficult to do.

"One of the reasons there was some disconnect with some of the boosters is because some of the boosters were upset," Nutt said. "There was a lot of disconnect when I first got there, because they hadn't won in a long time. When you're winning a lot, it solves a lot of problems. There wasn't much said the first two years, because we were winning Cotton Bowls.

"Then you had the Black Bear and the discounting of the Rebel. You've got a lot of things going on. There were a lot of sections there of disconnect. I wouldn't say that it was really about one group. There was a lot of it.

"I went back and I told our guys to focus on one thing, and let's worry about making a difference with an 18-year-old, and making them better academically, and in football, and let's win. That's where my focus and time was, but it's hard not to hear the outside noise, especially when things weren't going well that third and fourth year."

A pair of tough years coupled with an administration reluctant to commit to facility upgrades made it rough for everyone. It doesn't take long to fall even farther behind your SEC peers.

"We didn't get a weight room, and when you're rolling, that's the time you can jump on recruiting and make things better," Nutt said. "It's all about the eyes of an 18-year-old when they come in. You may think that weight room is fine, but compared to Alabama, LSU, and even the one we had at Arkansas, was so much bigger and nicer.

"You're competing. There was no team meeting room. The weight room wasn't up to par. The nutrition plan wasn't. All of those things changed immediately when I walked out the door."

Now several years removed from Ole Miss football, Nutt still finds himself talking about some of the things that have taken place. While the former guy always makes for a convenient fall guy, Nutt denies any knowledge of wrongdoing from his former staff members.

"I know how good of a recruiter that David (Saunders) was, but the reason I hired him was because he worked for Cellular South in the state of Mississippi prepping the ACT and helping the student athletes, because the reading was at such a low level for some of these young men," Nutt said. "He was really an expert. He had such unique qualifications, and I felt so good about it.

"There were two or three kids that he said he wanted to help get eligible. This was in July and I said, 'David, guess what, I am locked into the 105 (roster limit). They're not going to be in the 105, and you have to be at 105 on August 1. Good luck.'

"The next thing I know, about the first week of school, on the second day of class, David said, 'I've got good news. We got a couple of guys eligible.'

"Well, great, but in my mind, they were redshirted already, but here's the thing: I kicked them off in October. I kicked them off for urinating in the lobby. Then it starts coming back to me about the majority of the violations. It just makes you sick,"

Nutt is working towards making peace with the past, but he rests assured each night that he still has the admiration and respect from many of his former coaches and players.

After a recent article from the aforementioned Bruce Feldman pointed out that Nutt's name was nowhere to be found in the NCAA charges, many of his supporters reached out.

"The phone's been quiet. Diana made the comment, 'The phone doesn't ring as much'," Nutt said of being away from coaching. "During this time, the phone has picked up again. I've had former players and former coaches give a lot of feedback from that article. There was a lot of excitement on the other end of that, because the ones that know me know. They know."

I believe it to be apparent that everybody knows Nutt was innocent. No matter what folks may have told the national press, they simply knew better or they certainly should have.

Perhaps the most surprising detail in this story is the fact that the journalists on the national college football beat who were chasing the story didn't even call Nutt for his side of it. They simply ran with what Ole Miss gave them.

Nutt, who hasn't changed his phone number, thinks he might have gotten a call from ESPN, but he can't swear to it. If they did reach out to the guy being thrown under the "Rebel Express" driven by Bjork and Freeze, their story certainly didn't reflect it.

Chapter 22

Pushing Forward Back

The phrase "exemplary cooperation" has nearly been deemed profane here in the state of Mississippi. The Ole Miss NCAA legal team suggested it, Ole Miss administration believes they demonstrated it, and Ole Miss fans are tired of hearing it.

The NCAA defines exemplary cooperation as follows:

"Exemplary cooperation by an NCAA school or involved individual may be a mitigating factor when determining any penalties. Exemplary cooperation may include identifying individuals, documents and other information pertinent to the investigation; expending institutional resources to expedite a thorough and fair collection and disclosure of information; or bringing additional violations to the attention of the enforcement staff."

The Committee on Infractions will have the final say on whether Ole Miss' level of cooperation is worthy of the distinction. The Rebel legal team seems hopeful that the power of suggestion will aid in the effort to mitigate some of the pending sanctions.

Many supporters of Ole Miss Athletics scoff at the mere suggestion of cooperating with the NCAA. "Lawyer up, and make 'em prove it," is a common refrain. The biggest problem with that strategy is that the enforcement staff appears to have done a good job making their case.

Ole Miss has admitted to 14 of the 21 allegations against its football program. At issue are many of the charges leveled at the Rebels in the amended Notice of Allegations. Some of those allegations may be contested in a court of law.

Owner of Rebel Rags Terry Warren, the retail outlet owner, who is accused of providing free apparel to recruits, denied the charges vehemently, and went as far as filing a lawsuit against three of the witnesses, Kobe Jones, Leo Lewis, and Lindsey Miller, whom the owner alleges have made false statements.

Ole Miss is also disputing that charge as part of its defense against the allegations brought against them in the amended notice.

Warren filed the lawsuit in Lafayette County on Friday, June 9, and the defendants were served on Sunday, June 11.

The crux of the suit is that Warren denies all charges made against him personally and professionally. He also contends that the allegations made against him as a result of the probe are completely false.

While the University has disassociated several other boosters and businesses, to date, Rebel Rags is not one of them. This matter may not be settled for some time and likely not before Ole Miss has their hearing before the Committee on Infractions.

Rebel fans from around the country have been extremely supportive of Rebel Rags once news of the suit got out. Folks went shopping to show their support. Crowds of online social communities stepped up and provided the links and contact information for the store, so folks could purchase merchandise in a show of solidarity.

Some have seen Warren as a bit of a hero who's standing up for Ole Miss, and against the NCAA. Rebel fans have taken a beating, but the fact that Warren has gone to war has only galvanized the Red and Blue.

Fans from around Mississippi have made pilgrimages to Oxford to support their brothers-in-arms, and posted proof of their newly made purchases on social media.

Rumors about Jones and Lewis ran rampant on Ole Miss message boards with many suggesting that the two Bulldogs fabricated their testimony. Some supposed "insiders" hinted that the pair may recant their statements and that the Rebels will see most of the charges against them dropped.

Bear in mind, Ole Miss has already admitted to two-thirds of the allegations made against them.

As expected by those with reasonable intelligence, all accused parties sought legal representation of their own, and have prepared their answers to the claims made against them.

Warren wasn't the only person looking to take his claims to civil court. Former Ole Miss head coach Houston Nutt hired representation, and initially only asked for an apology.

At issue were the false reports fingering Nutt as the guilty party once news of the first NOA made the rounds. Nutt and his reps maintain that if the University had simply made a sincere public apology, everyone could have moved on with life.

With Ole Miss apparently unwilling to offer some measure of amends to their former coach, Nutt has elected to seek monetary damages in court.

Based on the information shared with me, it appears the veteran coach has a strong case against the Ole Miss administration.

In a brilliant stroke of "luck" for Ole Miss, one of the boosters, who's alleged to have provided payments to Leo Lewis, has sought through legal channels to prevent his name from being made public. For now, he's calling himself "John Doe."

For the first time in the history of the state of Mississippi, an individual sought to intervene in the proceedings. While I expect the final order to go my way yet again, I expect John Doe to seek injunctive remedy in chancery court to prevent his name from being released.

I feel confident that Ole Miss will once again use this side show as an excuse to delay the release of the names of those alleged of wrong doing. One would think a repentant program would want to sanctify itself, and distance itself from those who put the program in harm's way, but one would be wrong.

I believe the entire fiasco has been a shell game used to protect those who've run afoul of NCAA regulations, and a message to future wrong doers that the University will seek to protect their identities.

After all, Ole Miss was required by law to produce the first Notice of Allegations in January of 2016, and the amended notice in February of 2017.

Ole Miss has been aware of the ethics commission recommendations since May of 2017, and could have released the names of the boosters any day since then. Instead, the University negotiated in bad faith, and as their options ran short John Doe appeared with yet another legal trick to play.

It's an outrage that they have manipulated the process the way they have. Awash with late responses, flimsy excuses, last minute changes of heart and John Doe on his white horse are just some of the things that obstructed my quest. I was simply trying to get documents the state of Mississippi decrees I have a right to obtain.

The bottom line is Ole Miss' "commitment to transparency" is simply something that sounds good in a press release. There's no action behind it other than half ass, self-serving information dumps released to curry favor with fans.

Before "transparency" became an overused buzzword, in photography vernacular it meant a translucid 35mm Kodachrome slide. Due to transparency's over-use, the significance has been lost as it has become PR-speak, and now coach-speak.

Now the word transparency is thrown around like confetti in Hurricane Katrina. Its meaning is gone with the wind. Ole Miss's less-is-more approach to transparency has turned the word into a shadowy, worthless expression. Deception dodges transparency.

If a sentence starts with "we're making a commitment to transparency...." Get ready for the bullshit, because it's coming. Up until that point they've covered up, deflected, and deceived. Whatever happened to simply being open and honest from the get-go?

The only thing transparent about the Ole Miss administration during this investigation, is its "transparent dishonesty."

When this process finally winds down, you can expect another legal proceeding that reads "Robertson vs. The University of Mississippi."

It will be awfully interesting to see what, if any, action Barney Farrar takes. It's apparent he was prepared to be a good solider when he thought they were still all in it together.

Farrar's personal attorney, Bruse Lloyd, released a statement on behalf of his client once Ole Miss had released its response to the allegations from the NCAA. In that response, the Rebel defense team painted Farrar as a rogue coach who worked covertly against the instruction of, and without the direct knowledge of his supervisor, Freeze.

"Based upon credible, corroborated witness testimony and other objective evidence," Ole Miss' response to the NCAA said, "The University has concluded that former off-field staff member Barney Farrar committed significant violations during his recruitment of (Leo Lewis), intentionally hid this misconduct from the university's compliance staff and his head coach, and used multiple intermediaries in his scheme."

Lloyd countered the University response with some pointed words of his own.

"As I have stated over the last several days, the approach of decision makers at Ole Miss was to point the finger at my client, Barney Farrar," Lloyd shared. "Instead of standing together as one to face and fight the allegations, the decision was made to abandon and isolate one of Ole Miss's own.

"Until now, the Ole Miss Family was unaware that persons in positions of great responsibility, associated with the University, have lied to Coach Farrar for months and conspired against him.

"Apparently, these decision makers attempted to back Coach Farrar into a corner and leave him with one option, admit to things he did not do. This is my opinion and we do not know who made these decisions.

"I suspect it was at some point during this time University decision makers decided to lay blame on Coach Farrar in an attempt to deflect the NCAA's probe from them and offer up Coach Farrar as a sacrifice to curry favor with the NCAA."

My, how far we've come from the claims that it was "just women's basketball and track." Now we have Farrar, one of Freeze's first hires and most trusted lieutenants, claiming he was conspired against, and is being offered up as a sacrificial lamb to the powers that govern compliance in college athletics.

It's interesting to note that Farrar is painted as some criminal mastermind worthy of a Batman villain, but the only players he's alleged to have cut corners to get are the ones Ole Miss didn't sign.

How's that for exemplary cooperation?

Farrar paid with his job and reputation. His alleged accomplices in the plot to sign Leo Lewis have been disassociated by the University despite the fact that the Rebels are contesting some of the allegations against them.

The NCAA enforcement staff and the University have agreed that these boosters were involved with improper contact with Lewis and aided in the recruitment of him.

Ole Miss argues through both sides of the Rebel mouth

that Freeze promoted an atmosphere of compliance, and that no system of follow-up could've uncovered Farrar's actions.

Following that line of thinking, Freeze is either complicit in the matter or incompetent as a supervisor.

It might be both, but it can't be neither.

To further illustrate this "atmosphere of compliance," multiple Freeze assistants are charged with level one violations. Those allegations of wrong doing cover multiple recruiting classes. By their own admission some infractions took place while the University was already under NCAA investigation.

If there existed a strict adherence to NCAA recruiting guidelines, then how could this multitude of sins be so widespread? How could a coach looking to cut a corner feel comfortable if he felt his boss would be following up behind him?

The Ole Miss response to the NOA references a checklist as evidence of strong compliance. When the building burns down, the fire preparedness checklist hanging from the clip board generally goes with it. If the systems in place weren't able to prevent and uncover wrongdoing, then the systems weren't sufficient. Arguments of, "we tried, but they were just too sneaky for us" won't resonate with the committee on infractions.

I'd recommend not bringing up the checklist. Nobody cares what you did, if you didn't get the job done.

Many Rebel fans breathed a premature sigh of relief when the first Notice of Allegations stopped short of charging Ole Miss with the dreaded Lack of Institutional Control allegation.

Considering the scope of the charges against major athletic departments at Ole Miss, the charge certainly seems warranted. Major violations were uncovered in three Rebel sports, during the tenure of two different athletic directors and two different chancellors.

If this is "control" by the institution, I shudder to think what a lack of control would look like.

Women's basketball staffers paid for and completed on-line testing for recruits, lied to the NCAA, encouraged others to lie, and attempted to destroy evidence.

Track coaches cut corners with recruiting, violated rules regarding tryouts, and lied to the NCAA.

Football coaches had a hand in fixing the ACT, used boosters of the University to aid in the recruitment of student athletes; those boosters in turn provided impermissible benefits to prospects, lied about it, and that's just the infractions they've admitted to.

As I am sure you've noticed, there were charges in all three sports of Ole Miss coaches providing false and misleading statements to the NCAA enforcement staff.

Knowing what's already been admitted to and the number of third parties who've been disassociated by the University, it is difficult to give anyone involved the benefit of the doubt.

Cheaters are generally liars too. It's part of the job description. It appears that "Faith-based recruiting" didn't extend to bearing false witness to the NCAA.

Chapter 23

Freeze Escorted Out

July 5, 2017

As most Americans returned to work after a day of family, food, and fun celebrating our nation's independence, I was pecking away at my trusty keyboard mining for information.

Thanks to a new connection I had developed during the writing of this book, I had a ton of fresh information to sort through.

I met attorney Tom Mars through a mutual friend. I say a friend, but how many of your "friends" on Facebook are really your friends? In this case, my "friend" was a fan who looked me up on social media and clicked "Add Friend."

We were friendly, my Facebook friend and I, but we had never met. We talked on the phone just once, and that was when he contacted me about speaking with Mars.

Mars had been retained by Coach Houston Nutt to handle his conflict with Ole Miss involving the disparaging comments allegedly made in an effort to cast aspersions at the former Rebel coach and deflect blame away from Freeze.

I have to admit I was initially reluctant to speak with Mars. Quite frankly, as litigious as my home state has become, I don't really make a habit of speaking to lawyers, even my own.

For some reason I found a bit of a kinship with Mars from the very first phone call. My hope was that Mars would make Nutt available for an interview for this book if I was willing to compare notes with them.

The relationship continued even after I spoke with Nutt.

My first pass through the products of the FOIA request showed several phone calls to and from national media members the weekend of January 29, 2016. The date should seem familiar by now. It's the first time Ole Miss publicly acknowledged the receipt of the NCAA's Notice of Allegations and the focus of Nutt's civil suit.

The next group of records only contained the calls of Freeze from January 19 - 21 of 2016. Honestly, I was a little disappointed in the date range. I would've requested the records for that weekend. After all, Ole Miss received that first batch of allegations on Friday January 22.

I decided that it wouldn't hurt to look through them. If you have them, you may as well take a look to see what's there.

There were 84 phone calls on the spreadsheet provided by Ole Miss for that time period. It didn't take too long to find something of interest.

January 19, 2016, was a Tuesday. Like every other college coach in America, Freeze was on the road conducting in-person visits with recruiting targets.

The first business call of the day appears to have taken place at 2:51 p.m. when former Ole Miss football staffer Barney Farrar called for a two-minute chat, the first of four calls between the two that day.

There were several other calls that afternoon between Freeze and his staff as they looked to hit their final strides towards National Signing Day.

At 8:34 p.m. the phone records provided for Freeze's University cell phone show a call to a Verizon cell phone number with a 313 area code.

I plugged that number into the search engine and no record was returned. A quick Google search changed everything.

With that number plugged in, an assortment of exotic ads for escorts filled the screen. The same pictures and digits highlighted every single one of the online listings.

I double checked the number and tried again. I tried the

Bing search engine and it yielded the same results.

My wife walked into the house after an afternoon of yard work and I asked her to read the number from the records to me to ensure that my eyes weren't playing tricks on me. One-by-one she read back the same numbers.

I even asked her to click the search button and she jumped back startled as if the screen had become three dimensional. She asked, "What in the world is that?"

"A call from Hugh Freeze's phone records," I replied. "Let's check again."

I had a hard time believing what I was seeing, so I called Mars. I asked him to pull the records and double check. I already knew what the answer was going to be, but I just wanted someone outside of my house to confirm it.

As the products of his google search littered his computer monitor, his words appeared to leak out before his lips were ready, "Oh, Hell!" He didn't need to say anything else.

We sat their speechless trying to come to grips with what we were seeing.

Could this man who tweeted Biblical scriptures really be calling an escort service? I'm not sure who spoke first, but Mars and I agreed to speak again after taking some time to let it all sink in.

A 24-year-old Asian beauty stared back at me and my shell-shocked wife. I minimized the screen if for no other reason than to protect my wife and me from an awkward moment should one of the kids walk by.

If you talk to enough people you can hear anything you want. Sure there had been rumors of trouble in the house of Freeze, but he was a big target for things like that. Rivalries bring out the worst in people, and many want to see the worst in the other guys even if it takes a little creativity.

I fully appreciated the weight of it all. Even the mere

appearance of some sort of infidelity would have far reaching consequences for all involved. There are no family members removed from harm's way once allegations like these hit the streets.

The next time I spoke to Mars, I was a little spooked. I did my best to take a step back and take a deep breath. I said, "Well, all we really have is one call. The facts are that in the records they provided there was a call from his phone to a number associated with an escort service."

Yes, that was all factual, but alone it didn't prove a whole lot. I felt we needed a bigger sample size before anyone could go public with anything so scandalous. I wanted to give Freeze the benefit of the doubt, but my greater concern was for his wife and family. They didn't get a vote in any of this, but their lives would be impacted.

Did I want to break this news in the book, or did I want to let one of the national college football writers run with it and provide me a bit of cover in the end?

The bottom line is that I wanted to be right no matter what the truth turned out to be. This wasn't a recruiting violation, or an extra piece of cake at dinner, this was real world stuff. This was real life and hearts would be broken.

It was a very tough burden to carry. Yes, I uncovered the call, but I felt a little guilty about it. I leaned on my wife and spoke with my sponsor and literary agent daily about it.

What's the right thing?

It never left my thoughts. I agonized over it for several days. I barely ate or slept. I felt myself aging under the weight of it all. I tried to talk myself into publishing it, and I tried to talk myself into just leaving well enough alone.

I spoke with my attorney, Casey Lott, at length about it, and he told me that I deserved to break the story, because it was my discovery. That helped a little, but I just didn't feel right about it.

I also had an agent telling me how important this would be for the book and that "facts are facts." I agreed with all of that, but these facts were game changing. At times I felt perhaps the burden was more than I could carry, but I was finally ready to try.

Just as I had built up the resolve and words to add that juicy morsel to this book, I got a call out of left field that sort of changed things again.

A friend from Tupelo reached out and told me that Ole Miss was aware that I had the phone records and they were concerned about it. He also said that they were trying to "get out in front of it, before you break it."

How do you get out in front of a story like this without making a coaching change?

Later that day, I was informed that Ole Miss was prepared to take steps to protect Freeze if he was painted in a "false light." For those of you who don't know, that's the younger brother of a defamation of character lawsuit.

Not wanting to be sued, the phone call was out of the book once again.

I thought I'd be at peace with all of that, because it seemed like the responsible thing to do. There was no reason to come off half-cocked in a situation like this without more evidence, but the same feeling of anxiety returned.

No more sleep. No more appetite.

I started getting more and more phone calls from national and regional media folks. Somebody was sharing the rumor and it pissed me off to be quite honest. I didn't know who was talking, but someone clearly was. I felt like I was in a bad spot. People wanted to know what I had uncovered, but I really worried about sharing it.

I talked with a couple of in-staters. I told them both that

there was not enough to go on, and that they needed to do their own research. I admitted I had heard some rumors, but I didn't offer many specifics.

There were a few things about the phone call that kept haunting me. There were things that just didn't make sense with what I know about telephone communication.

Ole Miss had let it be known privately on Friday July 14 that the call was a "misdial."

I know when I misdial a number, I immediately hang up and call again. Either I get the right number or I dial the wrong number again. Maybe I've written it down wrong or something to that affect. I don't just move on with life. I had a call to make.

In Freeze's case, he didn't make another phone call after his "misdial" for 12 minutes. That final outgoing call of the night went to Farrar at 8:46 p.m., not an 813 number or a 313 number.

The spin on the message boards was that he missed a digit and then called the right number after the misdial. That's a complete fabrication. If Freeze made a follow-up call to an 813 number, then he did it using another phone. In the records provided, Freeze didn't make a single call to an 813 number.

Two days after making the call to the number associated with the escort service, Freeze received a call from an 813 phone number. That call appears to have been from a recruit and unrelated to the call in question.

There are nearly 673,000 people who live in Detroit, Michigan. What are the odds that Freeze just happened to call someone with a 313 phone number that just happened to be an escort based out of Sarasota, Florida, the night he was in Tampa, Florida, only an hour away?

Quite the coincidence!

Curiosity finally got the better of me, and I just called the number myself. It turns out that it was disconnected. With that looking like a dead end, I did some more on-line research and found that the number was listed in escort ads as early as 2015 and as late as May of 2017.

Freeze's phone records show the call originating from his University-issued cell phone took place in 2016, so there was no chance the number changed hands. If it had, the owners were clearly in the same line of work.

Content to simply ride it out and publish this book without mentioning the escort call, I started getting calls from media peers who were curious who was chasing the story. Everybody seemed to be close, but nobody seemed ready to roll.

Ole Miss *Rivals* writer Neal McCready incorrectly reported that I had shopped the story to others and found no takers. I never shopped it to anyone or picked up the phone to call anyone to write the story. The bottom line is that blood was in the water and the sharks were circling.

Sunday evening, I elected to share with my Twitter followers that I had the Freeze phone records and that I would discuss them on Monday's *Boneyard* show.

Social media exploded.

I got more threats and rumors began to run wild. The fact of the matter is people embellished a lot and by the time the show started some had built a house of cards suggesting the records revealed things that they didn't.

In the hours leading up the show, I had calls from people who had been contacted by attorneys hoping to stop me from discussing the records. I had no intention of discussing the escort call that day, but they didn't know that.

Hysteria grew as I started the show, but I wasn't about to say anything to get myself in trouble. I had my suspicions, the threat of lawsuits, and one phone call that lasted a minute.

Two days later, Mars informed me that he had filed another

FOIA request of Ole Miss. This time, the longtime attorney has requested every phone record, cell or landline, for Freeze from 2012 through the present.

I shared this on my Wednesday show and people went crazy. It became a watershed moment. It was clear that Nutt's legal team was playing for keeps and Mars was ready to put Ole Miss into a decision making process sooner rather than later.

On Thursday, July 20, things began to happen. I started getting texts that something was brewing in Oxford and that the leadership was hunkered down in afternoon meetings.

Pat Forde tweeted that "explosive" new developments had emerged and that Freeze's job was no longer secure.

Just as the buzz began to spread, Ole Miss released the following tweet:

Ole Miss Football ✓
@OleMissFB

&+ Follow ⌄

ANNOUNCEMENT | Hugh Freeze has resigned effective immediately. Matt Luke interim head coach. Press conference live at 7:30 PM CT on ESPNews.

Within minutes of this announcement, Dan Wolken of *USA Today* dropped the story about the mysterious call to Detroit Rock City that proved to be Freeze's undoing.

It felt so surreal watching it all unfold on social media. Nearly five months earlier, we had all watched the "hostage" video where the Ole Miss leadership shared the amended Notice of Allegations. Now another press conference would take place without Freeze making a statement.

Chancellor Jeff Vitter called it a "sad day" for the Ole Miss family and indeed it was. The coach they had supported throughout the NCAA investigation had now resigned in lieu of being terminated.

Faced with the reality of more personal indiscretions coming to light publicly, Freeze stepped down from his post as the Ole Miss head football coach. One week earlier, Freeze addressed the crowd at SEC Media days and discussed how the challenge of leading his team through the coming adversity was his "finest hour."

With the fake platitudes of that photo op now fading, a national audience watched as Bjork laid out the details of why their program was looking for a new head football coach.

"I'll walk you through how we got to where we are tonight," Bjork said. "Earlier this month, as is reported in response to a public record request, we released coach Freeze's work-related phone records for six days in January of 2016.

"Coach Freeze redacted personal calls from those phone records before they were released. There was a phone call that was not redacted and it was brought to our attention in the middle of last week.

"We did a quick assessment and determined that this was the only time that that particular number was ever called from Coach Freeze's phone since he started working here at Ole Miss in 2011. Because the call lasted less than one minute and did not appear at the time to be part of a pattern, we initially attributed this call to a misdialed number.

"As part of our core values in running the athletics program, we have an obligation to do the right thing, so we proactively looked into the rest of his phone records. In our analysis, we discovered a pattern of conduct that is not consistent with our expectations as the leader of our football program. As of yesterday, there appeared to be a concerning pattern.

"So, Chancellor Vitter and I spoke with Coach Freeze last night. We discussed the entire situation. Coach Freeze was very transparent, open, honest, and admitted to the conduct.

"Earlier this afternoon, Chancellor Vitter and I met with coach Freeze again. He offered his resignation, and we accepted. He has taken responsibility and is accountable to his actions. We will respect his privacy, and our thoughts and prayers are with him and his entire family."

There's a lot of mud to wash off the boots, but the crux of the matter is that the one-minute phone call uncovered by chance on records requested for the wrong dates led to a bigger concern once five years of phone records were requested.

Sources close to Freeze shared that the production of those records would be a "real problem for Hugh."

One of the biggest issues at play here is the fact that the University and Freeze had an opportunity to redact the records. Ole Miss attorneys provided the documents, and simply left that call on the log.

There were three calls removed from the January 19 records, but for some reason no one thought to check the other numbers to ensure there were no issues with them. The men charged with protecting the University of Mississippi simply handed over the smoking gun.

They just gave it up voluntarily.

With one stroke of the pen, the entire sordid tale could've been kept secret for at least a little while longer. It was that simple.

What's equally incredible is it all could've been avoided with a simple apology. Mars contacted Ole Miss lead counsel Lee Tyner and asked about an official apology to Nutt back during the spring.

Not only could the Rebels not be humbled enough to apologize, Tyner reportedly cut off contact with the Nutt legal team for two months.

Had that apology taken place, Mars would've never met me, I would have never received those phone records and the call to the Sarasota, Florida, escort would've never been uncovered.

The University spent millions of dollars defending itself in the NCAA investigation, but saved about $20 million through their own ineptitude. Due to Freeze's resignation, Ole Miss was no longer on the hook for a buyout or settlement of the remaining years on his contract.

Perhaps they can use some of that savings to settle the lawsuit with Nutt.

Freeze made the Rebels dream big dreams, but was now being ushered out of town on the business end of a personal nightmare. The Hugh Freeze era was over, but the Rebels still have some penance to pay once the NCAA decrees the price of their atonement.

Some have asked me about the possibility of the escorts being used as part of recruiting weekends in an attempt to entice recruits to sign on with Ole Miss. While something may come out in the future about that, there is nothing in the evidence that I have seen that suggests that is the case.

Of course, we only had six days' worth of phone records to work with. A larger sample size would certainly yield more information, but it's probably best to table that talk for now. Now that so many national publications are chasing the story, if there is a more sordid tale to be told, it will be.

The conspiracy theorists of the world have offered that Ole Miss may have wanted the call to be found. The belief being that the transgression was so scandalous that the Ole Miss administration would be able to cut Freeze loose without the golden parachute to cushion his fall.

As Bjork said in the press conference following Freeze's

resignation, the outgoing coach gets no settlement or buyout.

While interesting, I'm not sure it passes the smell test. A caper of this sort would take a Marvel Comics evil mastermind to enact.

Freeze's predecessor files an FOIA for phone records, shares them with a Mississippi State writer, who discovers the call and the national media runs with the story. It's diabolical. It's also not true.

I can't ever imagine a scenario where Ole Miss would have ever depended on Houston Nutt and Steve Robertson as wing men. Those are the things that sit-coms are based on.

The bottom line is that each man is responsible for his own actions. While Freeze has said in vain many times throughout this process that he took ownership of the mistakes that were made in his tenure, this time he meant it. It might have taken the threat of being fired to bring real personal accountability, but for the first time Freeze did the right thing.

Some will remember the two wins over Alabama, while critics will point to losses to Memphis and Vanderbilt.

Some will speak fondly of a the Sugar Bowl win over Oklahoma State, provided it doesn't end up vacated, while others will point to crippling NCAA sanctions.

No matter what took place on the field, Hugh Freeze's legacy is one of shame. Under his leadership, Ole Miss accrued some of the most egregious NCAA allegations since SMU. The entire era likely needs an asterisk signifying it was a special circumstance.

Much like the middle aged woman who pretended to be Analesa Presley in hopes of getting attention on social media, Freeze wasn't who he claimed to be. He professed to be a person of character and values, but ended up resigning in disgrace.

Freeze spoke of competing for championships and teaching boys to become men. In the end, he didn't have what it took to do either. Rather than providing young men with a role model to pattern themselves after, he demonstrated through his own conduct exactly what not to do.

Mei's Escort Resume

Sarasota, Florida
313-570-■■■

ESCORT CALLGIRL

ADVERTISING AND PROMOTIONS

CUSTOMER SATISFACTION

DATING AND MARRIAGE COUNSELING

SEXUAL SATISFACTION

GENITAL AND ORAL STIMULATION

PROFILE

Hello, my name is Mei. I'm a 24 yrs old sexxxy princess. This is my online career resume where you can see all the data about my career as a classy callgirl. I left Sarasota, FL the 1st of October and have been escorting in the Sarasota, Florida area ever since. I began my upscale escort career in October of 2015 in Sarasota, Florida. I am always seeking new dates all over.

If you wish to book an appointment please get ahold of me at 313-570-■■■

CAREER OVERVIEW

Visit http://■■■■■■■■ for more resumes

.***SeXy AsiAN PlAyMaTE***. - 23
Thu May 11th, 2017
Now that you found me don't lose mei will knock your socks off with my looks, my appeal, and ability to
entertain i aim to please baby. I am one of a kind & open to suggestions
i pr0vide an all about y0u experience that y0ull remember f0rever. You'll love my lips, and my sexy
curvy irresistable body, that's longing for you're touch. Lena 313. 570. ▓▓▓

CLAIM YOUR PRIZE *~MISS BaNGiNG BODY~ YUMMY. - 23
Thu March 23rd, 2017
Now that you found me don't lose me i will knock yoursocks offwith my looks, my appeal, and ability to
entertain i aim to please baby. I am one of a kind & open to suggestions

i pr0vide an all about y0u experiencethat y0ull remember f0rever. You'll love my lips, and my sexy curvy
irresistable body, that's longing for you're touch. Lena 313. 570. ▓▓▓

.***SeXy AsiAN PlAyMaTE***. - 23
Sun February 26th, 2017
Now that you found me don't lose me i will knock yoursocks offwith my looks, my appeal, and ability to
entertain i aim to please baby. I am one of a kind & open to suggestions

i pr0vide an all about y0u experiencethat y0ull remember f0rever. You'll love my lips, and my sexy curvy
irresistable body, that's longing for you're touch. Lena 313. 570. ▓▓▓

.***SeXy AsiAN PlAyMaTE***. - 23
Thu January 26th, 2017
Now that you found me don't lose me i will knock yoursocks offwith my looks, my appeal, and ability to
entertain i aim to please baby. I am one of a kind & open to suggestions i pr0vide an all about y0u
experiencethat y0ull remember f0rever. You'll love my lips, and my sexy curvy irresistable body, that's
longing for you're touch. Lena 313. 570. ▓▓▓

.***SeXy AsiAN PlAyMaTE***. - 23
Mon January 23rd, 2017
Now that you found me don't lose me i will knock yoursocks offwith my looks, my appeal, and ability to
entertain i aim to please baby. I am one of a kind & open to suggestions i pr0vide an all about y0u
experiencethat y0ull remember f0rever. You'll love my lips, and my sexy curvy irresistable body,that's
longing for you're touch. Lena 313. 570. ▓▓▓

:. : A ReAl PlaYFuL BrUnEtte BeAuTy *:. :*** - 24
Thu October 01st, 2015
New to town... Im classy and independent, with a wild side. Im the total package... Sweet.. And fun. I am
very friendly, caring and attentive to the needs of polite gentlemen. My sessions are very sensual, 100%
discreet and never rushed. I can assure that your quest for satisfaction will be fulfilled with me. If you
like my pics... You'll love me in person. Give me a call you won't be disappointed. I'm waiting. Incall

jessie 313. 570. ▓▓▓

ONLINE PROFILES

Online Resume
http://███████.com/313-570-███

Escort Ad History
http://███████.com/313-570-███

Review Profiles
http://████████/view.php?c=17&a=r

REFERENCES

Greg ███ ....*Jul, 2017*

1hr (Full Service Session)

"Was everything you can imagine and more. She does it all and leaves you feeling tired, wore out, and revived, if that makes any sense at all. Seriously, I will be seeing her again!"

Paul ███ ....*Jun, 2017*

1/2hr (Quickie Session)

"Not as good as the pics, but you know, that's how it always is with all the girls. She did what she was supposed to I guess. It was good, I would see her again but it was not something I would write home."

Raj ███ ....*Aug, 2016*

1hr (Full Service)

"She tell me she do many things before I pay and she be nice to me about all things. But after she not do everything like she say to me. She does sell me her panties which is very good and I like. I have better before and she good but I see better last week with Sheika but she is not longer available."

SEE ALL OF MY REVIEWS
http://escortresume.com/view.php?c=17&a=r

OTHER SKILLS

* Technical Skills: Windows XP| Microsoft Office
* Facebook , Twitter, Snapchat, Instagram
* Escort Ad Posting
* Criminal Court

* Customer Service
* Telephone Sales
* Hotel Booking
* Money Management

PORTFOLIO

Epilogue

I have the chance to speak at meetings around the state of Mississippi, and beyond at times. Over the course of the last two years, no matter what I spent my time talking about when I opened the floor for questions the first question was always the same.

"How bad is Ole Miss going to get hammered?"

That's the million-dollar question, isn't it? The sanctions are still to be determined, but some Ole Miss fans have shared with me that they're preparing for Armageddon.

That may be a little extreme, but I believe the penalties in this case will be severe and program changing.

A year ago, I was told that the USC sanctions may be a pretty good barometer of what Ole Miss may face once the Committee on Infractions hands down the penalties for Rebel non-compliance.

In 2010, USC was hit with sanctions in football, men's basketball, and women's tennis. The football portion of the penalties were severe. The Trojans were penalized with four years of probation, a two-year bowl ban, vacated wins, including the 2004 BCS National Title, and a loss of 30 scholarships.

The 30 scholarships were split evenly over three years. The Trojans were only allowed to sign 15 new players per year, and the total number of annual scholarships were reduced from 85 to 75.

While those numbers may ring true in the Rebel case, it's important to remember that the sanctions against USC were largely criticized as an over step by the NCAA.

USC's indiscretions are centered largely around former Heisman winner Reggie Bush, and basketball star O.J. Mayo, who were both alleged to have accepted gifts from agents. The Trojan allegations were more about amateurism and a lax attitude towards compliance. The University was also hit with a Lack of Institutional Control charge.

The core of the USC case involved Bush, and his parents being showered with gifts by agents seeking to sign Bush as a professional client. While the university was not involved with the wrongdoing, the committee on infractions ruled that the school didn't do enough to stop it, and that a coach with knowledge of the benefits failed to report the issues.

In all, USC was charged with seven total violations including the LOIC. Two of the remaining six allegations involved exceeding the approved number of football coaches, and 123 impermissible international phone calls by a women's tennis player that totaled $7,535.

Ole Miss has five times the number of total allegations that USC had, and 21 allegations against Rebel football alone.

Some of the factors that are expected to aggravate the charges against Ole Miss involve substantial booster involvement with the recruitment of several student athletes, and the admission that members of the Rebel football staff were aware, and in some cases, accused of conspiring with the boosters to gain a competitive advantage.

Since the 2010 NCAA public report on USC, there have been 47 major infractions cases that involve football. One would be hard pressed to find one more serious than the Ole Miss case.

Nine of those 47 cases resulted in at least a one-year bowl ban with three member institutions receiving a two-year post season penalty.

Ole Miss has already self-imposed a year bowl ban for the 2017 season. Based on recent rulings, a two-year ban is likely, and I wouldn't rule out a third year if the committee accepts the enforcement staff's case in full.

If the new NCAA penalty structure is followed to the letter of the law, we may see some real fireworks when it comes to the Ole Miss post season penalty.

Also of note was this comment from the COI after the football case was severed from the women's basketball and track issues. "Too many institutions appear to be timing their self-imposed bans as a matter of convenience and strategy," the report read.

The three cases where a multi-year post season penalty was levied since USC (Texas Southern: 2012, Miami: 2013, Syracuse: 2015) all involved extensive booster involvement, but not as widespread as alleged by the NCAA in the Ole Miss case.

There've been eight football programs banned from post season play for three years in NCAA history. Texas Southern was the last school to suffer through that back in 1996. The last Power Five team to see a three-year ban was Oklahoma State in 1989.

If you're looking for a real sense of history, there've been two FBS programs hit with four-year bowl bans, Indiana (1960) and North Carolina State (1957).

In 26 of the 47 cases, the committee on infractions elected to use the show cause penalty when there was evidence of football staffers involved in the indiscretions.

The enforcement staff is now seeking show cause penalties for several current and former Ole Miss football coaches including former head coach Hugh Freeze.

On October 7, 2016, the committee on infractions issued its final report regarding the allegations against Ole Miss women's basketball and track. Included in those sanctions were show cause penalties for all six Ole Miss staffers named in the January 22, 2016, Notice of Allegations.

The enforcement staff went a solid six for six in their first round of sanctions with the University of Mississippi case.

Another important factor to consider from that final report is that the NCAA charged former women's basketball coach Adrian Wiggins, and former track coach Brian O'Neal with failure to monitor their assistants. Those charges were upheld by the COI.

Freeze is charged under some of the same NCAA legislation. Considering that multiple assistant coaches under his direct supervision are charged with Level 1 violations in this case, the Freeze legal team has some serious work to do to mitigate the charges against their client.

Again, everybody can't be rogue.

Six programs since USC felt the pulverizing impact of the NCAA hammer have been cited for Lack of Institutional Control. Ole Miss is expected to be the seventh.

The LOIC is essentially the "Scarlet Letter" in college athletics. The penalty is reserved for athletic departments that are complicit in wrong doing or are asleep at the switch when it comes to compliance.

Ole Miss is facing a scenario where three head coaches were derelict in their duties as supervisors, multiple athletic staffers had a hand in the wrong doing, and the athletic department's safe guards proved largely ineffective.

When the Rebels announced their initial answer the NCAA's charges against them, some self-imposed sanctions were revealed as well.

There were some suspensions, some reductions in evaluation days, and a prohibition on unofficial visits from February 21, 2016, through March 31, 2016, but the more important items were a bit half measured.

Ole Miss offered to impose three years of probation, reduce scholarships by 11 over four years, and pay a fine of $159,325.

Considering what the Rebels are charged with, those sanctions imposed by the University will certainly be accepted and added to.

In the 2016 University of Louisiana-Lafayette case, a spinoff of the Ole Miss probe, the Ragin' Cajuns were hit with two years of probation, and a reduction of 11 scholarships over the course of three seasons.

ULL was charged with a total of four violations all related to the alleged conduct of former staffer David Saunders, who is also named in the Ole Miss case as part of the ACT fraud charges.

To suggest that Louisiana-Lafayette and Ole Miss deserve comparable penalties is completely absurd. The case against the Cajuns was truly limited to a rogue coach not seven "rogue" coaches and a dozen or so "rogue" boosters as is alleged in the matter against Ole Miss.

If we want to get down to the brass tacks of the matter, one could make a solid case that Ole Miss is a rogue program. It's a cultural problem, and not a coaching one.

Many of the third parties now disassociated by Ole Miss were Rebel fans long before Hugh Freeze came along. Some of the boosters exiled by former A.D. Pete Boone as part of the Billy Brewer NCAA issues are back in the fold, one famously posing for a picture with Ross Bjork.

The more things change, the more they stay the same.

Ole Miss is charged with some institutional issues as part of their NCAA woes. One would expect those to be cleared up as the University clamps down on compliance in the coming probation years, but what about the boosters?

By their own admission, Ole Miss has revealed that they were essentially powerless to prevent boosters acting on their behalf from involving themselves in the recruiting process.

And what have they done to show those boosters and others that those actions will not be tolerated going forward? Well, as I can personally attest, they've fought to protect the identities of those named in the allegations against the University.

Maybe they're afraid it will hurt their feelings if they took a strong stance against them.

Many Rebel fans have said that Freeze is being personally attacked. Let me offer some assurances that this is not totally about Freeze. He's the guy who just happened to be the head coach. There have been coaches before him, and there will be coaches after him.

The core problem is a culture built on privilege, shortcuts, and self-entitlement. "They have it, so we have to have it. Daddy, go buy that for me."

There is a segment of Ole Miss fans who feel it's their duty, and in some cases their right to be involved. It's not enough to cheer the Rebels on to victory. Many of them get drunk on the access, and share their experiences with others who then become envious and want in on the action.

A close friend who associates with some fans of that sort shared with me that now that the new generation of Rebs have had a taste of success they won't stop. Despite pending sanctions, and a new home on the center of the NCAA radar, they'll double down.

The hundred-dollar handshakes won't stop. They'll just take place farther under the table.

I can speculate on what sanctions may be, but we're all simply guessing. What they have to be are penalties so serious that hangers on have to feel that it's simply not worth it, and scary enough that real fans of the program will partner with the University to root the offenders out.

This story is bigger than one coach, one case, one moment in time, or one chapter in the Egg Bowl rivalry. It's about a mentality that won't die out easily.

Some have elected to put the black hat on Freeze and paint him out to be the villain. I believe he could've done more to curtail the activities that didn't match his value system, but he's far from the only one to blame.

Over time, I believe he simply became a product of his environment.

When Freeze was introduced as the new head man on December 5, 2011, he spoke of clean slates, getting to the SEC championship, and doing things the right way.

It's obvious by now that Freeze's sixth season was over before it started. Due to the post season ban the Rebels are ineligible for the SEC title game, so their players won't make it to Atlanta, either.

It is unclear today if Ole Miss is ready for a clean slate when it comes to Rebel football, but is abundantly clear that things haven't been done the right way.

"Power doesn't always corrupt. Power can cleanse. What I believe is always true about power is that power always reveals."

– Robert Caro

Acknowledgements

There are so many people worthy of inclusion in this section. Above all, I want to thank God for second chances, the love of a good woman and the gift of a wonderful family.

I cannot express how grateful I am to my wife, Dana, who spent countless hours listening to me talk on the phone. Many times, she heard the same story over and over and over. She'd come in after working a 12-hour shift and proof read for me, because she loved me, and she believed in this book. I love her with all I have.

My children, Oni, Audrey, Mia and Ian have heard about the book for months. They're the reason I work as hard as I do. I hope I've made them all proud with this effort.

Special thanks to Gene Swindoll who saw something in me, and gave me the chance to become a professional writer. Gene has probably worked harder on the site this year than ever, because he wanted me to be able to devote the time needed to produce this book.

David Murray has served as sounding board and adviser to me throughout the process. When I was teenager, I wanted to do what David did, which was write about Mississippi State. It's funny how life works out.

Brian Hadad and all of the folks with Bulldog Sports Radio gave me the chance to host my own show, The Boneyard. The show has been more fun than I ever imagined it would be. Brian had a front row seat to a lot of this story, and served as a confidant when I simply had to share something with somebody.

There were several people who shared their experiences with me privately in an effort to help me get to the truth. They know who they are. I hope I've done their stories justice.

I'd like to thank Alterbridge, Black Stone Cherry, the Foo Fighters, Guns N' Roses, Korn, Lynch Mob, Motley Crue, Nonpoint, Nothing More, Ozzy, RATT, Seether, Shaman's Harvest, Shinedown, 10 Years, Tesla, Whitesnake, and many other bands that provided the soundtrack to my life, especially on the days I sat there staring at a computer screen trying to get inspired.

God bless the family of Chris Cornell.

There have been days in my life when I felt like music was my only friend. It provided some shelter from the rain when the storms of the human condition rolled in. Music's a living thing. Enjoy every note.

I love all of those who loved me through the good times and bad, my Mama, Shorty, Mama D, Pat, Kim, Nikki, Tara, and their families.

I'd be remiss if I didn't thank all of mine and Bill W.'s mutual friends. You guys have helped me learn a new way to live, and I love you all.

Extra special thanks to the Count of Purple Crisco and Mark Fulton.

Finally, for all of those people who contacted me in person or on-line with words of encouragement, I appreciated that more than you'll ever know. Every time I found an emotional valley, your kindness gave me the strength to keep going. This book is yours, and it was written with you in mind. I hope you enjoy it for years to come.